Kill the EPA

2nd Edition

So Humans Can Live!

B R I A N W. K E L L Y

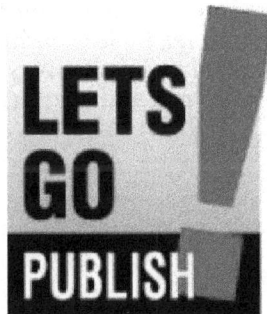

Published by: LETS GO PUBLISH!
                  Brian P. Kelly, Publisher
                  P.O. Box 261
                  Wilkes-Barre, PA 18703
                  brian@brianpkelly.com
                  www.letsgopublish.com

Book Cover Design by Michele Thomas

ISBN Information: The International Standard Book Number (ISBN) is a unique machine-readable identification number, which marks any book unmistakably. The ISBN is the clear standard in the book industry. 159 countries and territories are officially ISBN members. The Official ISBN For this book is:

978-0-9962454-1-8

Release Date: June 2016

LETS GO PUBLISH!

Dedication

To Brian Patrick, Michael Patrick, Kathleen Patricia

My Wonderful Children

At the Top of All My Lists for a Long Time!

And Forever!

Acknowledgments

I would like to thank many, many people for helping me in this effort to produce my 59th book.

To all the people that I have ever mentioned in the Acknowledgments of any book, I continue to appreciate your contributions. For those new to the experience of helping me bring in my book projects and/or who help me in my life, I want to thank you all from the bottom of my heart.

Please check out www.letsgopublish.com Acknowledgments to read the latest version of what once was the largest acknowledgments in the world, though the rigors of the Guinness Book were too time consuming for us to apply.

You are listed online and if not please send me a spirited, yet irritated response. I do appreciate your great work in my publishing efforts.

God Bless all the helpers!

Thank you so very much!

Table of Contents

Chapter 1 The "God" of the EPA is Mother Nature 1
Chapter 2 Barack Obama Has Awakened a Sleeping Nation?.. 15
Chapter 3 Was Silent Spring Too Loud? 23
Chapter 4 How Did the EPA Get So Bad? 31
Chapter 5 No More Killing the Environment 39
Chapter 6 Who Do Chemical Corporations Care About? 45
Chapter 7 A Few Outrageous Environment Responses 53
Chapter 8 A few More Outrageous Responses 63
Chapter 9 Snake Oil & Honeybees 73
Chapter 10 EPA Hates Farmers 81
Chapter 11 EPA Hates Energy & Keystone XL Pipeline 85
Chapter 12 BP Oil Spill—Not Obama's Finest Moment 95
Chapter 13 The Infamous Delta Smelt 109
Chapter 14 The EPA Is Obama's Tool to Marginalize America 117
Chapter 15 Who Thinks the EPA Should Die? 129
Chapter 16 Our President Is the EPA! 135
Chapter 17 Is Obama's EPA a Rogue Agency? 143
Chapter 18 The End of Incandescent Light Part I 151
Chapter 19 The End of Incandescent Light Part II 159
Chapter 20 Humans are EPA Enemy # 1 169
Chapter 21 Master Game Player Uses EPA to Make His Moves 179
Chapter 22 We're Broke! Part I of IV 189
Chapter 23 We're Broke! Part II of IV 195
Chapter 24 We're Broke! Part III of IV 203
Chapter 25 We're Broke! Part IV of IV 209
Chapter 26 Turn EPA Role Over to States Part I 217
Chapter 27 Turn EPA Role Over to States Part I 227
Chapter 28 DDT & World Population Control Part I 237
Chapter 29 DDT & World Population Control Part II 253
Chapter 30 The Truth about CFCs 265
Chapter 31 The Best Solution to the Freon Non-Problem Part I.... 279
Chapter 32 The Best Solution to the Freon Non-Problem Part II... 287
Chapter 33 The EPA Kills Asthmatic Children 297
Chapter 34 Some Final Thoughts 307
Books by Brian Kelly 319

Preface:

This is the second edition of the very popular book, Kill the EPA! The book has already been read by thousands and thousands. Nothing stands still in time including the EPA, though it surely should. Thus this book in its second edition is refreshed with over 100 pages of new facts, and outrageous stories about how the EPA, a killer agency itself, must be killed so that people all over the world will be able to live their lives to completion.

When George Bush lost power, the unemployment rate was 4.6 percent and the US was doing reasonably well, other than the trumped up market crisis of 2008. Unemployment in 2016 is listed as 4.7%. Ypu'd think everything was almost OK again but then again, you would be wrong.

Although the country's U-3 unemployment rate, as it's officially known, currently sits at 4.7 percent (which is considered to be a historically low percentage), that number only accounts for a small subset of Americans – those without jobs who have actively looked for work in the last four weeks.

If the Labor Dept wanted to be honest, they would tell you that George Bush's 4.6 percent was a lot better than Obama's 4.7 than just .1 percent. But then again, Obma is happy that you do not have the right perspective when it makes him look better than Bush. .

This book is about the EPA not about the problems facing workers in America but you can get an idea of the EPA lies by looking at the labor statistic lies. Discouraged workers are considered to be among those not included in the labor force.

It's not that they do not want to work, it's that Obama's stats look better when they are not included.

It gets even more discouraging for those of us looking for truth from government. Discouraged workers are cleverly suggested to be a subdivision of "marginally attached workers," who have looked for work at some point in the past year but hadn't in the last four weeks.

Of the 1.8 million marginally attached workers in the U.S. in a recent month for example, 563,000 were considered discouraged workers. But millions of others are simply considered out of the labor market and just aren't looking for work, for one reason or another. They do not make it into Obama's stats simply because they make his stats look bad. EPA stats are even worse as you will learn in this book.

During the Obama period, you and I have heard that unemployment went from over 10% in 2009 to 5.5 % in 2015 and now 4.7% in 2016. And, of course that Brooklyn Bridge is still for sale cheap!

Many economists, including the experts at marketwatch.com say that the Team Obama reported numbers are simply a hoax. The President cannot be believed. He'd like to tell the truth but simply cannot. The President's team therefore cannot be believed, and the modern media cannot be believed because they are owned by Obama. None of what is reported is true. They are all liars. I am probably the only guy speaking about the government who has told you the truth and nothing but the truth in many years.

Right now as I write this line, there are 94 million Americans who have simply dropped out of the labor market, refusing to work or even look for a job. And if you didn't look for a job in the past month, Team Obama chooses to no longer count you as unemployed. This little trick makes this President look like a better economic leader and a better economist than even the great Adam Smith. It is chicanery at its best.

The unemployment rate is not 4.7%, as the government claims. The real unemployment rate is over 35%, experts say. More than 103 million people aren't working in the Obama economy. That includes the 9 million who are officially counted by the administration as unemployed as well as the other 94 million who've just given up because there are no good jobs left.

Jobs are hard to come by everywhere in the world today including the United States. Even some liberals are starting to say that "you can blame the government for that." In this day and age, you can blame the government for lots more than that, and nobody would think you were kidding.

Despite no jobs for anybody else, the US government workforce itself is growing in terms of employees at a record pace. Yet, there is less and less real work even for government workers. And, so agencies such as the Environmental Protection Agency (EPA), a group that once did good work in its advisory role to the President, have taken more than one step into what Rod Serling would call the Twilight Zone of "regulation theory."

There are about 18,000 employees taking a salary from the EPA. Few Americans who *still can think*, find little value provided for the pay.

The EPA, when formed, was just a small agency that cared about humans first. The original EPA took its charter seriously and did its best to do all it could for America and Americans. Those days are long gone.

This new EPA cares very little for you or for our country. The EPA of today is working on a number of new best sellers; one edition is even more silly than the next, but equally harmful.

When you are introduced to the new EPA regulations in detail in this book, in the media, or on the Internet, they will appear to be even sillier than the list of "about to be released" EPA best seller titles that we show immediately below.

The list of titles is facetious but telling. The real list is dangerous and it threatens our freedom and our sustenance as a country. Ask the EPA about it while they still exist. My objective is that this second edition book; a more blistering indictment of a nightmare agency, will place the EPA on the endangered species list forever. However, this species is one that would serve mankind more by being eliminated.

Once an only hope that a great man like Donald Trump will unmask the Nixonesque façade from the EPA so that the smell you think you are smelling from the EPA actions can be visualized when the mask is taken away.

You simply won't believe how bad the EPA has become.

Check out this list of top tenners in the EPA with an extra one added because the EPA can't even count :

The EPA's Top 11 Hits
The Clean Toilet Act
The Better Urine than Mine (pronounced my-in) Act
The Mother Nature First Act
The Single Ply Toilet Paper Act of 2016
The Don't Drive after Midnight or Noon Act.
The Chinese Light Bulb Act
The Greenhouse Gases Are Not Found in Greenhouses Act
The Sulfur Dioxide Restroom Purity Act.
The Rotten Egg Act.
The Rotten Tomato Act a.k.a. the Leachate Act of 1979
The My Globe Is Warming Act
And many others.

So much for EPA humor for now!

The EPA has become a monster in size and in its intrusive tactics. The typical victims of the EPA are small businesses without enough legal staff to withstand the continual onslaught. People had been affected indirectly by the EPA through increased costs but with the Light Bulb act, and actions threatening to make home heating a luxury, the EPA now even terrorizes US households.

To get its dirty work done; the EPA enlists the help of other large agencies such as the Department of Transportation (DOT), the Department of Energy (DOE), and others. In addition to other missions, the DOT is responsible for minimizing the exhaust gas emissions of automobiles and other vehicles. All of this sounds good but when the EPA is in your sock drawer for no reason, it will be easier to tell they are up to no good. The EPA stepped in recently and gave DOT a new assignment.

DOT was forced to add greenhouse gases to its list of things that must be OK with an automobile when it is inspected. Considering the science on greenhouse gases is incomplete and far from perfect, many wonder exactly what will be measured.

As hard as it is for mere humans to believe, CO_2, a gas humans naturally and freely exhale while breathing, has been declared a noxious greenhouse gas by the human-hating EPA. Please pause to think about that. Breathing has been declared harmful to Ma Nature. Clearly the EPA has gone mad?

They do not discuss whether the exhalant must contain garlic or other malodorous scents in addition to the CO_2 for it to be declared noxious. For right now, CO_2 exhalant may be just enough for anybody's car to have a problem passing inspection with this pesky set of regulations.

You may recall the government-sponsored Car Allowance Rebate System (CARS). You and I knew this seven years ago as "Cash for Clunkers." It was an economic porkulus program that ran between July and August 2009. It was an EPA boondoggle event.

Owners of drivable, registered vehicles less than 25 years old and rated at 18 mpg or less (EPA combined) were able to scrap those cars and trucks in exchange for $3,500 or $4,500 credits toward the purchase of more fuel-efficient new vehicles. The only sure long-term winners were those who cashed in low-value clunkers for $3,500 or $4,500 new-car credits. The air sure does not seem any better.

Quite suddenly during the program, you may recall that the EPA had underestimated its requirement for cash and the agency ran out of funding. Americans may not have fought the program in a meaningful way, because it put cash in many pockets. It did not accomplish its goals of taking older, cheaper, working cars off the road, but it incented people to do meaningless things to make money.

As a country, we did learn one thing for sure. Americans can recognize a deal when they see one. People from the East Coast to the West Coast continue to thank the EPA for "saving the air" from all those clunkers.

The EPA ordered all of the cars traded to be crushed. They thus stole money from taxpayers to accomplish nothing. They did take out a lot of fine working automobiles that the poorest Americans could have effectively afforded and used. It was a bogus program. The new EPA is bogus!

Why did I write this book? The quick answer is because it needed to be written. The bogus EPA must be stopped. They do not like Americans. Actually they are not happy with people in general.

In all my years of eligibility to vote, I cannot recall voting for any of the powerful brood of 18,000 members of the EPA.

Yet, they have become more important than the president and the Congress in 2015. That is simply unconstitutional.

With little regard for the Constitution, the President has decided that the founders had it wrong. Perhaps he is the first of many to come who never received the proper grounding in American History.

I wrote this book not because of any nice executive orders and regulations that are daily spewing out of Washington. Progressive Marxist actions from the top show little concern for our country. There are unconstitutional executive orders, unaccountable czars, and many agencies mindlessly doing the government's bidding while intentionally usurping the powers of the Congress. This has permitted a major policy enforcer agency, the EPA "brownshirts" to accomplish what it never could accomplish if it were held accountable by the Congress.

As you read this book, and you ask how we can best help America to be saved; think of these two choices. In our future, we have just these choices: 1 "Kill the EPA," or (2) Bring on the Donald and "Fire the EPA!" Either choice works for me.

I hope you enjoy this book and I hope that it inspires you to take action to help change the members of Congress who choose to defy the American Constitution. If need be, replace every member of Congress and the Senate (up for reelection) unless we can find verifiable statements that they are not responsible for perpetrations against the people. In addition to Congress, it is also necessary to replace the head of the EPA, today's President, by a candidate who loves America and wants America to succeed. This will help make the US a far better country. All of this please while totally eliminating the EPA.

I wish you the best

Brian Kelly

About the Author

Brian W. Kelly retired as an Assistant Professor in the Business Information Technology (BIT) program at Marywood University, where he also served as the IBM i; and Midrange Systems technical advisor to the IT faculty. Kelly has designed, developed, and taught many college and professional courses. He is also a contributing technical editor to a number of IT industry magazines, including "The Four Hundred" and "Four Hundred Guru" published by IT Jungle.

Kelly is a former IBM Senior Systems Engineer and he still has an active information technology consultancy. He is the author of 59 books and numerous articles. Kelly has been a frequent speaker at COMMON, IBM conferences, and other technical conferences.

In 2010, Kelly ran for Congress as a Democrat against a 13-term Democrat and, took no campaign contributions, spent enough to buy signs and T-shirts, and as a virtual unknown, he captured 17% of the vote.

In 2015, Brian Kelly ran for Mayor of Wilkes-Barre, PA, his home town. Feel free to help him in whatever way you can to assure a Return to Glory for all Wilkes-Barre PA residents. He asks Democrats to vote for him on the ballot, and for Republicans to write him in.
www.briankellyformayor.com.

Chapter 1   The "God" of the EPA is Mother Nature

Mother Nature Über Alles

Terms such as hypocritical and a few other contemptible non-virtues at first may appear to be over-kill in describing the Environmental Protection Agency until you look just under the covers to find that the EPA is simply outrageous. The EPA is malevolent and their decisions are shockingly corrupt, biased, and almost always anti-American. The EPA has a god. Its name is Mother Nature.

When the EPA sees man punishing their god in any way through pollution or even perceived pollution, EPA regulations are cast to punish humankind to the point of death. Ask the millions who have died or almost died in poor third world countries because the EPA believes that DDT negatively affects Mother Nature. Then ask the real scientists who have proven that DDT is safe. You will learn about this issue in detail in this book.

The EPA Is Born

The Environmental Protection Agency (EPA) was formed in December, 1970 in the US by the Nixon administration to deal with pollution.

Nixon was certainly not an environmental whacko and there were lots of reasons at the time to create an agency to advise the president on matters of the environment and pollution. The stated mission of the EPA was to "conduct environmental research, provide assistance...[in] combating environmental pollution, and assist the Council on Environmental Quality in developing and recommending...new policies for environmental protection...to the President." That's it. The EPA was not supposed to become a guerilla anti-capitalist, pro-Mother Nature stand-alone army engaging war against all humans and all businesses run by humans.

For those who remember the Nixon years, there is no way our President Richard Nixon would have put an agency in place that would serve as an ideologically driven monstrosity with a mission to usurp executive power to mandate the most severe eco-centered, brazenly anti-capitalist environmental regulations imaginable. Even the EPA guidelines are off the wall. The regulations have become deadly. All Richard Nixon hoped to achieve in the creation of this agency was a research and advisory role for both himself and future presidents. Nixon's EPA were not enforcers.

The slippery slope is alive and well and it is fully manifest today in the EPA, and agency that at least in its present form, simply should not exist. The EPA is a case study in mission creep. If you are wondering who the EPA's next victim will be look no further than the closest mirror. Forget about Uncle Sam, the EPA wants Y-O-U.

Ron Paul: Pollution exists because of EPA

In late 2011, Ron Paul had demonstrated how, in his presidential administration the budget would be balanced in three years by eliminating five federal agencies. Specifically, he wants to eliminate the departments of Energy, Housing and Urban Development, Commerce, Interior and Education. Ironically, of the five huge agencies that Paul targeted, the EPA was not on his list. So, many of us are very interested in how the champion of liberty views this rogue agency.

On the Ron Paul forum, a blogger by the name of GoodA$Gold asked a question about Dr. Paul's position on the EPA. His forum question follows:

"What will Ron Paul try to do with the Environmental Protection Agency and what are his reasonings? Thank you."

The Ron Paul forum answer is as follows:

"As with any federal agency, it [the EPA] is not authorized by the Constitution and is therefore not to be funded by your money. If you wish to fund a private organization, then that is your prerogative.

"His way of dealing with pollution is to examine and respect property rights within the courts. That means that if someone pollutes on your property, you sue them. Private property ownership is always better maintained then public ownership. By recognizing in the courts that you can sue the government or a company that pollutes on your land will cause the polluters to be hurt by pollution instead of taxpayers. This will create incentive to eliminate pollution instead of just creating rhetoric and doing nothing about the problem.

"The EPA stands to lose their jobs if they solve this problem so they are on a tight wire of having to make it seem like they are working to fight pollution but having every motivation for pollution to continue to be a problem."

Don't Breathe! Literally!

Among items that should make the late talk shows get a real chuckle, the Environmental Protection Agency (EPA) recently (so to speak) declared Carbon Dioxide (CO_2) as harmful to humans. What joke was ever told on late-night TV in which the exhaled carbon dioxide was less than the normal emission? When a talent is hitting crescendo on a hot joke, you can hear the extra breathing and of course that means more exhaled pollution in the form of CO_2. So, does that make late-night TV hazardous to the health of the studio audience? Maybe so! Check the fine print in the EPA's greenhouse gas regulations.

Can it be that the EPA checked its own CO_2 emissions with a government provided meter and the readings got them concerned about the action they would have been forced to take if it had been us, instead of them? The evidence from their website is inconclusive.

A trip to the EPA website says that CO_2 is naturally occurring, as well as man-made. I don't have a problem with that statement. What I have a problem with and what you should have a problem with regarding the EPA is their claim that CO_2 is harmful. If so, to whom? Without CO_2, we would have no plants as they breathe in CO_2 and exhale oxygen.

By the way, only a small percentage of the CO_2 produced on earth is man-made. The oceans are the largest contributor and most of the "emissions," therefore are natural, unless, of course the EPA figures out how to ban the oceans from producing waves.

EPA ignores own rules

The Daily Caller on September 28, 2011 announced that there was an EPA report available dating back to April 2011. It was about how the agency ignored their own rules to push out damaging regulations. Yet, somehow the report was kept a secret until Oklahoma Republican Senator James Inhofe demanded its release.

The inspector general had found that the EPA had failed to follow the Data Quality Act and its own peer review process. Therefore, it did not have the authority to take any action on greenhouse gases. Yet, it did anyway. Under its own rules, it did not have enough proof that it could issue the determination that greenhouse gases cause harm to "public health and welfare." Since it did not have enough proof, it did not have enough authority by law, yet they chose to proceed without having sufficient evidence. They were above their own rules. Sorry EPA, that is just not good enough for what we pay you.

Inhofe said. "This report confirms that the endangerment finding, the very foundation of President Obama's job-destroying regulatory agenda, was rushed, biased, and flawed. It calls the scientific integrity of EPA's decision-making process into question and undermines the credibility of the endangerment finding."

The Obama administration blamed Congress for inaction about a greenhouse gas claim that the EPA had not ever proven. Obama actually threatens to go around the Congress against the Constitution and take matters into its own hands. Obama would more than bless the undertaking. He would order it. His executive orders would permit the EPA to directly regulate greenhouse gases despite it not having completed its work. In essence, Obama has challenged the Congress to act on its own, or his plan would empower his agency, the EPA, full of government loving bureaucrats, to do it for the Congress. And, all Americans as well as our Constitutional Republic would suffer.

If you want to reduce government spending, one key accomplishment and the major recommendation in this book is to eliminate the entire department. More and more conservatives are convinced the solution is a big roll back in power or a full elimination of the agency. "The EPA has got to go!" We show you how to eliminate these tyrants in this book.

The EPA is not the only waste

While we are eliminating waste, we should also consider for that matter, eliminating the government's youth propaganda machine, the Department of Education. Future members of the EPA breed from the propaganda spewed from the Education Department.

There are a number of other governmental agencies on my short list of things to go, all of which can be eliminated or at least severely shrunken. They are literally killing us. Getting rid of a ton of them would help Americans breathe easier. It would also help us get our fiscal house in order. Our breath is not something that is owned by any governmental agency.

If we were to work hard to reduce our multi-trillion dollar debt, and if we decided that one good way would be to provide an environment in which corporations would not have to be prodded to participate, we would need to eliminate those government agencies that scurrilously, intentionally and directly hurt the private industries in the United States without really providing any countervailing benefit to the people. The EPA is the chief culprit. It is simply outrageous.

A brief EPA abuse egregious example:

California farmers know how contemptible and outrageous the EPA can be. The farmers of the highly fertile Central Valley are being starved out of existence and denied water for growing crops because of a small fish called the delta smelt.

The EPA offers no compromises; this bait fish used by salmon fishermen, is winning in the courts for the EPA. California farmers who can no longer provide irrigation for their crops and all other Americans lost as food is in shorter supply and it is more expensive. The progressive courts in California always take the fish's side against the farmers. The fish lives on but the crops died, and the farmers are on welfare. So, who really won that battle?

If it were a nasty mosquito instead of a stinky little smelt, the EPA would still have insisted the farmers pay the price with their livelihoods. Meanwhile American food prices are skyrocketing. The key fact here is that farmers are human, and mosquitoes, nasty as they are, exist in Mother Nature's domain. The EPA loves Mother Nature and as a rule does not like humans.

The Endangered Species Act (ESA) had done positive things in the past, but in recent times it has been putting people out of work while increasing the price of food. So, if the EPA loves you and your family, why do they favor little fish over humans and why do they try to regulate CO2, which is a human exhalent? The EPA says it is a greenhouse gas and al such gasses are bad? Knowledgeable scientists, not those on the EPA payroll, see the EPA's callous disregard for humankind as impacting about every industry in the United States.

Natural transition--coal to other energy

The earth is neither always warm nor always cold. Before the EPA came into existence, people on their own had begun to gravitate to electric heat and / or gas or oil heat from individual coal fired stoves and furnaces.

Before the EPA came into existence, people lived productive lives without the threat of their power being turned off by some biased, fact-less bureaucrat. The move of the American population over many years to oil, gas, and electric energy happened because it was more convenient and it was overall cheaper to burn than coal. The EPA did not inform

Americans that coal was not the best bet for their homes as the EPA did not exist when the transition began.

In the home, the transition from coal to other energy sources was one little furnace at a time. One family replaced their coal fired units at a time though the conversion cost them a substantial percentage of their take-home pay.

They did it because it was good for them in the long haul. Uncle Sam had no input as it should be in America. People are not dummies. Yes, it was a lot of dollars in future savings for each and every family that convinced them to make the costly move. The environmental result was that over time, less and less pollution from coal occurred without the EPA guiding the people's every move.

My family and my parents' families never even had coal furnaces. We had two coal stoves on the first floor of my parents' home. One was a Heatrola which stood in the Dining Room and provided the major heat for the house. There was also a kitchen stove that heated part of the house and the water, and it also provided a means of cooking things on the top or the middle sections. In retrospect, it was impressive.

Anything needing to be boiled sat on top of the old Wilkes-Barre or Pittston Stoves in my home town and anything that needed to be baked went in the oven. We had both brands of stove over the years in our home as one would die and another would replace it.

An innovative invention called a "hot water back" permitted water to circulate within the stove and the house's plumbing system carried that "heated" water to the bathtub upstairs. We did not know that it was unusual at the time, but all nine of us in the six room home brushed our teeth and washed our faces from the water running in the upstairs bathtub. There was no bathroom sink in our house – ever. There was just one commode and yes, patience is a virtue.

The hot water back permitted people like me in the 1950's and 1960's to bathe in hot water. In the summer, when all stoves were off it was a bit tougher but we managed. Eventuallly, we got gas and a gas stove. So, we bought some galvanized buckets and two buckets of hot water drug up to the tub made a reasonably OK bath. Showers? What were they? We did not find out about them til we went to high school. No, I am not kidding.

People moving from coal to gas, to electricity, and even to oil were better deals for the environment than the coal and wood smokestacks of every house in every city sending up their own emissions to the chagrin of Mother Nature.

As desirable as the move might have been, there were a lot of hard working parents who could not afford the move to other technology and so coal was a way of life and for some it remained their only means of cooking and heating for some time to come. For some, it still is.

In this book, you will see that the EPA is not concerned about life as we know it and care about it. The EPA cares little about the struggles of humans and so don't trust that their clean air mantra means that they hope you are around to breathe it.

We all want to breathe fresh air and drink clean water but we also must live first. Regardless of the impact on humans, the EPA, if it could, and it is trying like hell, would force all to go either cold or go totally green. I think they would prefer us to go cold, because no energy use has less impact on the environment than even a green home.

Looking at it objectively, you would conclude that the desire of the EPA is un-American and unconstitutional to boot. An agency whose 18,000 workers collect paychecks because their charter is that they work for the needs of Americans, should not be paying homage only to Mother Nature and Barack Obama. As quickly as possible, the EPA, an agency gone badly, must die or they will enact legislation that forces us to die quietly so there is no noise pollution.

EPA says wear thick clothing in bed

Some say that we must rely on foreign oil because we "cannot" drill for it here in our own country. Much of our energy problems would be solved just by allowing oil drilling. The EPA bristles at the thought of us having enough energy because of its impact on Mother Nature. The "cannot" part of that sentence is because there are people in the US who would be warm regardless of the EPA policies. They are OK with regular people like you and I, no longer being warm as long as Mother Nature is happy. Most of these people are part of the EPA, and the others are big rich Democrats who know their tax policies will not cost them.

The EPA abhors fossil fuels. They like the so-called renewable fuels, such as solar, geothermal, and of course, their onetime fav, Ethanol. This inefficient fuel is mixed with gasoline at a 10% level. The EPA does not send out email blasts, however, to notify the American customer that they are being cheated at the gas pump as Ethanol does not burn as efficiently as gasoline. In other words, you need more of it to go each mile.

Moreover, Ethanol is made mostly from our corn crop. So, this little trick by the EPA hurts us in automobile efficiency and it hurts us by increasing pressure on food prices. With all the farmers bustling to get on the Ethanol bandwagon, 40% of US corn is now burned in automobiles. With people starving across the world, we simply should not be burning food.

Permit me to offer a corollary to the notion that small town farmers are the culprits. Nope! It is the corporate farms who have figured out how to make a huge amount of dollars by sending their huge farm crops to the oil companies while the price of corn for Americans skyrockets. Why is the EPA in bed with the corporate farmers? Good question. The EPA is impure and Ethanol is less pure but the EPA, even though they now know their notion was wrong, insists that Ethanol is a good deal. Unfortunately, the dollar still rules even in large farm corporations. Which member of Congress will vote against the farmers? What if I said which member of Congress will vote against the blood sucking corporations that grow corn for Ethanol?

Respected scientists say global warming is a hoax!

But, Al Gore, who is quickly heading to be the first green billionaire, disagrees. No matter what the commoners, like Al Gore speculate, the scientists know better. The scientists that I read say that Global Warming is a hoax. More and more scientific evidence says it is a hoax. Even the EPA bypassed its own data to release their greenhouse gas warning. Why would they do that if their warning were accurate?

In the last several years we have all seen the documentation about the dishonesty from the mainstream environmentalists trying to scare us all into dying early so they can save Mother Nature. There were forged emails, and even raw data was manipulated (and then lost) to fit the testing constraints. Some data was fabricated from thin air to hit on target with the premise that the earth was in peril and the EPA had the only solution. Hogwash! This is a hoax perpetrated by environmental zealots who want it to be so. But, despite their best wishes, it is not so.

On the far-out side, I think it will be a long time before we see the zealots one day trying to make human sacrifices to Mother Nature. That is good. On the contrary, when we examine the callous disregard for the thousands of children across the world, dying of malaria and other preventable diseases each day, we can easily conclude that the human sacrifices have already begun.

Evidence has been continually mounting against the notion that global warming is real. So, faced with an eternity of not understanding simple thermometer logic, the environmentalists, including our beloved EPA, decided to fight the truth, rather than switch their basic thinking.

They had been defeated and proven to be corrupt cheats in the environment game, though Al Gore, getting richer every day, continually vouched that the data was right. They could not find real proof but their zeal for Mother Nature caused them to continue their cause when they should have packed it up and left town. But, what would they do for a living. So, they had no choice but to keep the myths alive.

To help them out once the term, "global warming," fell into disrepute, they changed the name of the war to "climate change." It makes me want to laugh out loud! This literally means if it is cold, it is caused by "climate change" and if it is warm it is caused by "climate change." Climate change is their new villain. They don't really want to comment on the notion of the four seasons as that is "weather change," but they also do not want to prove climate change to be able to declare that the climate is changing. Their ideology cannot exist unless they purport the preposterous to be true. And, so they do.

I urge you to not let them win the semantics battle. Let us keep using the term, "global warming." The semantic and the real battle continue on the Internet as mankind tackles the ever present fraud in the global warmer mentality. "Tonyhubble" netted it out perfectly when he said, "It [the rename] means that they cannot be proven wrong, regardless of what actually occurs." Amen! And, that is their goal. So, why do we need the EPA? Why should we pay them $10.5 Billion per year to exist and torment us?

Here we are in 2015, and no matter how hard the laughter comes, nobody on the eco side has admitted that the thesis was incorrect in the first place. Besides, zeal there is funding and of course, the very jobs of the EPA proponents are at stake. Funding would stop if they told the truth. Good environmentalists, even those "fine" people in the EPA, would be forced to discover another hoax if funding stopped.

So, let's stop the EPA funding!

What a great idea!

Chapter 2   Barack Obama Has Awakened a Sleeping Nation?

Gary Hubbell Via Email

When this came into my email box, I was impressed as now I am hard pressed to explain to those not as deeply into what is happening, how the President is quickly destroying America on many fronts. This could be any chapter of any political book about this historical period. It is not specific to the EPA but it sure is a quick look-see into what is going on while we contemplate whether the EPA is bad or good for America.

I need to tell you that I had not intended to write a book about the EPA. I was running for the US Senate in 2012 and to help me understand why things are as bad as they are, I knew that I needed to deeply examine the EPA and its job killing regulations. It was a must as a topic so I could be prepared for my Senate candidacy. The research was the beginning of the prep work for this book.

I already knew a lot about the EPA, but like many of us, I needed to verify my facts. My best avenue for research was to read a lot and then synthesize what I read along with my prior knowledge. My idea was that I would put it into text form that would make it easy to examine and test my hypotheses.

"Kill the EPA" was the natural title of every segment of every essay that I wrote on this topic before this was a book. My intention originally was to stop after just one essay. I naively thought that I could describe the total fallacy of the EPA in just one essay. For a writer, the topic of the "EPA" was a gift that just kept on giving as their faults are so egregious that my research turned out to be far more fruitful than I could ever have imagined.

This second edition book has thirty-four chapters in total and a number of them have multiple parts.

I first verified my original thesis that the agency hurts Americans and that became the major premise. From that I concluded that such an agency does not deserve to exist, and I share the opinion of Ron Paul, in that I too believe the agency should be completely eliminated.

Humans certainly deserve to breathe clean air and eat safe food but this EPA has too many other items in its agenda. Control of the citizenry is at the top of its list. I have concluded that the EPA cannot be trusted to do what is right for America. I am not alone in this belief.

Along the way to this book, I wrote ten original essays to explain this phenomenon known as the EPA. When placed in book form along with some other material, the work blossomed into thirteen chapters. You are reading Chapter 2 of the second edition, which clarifies items from the first edition and contains substantially more important material. Thank you for selecting this book.

The chapters are all here in the hard copy for you to read. There are lots more after this one. In addition to the printed version of the book, during my brief Senate run in 2012, I hosted some of the text for the book on the website, www.kellyforussenate.com. In 2014, this full book in an earlier incarnation could be downloaded for free, one chapter at a time at – one per week, at www.conservativeactionalerts.com. You were also able to read it online at their site. If you tried the link today, you now know it is gone. I will make the book again available online after I get this edition edited and approved for printing.

All pages are copyrighted but you are all welcome to use this book for any non-commercial endeavors that you may choose. My objective is to spread the word and have as many Americans write their Congress as possible to get this agency out of our hair.

If you want your own hard copy of the book in its paper form, it is available at www.conservativebookshop.com Lets Go Publish! is the main publisher of the book.

It will not take you long from here on in to see that I have little regard for the EPA and from my research, I now am sure that they have little regard for you or for me. The difference between us, of course is that they do not pay $10.5 billion per year for your existence or my existence.

My cohorts and I (fellow citizens such as you) pay a whopping $10.5 billion for these charlatan EPA employees to do their best to make life miserable for all of us. If I had been elected senator, I would have done my best to end this travesty. Now, through my books and my writings and my continual pleadings to my representatives from Pennsylvania, I personally lobby for their elimination—so humans can live.

The guerrillas in the EPA will have to leave their Obama fatigues behind and be re-clothed when they come back on the streets after we fire them. Perhaps we can send the tailor who creates Obama's new outfits to help make the EPA's new civilian duds?

By the way, you know who that tailor is—the one who prepares Obama's clothing. It is the tailor who masqueraded and then created the Emperor's clothes with no threads at all. This tailor is highlighted in the Hans Christian Andersen classic, The Emperor's New Clothes. Can you imagine President Obama wearing the tailor's latest designs? He would look just as proud as the Emperor did in the story, which I saw years ago on b/w TV.

We are going to close out this chapter with a tremendously popular email sent around the Internet, forwarded by hundreds of thousands of geeks and/or ordinary users every day. It is that good. This is Gary Hubbell's classic email on Obama waking up the public in the US. Remember, as you read this: Everybody in the EPA works for President Obama.

This President is made of Teflon for sure. He does not want to accept guilt for anything, and he does a good job of staying out of range from the blame. Yet the fact is that when a company puts out a bum product, the CEO, if he or she chooses to be brave, takes the blame. As the CEO of America, this President has not showed any cojones, and instead has blamed others for his failings. I am as surprised as most conservative Americans that this technique has worked so well for him.

Anybody ready for some TEA?

"Barack Obama has awakened a sleeping nation" by Gary Hubbell

The original piece was published by the Aspen Times Weekly in February 2010, just a year after Obama took full control of the government. I requested permission to run this piece from Gary several years ago. Enjoy!

Figure 2-1 – The Aspen Times Web Look

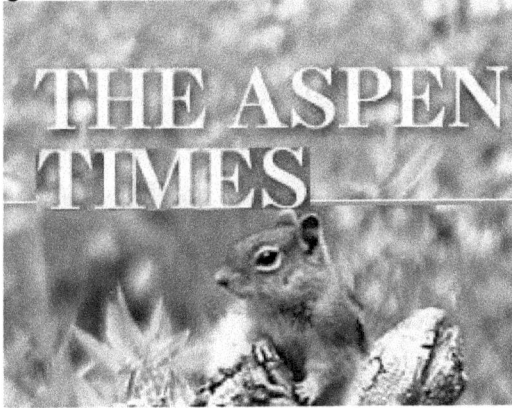

Thank You BHO

Here is Gary's email:

"Barack Obama is the best thing that has happened to America in the last 100 years. Truly, he is the savior of America's future.

Despite the fact that he has some of the lowest approval ratings among recent presidents, history will see Barack Obama as the source of America's resurrection. Barack Obama has plunged the country into levels of debt that we could not have previously imagined; his efforts to nationalize health care have been met with fierce resistance nationwide; TARP bailouts and stimulus spending have shown little positive effect on the national economy; unemployment is unacceptably high and looks to remain that way for most of a decade; legacy entitlement programs have ballooned to unsustainable levels, and there is a seething anger in the populace.

That's why Barack Obama is such a good thing for America. Here's why.

Obama is the symbol of a creeping liberalism that has infected our society like a cancer for the last 100 years. Just as Hitler is the face of fascism, Obama will go down in history as the face of unchecked liberalism. The cancer metastasized to the point where it could no longer be ignored.

Average Americans who have quietly gone about their lives, earning a paycheck, contributing to their favorite charities, going to high school football games on Friday night, spending their weekends at the beach or on hunting trips - they've gotten off the fence. They've woken up. There is a level of political activism in this country that we haven't seen since the American Revolution, and Barack Obama has been the catalyst that has sparked a restructuring of the American political and social consciousness.

Think of the crap we've slowly learned to tolerate over the past 50 years as liberalism sought to re-structure the America that was the symbol of freedom and liberty to all the people of the world. Immigration laws were ignored on the basis of compassion. Welfare policies encouraged irresponsibility, the fracturing of families, and a cycle of generations of dependency. Debt was regarded as a tonic to lubricate the economy. Our children left school having been taught that they are exceptional and special, while great numbers of them cannot perform basic functions of mathematics and literacy. Legislators decided that people could not be trusted to defend their own homes, and stripped citizens of their rights to own firearms.

Productive members of society have been penalized with a heavy burden of taxes in order to support legions of do-nothings who loll around, reveling in their addictions, obesity, indolence, ignorance and "disabilities." Criminals have been arrested and re-arrested, coddled and set free to pillage the citizenry yet again. Lawyers routinely extort fortunes from doctors, contractors and business people with dubious torts.

We slowly learned to tolerate these outrages, shaking our heads in disbelief, and we went on with our lives.
But Barack Obama has ripped the lid off a seething cauldron of dissatisfaction and unrest.

A former Communist is given a paid government position in the White House as an advisor to the president. Auto companies are taken over by the government, and the auto workers' union - whose contracts are completely insupportable in any economic sense - is rewarded with a stake in the company. Government bails out Wall Street investment bankers and insurance companies, who pay their executives outrageous bonuses as thanks for the public support. Terrorists are read their Miranda rights and given free lawyers. And, despite overwhelming public disapproval, Barack Obama has pushed forward with a health care plan that would re-structure one-sixth of the American economy.

Literally millions of Americans have had enough. They're organizing, they're studying the Constitution and the Federalist Papers, they're reading history and case law, they're showing up at rallies and meetings, and a slew of conservative candidates are throwing their hats into the ring. Is there a revolution brewing? Yes, in the sense that there is a keen awareness that our priorities and sensibilities must be radically re-structured. Will it be a violent revolution?

No!.

It will be done through the interpretation of the original document that has guided us for 220 "FANTASTIC" years--- the Constitution. Just as the pendulum swung to embrace political correctness and liberalism, there will be a backlash, a complete repudiation of a hundred years of nonsense. A hundred years from now, history will perceive the year 2010 as the time when America got back on the right track. And for that, we can thank Barack Hussein Obama."

Gary Hubbell is a hunter, rancher, and former hunting and fly-fishing guide. Gary works as a Colorado ranch real estate broker. He can be reached through his website, aspenranchrealestate.com"

In my email, it said: IF YOU AGREE, FEEL FREE TO SHARE THIS

Hubbell's email is not intended to be a history lesson. It is one man's opinion about how bad things have gotten. It does that quite well. I thank Gary Hubbel for writing this and for sending it along on the Internet for us all to enjoy.

Feel free to visit

http://www.aspentimes.com/article/20100228/ASPENWEE
KLY/100229854 for this article and for others you may
enjoy.   On Wednesday October 12, 2011, I contacted
Gary to gain his permission to reprint this article in its
entirety and to credit him and the Aspen Times. His web
site responded at 13:14:19 -0600 (MDT)

Chapter 3 Was Silent Spring Too Loud?

Are good solutions always bad?

There is no question that Rachel Carson's Silent Spring led to greater public awareness of pollution in the 1960s. Was there pollution? Absolutely there was pollution and there still is. Americans and other citizens of the world do need protection from dispassionate corporations who would unscrupulously create an environment in which carcinogens are produced in the industrial process, and there is no accountability.

Rachel Carson's book Silent Spring, way back in 1962 created an awareness of potential hazards of the pesticide DDT. Carson passionately and eloquently questioned humanity's faith in technological progress and she helped set the stage for the environmental movement.

Unfortunately, though environmentalists are always very passionate in saving birds, little fish, and nasty mosquitos, most hold great disdain for humankind as we are the world's greatest polluters. In a world without DDT, thanks to Carson scaring the crap out of the whole world with her book, millions of children all over the world die from malaria each year.

We discuss this in detail in later chapters. The irony is that the scientist who discovered DDT received the Nobel Prize, and the person who took him down was a journalist with an A.B. degree and a huge opinion and an even bigger following. The truth, however, is not something upon which the people have a vote.

Can you be anti-EPA and anti-pollution and "trust but verify" on corporations all at the same time? Absolutely! That describes who I am perfectly. The sins of the EPA are so egregious; however, it has not only outlived its usefulness; it continues to kill children every day.

It kills children by malaria in African, South American, and other third world countries; and it kills asthmatic American children in the USA by denying them the propellant CFC so they can quickly gain the beneficial medicines from their once trusty inhalers.

The EPA as a response to Rachel Carson's Silent Spring has become the moral equivalent of killing a mouse with an A-bomb. Ironically, the EPA would fight for the mouse to be saved even if humans would die. The EPA is a plague worse than the worst plague that could be delivered by a huge herd of mice and rats. You know the names of the plagues. Please include the name EPA among those other killer names.

My position remains that we need to kill the EPA partly because it continues to work on the wrong problems. But, more so than that, the agency has little regard for humankind. They devise cures for prevaricated illnesses. The cures create more havoc and devastation than the supposed diseases.

The EPA is not a people-first agency. People do not even have a ranking in the EPA priority list. As nature first, people come last. The EPA is always concerned about what man is doing to nature and not whether man can survive in nature. One thing for sure, man cannot depend on the EPA for help in surviving. This one man and many others think we should not fund an organization that would prefer we be dead.

Corporate thugs, union thugs, EPA thugs, government thugs, and all political thugs, must be kept tame by the people. Yes, it is a tough task but more and more people are signing up. More and more Americans have simply had enough. Many people I meet every day want to scream out loud, "Get off our backs!" How about you?

The truth about the lies of Silent Spring

Dr. J. Gordon Edwards notes in his powerful expose on Silent Spring, which he titles, "The Lies of Rachel Carson," that despite environmentalists wanting so much for her words to be all true, Rachel Carson did not measure up on the scientific side.

Her words were well-written but not true and in many ways they were intentionally deceitful. Rachel Carson is the patron saint of the EPA, and they take her lying license for granted in the major body of their work. If you are looking for nothing but the truth, do not read Silent Spring and do not visit the EPA web site.

Dr. Edwards and many environmentalists in his camp were delighted that somebody had finally addressed the environment in a meaningful way. However, as he was moving through Carson's book, his enthusiasm diminished. He began to clearly see the big holes in Carson's story. But, Carson made a lot of money promulgating her untruths.

Dr. Edwards is an environmentalist. He is not a conservative as many of us who read this book may be. He is not a journalist like Rachel Carson. He is the real deal. He has been published by the Sierra Club, The Indiana Waltonian, Audubon Magazine, and other environmental magazines. A well-known entomologist, Edwards is not a lightweight on environmental topics.

The following are direct quotes of Dr. J. Gordon Edwards from the cover story in:

http://www.21stcenturysciencetech.com/articles/summ02/ Carson.html

"...As I read the first several chapters I noticed many statements that I realized were false; however, one can overlook such things when they are produced by one's cohorts, and I did just that.

"As I neared the middle of the book, the feeling grew in my mind that Rachel Carson was really playing loose with the facts and was also deliberately wording many sentences in such a way as to make them imply certain things without actually saying them. She was carefully omitting everything that failed to support her thesis that pesticides were bad, that industry was bad, and that any scientists who did not support her views were bad.

"I then took notice of her bibliography and realized that it was filled with references from very unscientific sources. Also, each reference was cited separately each time it appeared in the book, thus producing an impressive array of "references" even though not many different sources were actually cited. I began to lose confidence in Rachel Carson, even though I thought that as an environmentalist I really should continue to support her

"I next looked up some of the references that Carson cited and quickly found that they did not support her contentions about the harm caused by pesticides. When leading scientists began to publish harsh criticisms of her methods and her allegations, it slowly dawned on me that Rachel Carson was not interested in the truth about those topics, and that I really was being duped, along with millions of other Americans.

"As a result, I went back to the beginning of the book and read it all again, but this time my eyes were open and I was not lulled into believing that her motives were noble and that her statements could be supported by logic and by scientific fact. I wrote my comments down in rough draft style, and gathered together the scientific articles that refuted what Carson had reported the articles indicated. It was a most frustrating experience.

"Finally, I began to join the detractors of Silent Spring, and when hearings were held to determine the fate of DDT in various states of this nation, I paid my own way to some of them so that I could testify against the efforts to ban that life-saving insecticide."

…

In coming chapters, we examine much of the underlying evidence that proves Carson was well off the mark. Her main proof comes from begging the argument. Yet, the EPA continues to remain one of her devout disciples.

The quick case for the EPA

It really is stretching truth to find something good about the EPA but let's go. At 18,000 people strong, the EPA is dedicated to destroying the economy of the United States. The choice for those who love America is clear: "The EPA must go." Let's say for argument reasons that we keep the EPA, which is Obama's primo regulatory instrument against the American people. What happens next?

The answer is clear. We would get 18,000 people working against John / Jane Q. Public. But, they would all have jobs. Isn't that enough to keep the employees of the EPA safe from hardship?

But, John Q. Public is US! That's us! How is it a good deal for any of us to keep an agency that wants to eliminate people and protect nature?

Most American people would not even be aware there was a war going on between the EPA and the people. When you are unaware, you most often lose big time. Yet, the EPA would still get its $10.5 billion in salaries and costs per year.

The people would have to deal with things like large fertile farmland areas being banned from using available irrigation. We would get a few more endangered little fish and perhaps a few more bug species that we are prohibited from eating or swatting.

And to help matters if you like the EPA, we would get brownouts and a group of bureaucrats determining how much water, gas, and oil, we are permitted to use. They would also determine how much CO_2 we could exhale. It might be good for them to have the power but not good for US to have to comply with their arbitrary and capricious nature.

In addition to Obamacare's rationing, the EPA would see to it that a lot of other precious items on their lists were rationed. Forget about double dipping. The EPA might not let you get even the first dip. But, they would still be in existence. So, the best reason to keep the EPA is that they will still be in existence. This, ironically is the reason why sane people want them gone.

As a bonus, we would get to turn off our lights because there would be no power available. The EPA hates coal fired electrical plants even if they warm people who otherwise would freeze.

We would get seven to ten percent more unemployment because businesses would have no choice but to close. We would find asthmatic children being denied the use of the best-made inhalers, while permitted to use sub-quality EPA approved inhalers that are just a bit more effective than a placebo. You may not believe me yet, but, please keep reading this whole book, and you will.

Overall, we would get more than we bargained for from an agency commissioned in its formation to help the people. The more research I did for this book, the more I was convinced that this agency has no use for people. It is time to return the favor by electing representatives strong enough to take them on. If your representative likes the EPA, you should not like your representative.

The quick case against the EPA

Now, if we get rid of the EPA, what do we get? We get a bunch of thick headed dinosaurs (the EPA staff) that immediately get pink slips and need new jobs. We also get a lot more happy and productive people (US). We get more jobs and we get businesses that can grow instead of being forced to stagnate and die.

We also get farmers who again can farm on rich, irrigated soil without requiring driver's permits and major government tests to work with tractors and other typical farm equipment. We get a country full of people who are permitted to heat their homes in the winter, cool them in the summer, and light them with Edison's own incandescent light bulb any time when there is darkness.

And, on top of that, we get energy independence from people who want to kill us. Perhaps more importantly, we escape the outright tyranny of the EPA. How does that sound?

Chapter 4   How Did the EPA Get So Bad?

Corporations are not princes either!

Let's take a break from Rachel Carson and the EPA, and take a look at the role of the corporation in government today. The EPA has a habit of defaming many corporations yet it crawls unashamedly into bed with others. We'll eventually talk about all of that. Eventually, we take a look at major legislation such as The Clean Air Act, one of the magical acts of Congress that worked, which brought about the EPA.

Life is a balancing act. Corporations were not even permitted to exist as we know them today in early America because they had previously worn out their welcome in old world civilization. Huge corporations such as the British East India Company had dominated trade in the new world before the revolution. Colonists had long decided from this experience that they wanted no corporations in the New World.

The colonists not only freed themselves from England; they got out from under the yoke of English corporations. You remember the Boston Tea Party and the British East India Company. Such corporations decreased the wealth of the people and controlled everyday activity. As you would expect, they were not held in high regard by early Americans. Until our corporations choose to favor America, Americans should not defer to the wishes of corporations.

The founders were very smart and caring about the people (US) to come. Therefore, they had a healthy respect for the capability of corporations to dominate all business through ruthless, nasty practices. So, after fighting a revolution to end their exploitation by corporate powers and huge governments, the colonists wisely limited the role of corporations and governments in America. No longer were corporations permitted to have a role in elections, public policy and other aspects of life. But, later politicians reversed much of their work.

Even in the beginning of the nation, corporations were permitted to conduct business only which benefitted the public. As for the government, legislators held fast to the Constitution so that bad men could never appear in the future and claim they were good men.

Besides God's Bible for "we the people," the Constitution became America's credo for all citizens, one by one. It is not for the powerful. The Constitution was created to protect the least of Americans, most of US, especially the poor from the more powerful, especially those whose power comes from groups of people who have formed corporations.

To assure that citizens, not collectives or agencies or other artificial entities controlled our country, the founders carved out very limiting rules, which corporations were required to follow. In essence, they reluctantly permitted corporations to exist but not on their own terms.

The rules made corporations diminutive participants in US trade. They were not permitted to gain the power that they hold today.

You may know the story of the legal slippery slope. It also applies in most aspects of life. Any lawyer will remind us that once in, an entity gains power. Stopping the "getting in" is the job of those wanting to protect an organization. Most often the newly admitted become more and more powerful until eventually, their power is a burden on the population that permitted them to exist.

Because of this fear, for the first 100 years after the US revolution v England, corporations were kept in check by honest legislators. Today, most people think the term "honest legislators" is not much more than an oxymoron. Because we elect thieves and scoundrels into office continually, we Americans unfortunately do get the government we deserve.

The early public still had memories passed down about the issues with the English corporations and they wanted none of that for America. The founders assured that. Citizens controlled corporations; and through their legislatures, they prohibited corporations from taking any action that legislators did not specifically allow.

Much control over corporations came from the corporate charters, which are still granted by the states and not by the federal government. It was the states, and not the federal government that were in control of corporations.

The most effective tool in the founding days was the notion of an expiration date or as it was called, a time limit. Corporations had an expiration date and were therefore forced out of business after being operational for a set time period.

They were chartered to exist for only a specific period of time and when the time was up, they ceased to exist. Their assets were then divided among the shareholders. This is a great idea even today.

There were lots of other controls, which kept corporate power to a minimum. In many ways, they were the good old days. Greed, however, is a powerful force of change.

During the first half of the 19th Century, the Supreme Court tried numerous times to usurp the power of the states' charters in regulating corporations. The public was outraged and the states fought back with modifications to their Constitutions and other measures to assure that the federal government would not steal their power.

Eventually, it seemed that the Supreme Court had heard the people and the states. In the 1855 case of Dodge v. Woolsey, for example, the court reaffirmed state's powers over "artificial bodies." Of course these artificial bodies were known to the citizens of the day as corporations.

The Captains of Industry continued to enrich themselves and expand their businesses by forming more and more corporations and industry alliances. They were not about to be stopped. They kept pressing in one way or another for politicians to view the corporate light in their favor.

They worked subtly and openly with politicians and crooked legislators and eventually they were able to gain more legitimate power for their corporate entities.

Though it is unpleasant to consider, they gained much power through quid pro quo actions with those corrupt officials, which they could buy-off. These corporate moguls were able to "hire" legislators and judges who believed the limits of corporate power could and should be expanded. How convenient!

Eventually, the courts and the legislatures acknowledged the power of the well-to-do chieftains and granted their wishes. Corporate power was on the rise. Only an educated and active public could have kept its power in check. Unfortunately for America today, the public chooses to not understand the things that have secured its survival for so many years. And, so we get the government we deserve.

Why do people go bad?

Greed is a powerful motivator and lust for power is a close second. Early Americans had an America almost as exactly as they had wanted it, without major league important entities like corporations or huge government agencies such as the EPA.

The early colonists were not interested in giving up the sovereignty of the people to forces more powerful than ordinary citizens. Once the powerful band together to control the people's government, the people are inevitably left behind.

Without a vigilant watchdog against the government, corporations in the late 1800 period gained substantial power inch by inch. They had patience and they bought off as many legislators as they could afford.

They grew stronger, and for the most part, ordinary people were unaware of the slippery slope of the power creep, and the nasty ways the titans used their power.

When power is not in the hands of the people, the government and the courts become easier prey. The industry captains about 100 years or more ago had their way.

By keeping lawmakers and judges squarely in their hip pockets, corporate mahoffs were able to freely reinterpret the US Constitution to transform the meaning of common law doctrines to suit their selfish purposes, rather than serve the common good.

Unfortunately for us all, it got even worse. In 1886, the Supreme Court stole more states' rights when it noted that a corporation henceforth was to be treated as a "natural person."

Once corporations had the right of personhood, they increased their control over resources, jobs, commerce, politicians, even judges and the law. For 100 years after the founding, the corporate powers were kept in check, but ultimately corruption and powerful corporate titans ruled the day.

Corruption of public officials is one of the most insidious enemies of freedom and liberty. Corporations have the resources to buy people who are weak. As the first means of preserving the Republic for as long as possible, the Founders protected the people against such huge sources of power.

Unfortunately, since that time, the people's representatives, the later congresses of our nation sold out the people to the corporations and permitted the rich and powerful to gain control of the government. Today's Congresses seem to continue the tradition that America and Americans are on the auction block.

As another means of guaranteeing the Republic, the founders provided elections to assure that the people were in control of the government.

The Founders did not believe that the people would be hoodwinked. They believed that the people would elect the best citizens to hold office for brief periods and that the citizens would then go back to their farms or work places after serving in Congress. They did not expect that the people would reelect thieves into office.

The Founders perhaps did not realize that when the thieves gained power, they could grant privileges to the commoners. Then, who would stop them?

A problem with human nature is that there are many people who like to pick the thief they know and permit them to represent their needs to the government. For helping the cheats get elected, the people are then rewarded by the thieves with largesse, such as jobs for their children and other important benefits. None of this helps America. Consequently, bad agencies such as the EPA can thrive by threat or by promise.

To keep such political favors coming their way, the people can become as corrupt as the rascals they elect to assure that spoils and largesse continue to come their way. It is a shame but we all know it is true. We get the government we deserve.

Giving up one's vote and taking favors that are not justified is just as corrupt as politicians taking from the corporations. So, to straighten out this mess, and to defang the EPA, and the corporations and the causes the EPA represents, we must all become better people. Only then can we the people be worthy of better representation and therefore better representatives. Only then will we choose the best representatives for the country.

As another major means of assuring the Republic, the Founders gave us the second most profound document of all time after the Bible – the Constitution. Like other constitutions, the Constitution of the United States of America is a set of fundamental principles and/or established precedents according to which a state or other organization is governed.

Our Constitution is a most eloquent document and though short, it is very comprehensive. It has been amended twenty-seven times over 200+ years. The first ten amendments, including freedom of speech, are known as the Bill of Rights.

The Constitution, when strictly adhered to by government, is intended to control even the most corrupt of politicians. But, the people are not absolved of participation. We must pay attention!

As we have seen, even with all these instruments of excellent government, as provided by the Founders, we continue to foster greed and corruption. Humans are not perfect, and we are prone to sin. We, the citizenry, must become better people to deserve a better government. I believe we can do that if we choose to do so.

I have introduced the rise of corporate power in this essay because they are a corrupting influence on our politicians. If the corporations were not so powerful and so self-serving, the people would be able to again control them and keep them from committing acts against the people, including acts against the environment.

Chapter 5   No More Killing the Environment

Yes, the air must be clean and breathable

In the 1960's in the post-war boom, more and more people were driving those magnificent automobiles of those times and the air quality, from exhaust emissions along with corporate smokestacks was becoming noticeably bad. In Los Angeles, for example, on a few particularly bad days, it was so bad that some people even died. They could not breathe with all the smog— (aka smoke that hovered like fog).

Congress took action at the time. They passed the Air Quality Act first in 1967 and later the Clean Air Act in 1970. In many ways, enforcement of the Clean Air Act made the air much better though nothing good ever happens over night. It takes time for improvements. And, improvements did come and the air became very breathable in California again.

The rest of the nation was not suffering as the people were in California. But, all states benefitted from this mostly good legislation. This was one of the greatest acts of Congress for all Americans. No argument here!

The formal objective of the acts were:

(1) to protect and enhance the quality of the Nation's air to promote the public health and welfare and the productive capacity of its population;

(2) to initiate and accelerate a national research and development program to achieve the prevention and control of air pollution;

(3) to provide technical and financial assistance to state and local governments in connection with the development and execution of their air pollution prevention and control programs; and

(4) to encourage and assist the development and operation of regional air pollution prevention and control programs.

Clearly the most important of these acts was # 1 and because of this act, the air several years after the legislation and even today is much better. It got better fairly quickly in a five year period after the act had become law. Air quality can always get better but from this experience we learned that we could whack out the real bad problems, but then we should move in incremental steps.

For years after this act, people no longer died from bad air, even in Los Angeles. The predecessor of the "EPA" had solved the problem. Yet, after the problem was solved and the EPA came into existence, the EPA would not go away!

In today's world, while we are all breathing major improvements in air quality from Nixon's actions, there is no reason to punish companies who are negligibly affecting our breathing if at all. The EPA, a survivalist and power seeking organization should have taken a victory lap and had a party for it had done good! Instead they decided to put businesses out of businesses with their new found power.

Why should it serve the EPA well to put farmers out of business and create food shortages; to put coal and oil and gas companies out of business and create energy shortages; or to wreak other havoc on Americans that is unjustified? You have to ask them. Once their success was glorified, why did they want to ruin America?

The answer is simple. The EPA have become the spokespeople for the ideologues who are also the environmental doomsayers. Like jihadists ready to blow themselves up for a good cause, these people are ready to sacrifice all of humanity for Mother Nature. Being part of humanity, they too must go! They are whackos. Sorry if I was the first to say it!

Their mantra and credo is that if humans cannot be eliminated, this planet, the good earth, is doomed. Yet, they choose not to release their short survivor list and with abortion as a major credo, maybe they have already gained communications with the plants and animals who will take over when they strap themselves at the end with explosives when they finally eradicate the plague of humans on EARTH.

The Congress gave no constraints to the power of the EPA, and Obama has given them full power. And so, the whackos seemingly have no constraints. Thus, the EPA believes there should be no countervailing authority to their power, and they simply should be permitted to do as they please. The needs of people do not matter to this agency, since people do not matter, period. Just the earth!

The Clean Air Act

The Clean Air Act came out in 1970. It evolved from the Air Quality Act of 1967 and it has been "improved" by a series of detailed control requirement amendments in 1970, 1977, and 1990. The regulatory parts of the Clean Air Act are as follows:

(1) All new and existing sources are prohibited from emitting pollution that exceeds ambient air quality levels.

(2) Ambient air quality program is implemented through state implementation plans (SIPs).

(3) New sources are subject to more stringent control technology and permitting requirements.

The Act addressed specific pollution problems, most of which scientists agreed were real. These included hazardous air pollution and visibility impairment.

(4) In 1990, a fourth program was added - a comprehensive operating permit program to focus in one place, all of the Clean Air Act requirements that apply to a given source of pollution.

Man and Nature Together

A balance must be made between the requirements of environmental acts and the ability to live. When man and nature conflict, it is not man that should choose to die.

Please note this major Act was not passed by the EPA. It was passed by our US Congress to help the people gain clean air. It was a good idea. We should not kill Congress; just the EPA, which has gotten way out of hand.

Congress is vital to our nation's health and survival but we could use a nice new broom to sweep many of the most entrenched and corrupt politicians out the door.

Quite often we don't know why the EPA does what it does. The Clean Air Act was and continues to be good for America. Most of the good in the act, however, has already been completed, and it was done well. The EPA has done nothing so substantial in comparison.

Having a group of guerrillas, such as the EPA using semi-terroristic acts to harass Americans at home or in their businesses is not a good idea and it was never the intention of President Nixon or the institution of the EPA. What of the EPA said you cannot grow hybrid corn or tomatoes or lettuce in your personal garden? Would that be OK?

That is the big problem with the EPA. Now that the air is reasonably clean and states have huge environmental departments themselves, the people can breathe without the job-killing, and people killing EPA. Keep the feds out of the states. Don't we all agree?

Clean Air Update to 2016

JunkScience.com is a group of real scientists with a mission to debunk the opinions of pseudoscientists and biased Marxists from the EPA. If the EPA were not so dangerous and dishonest, it might be fun reading about how junkscience.com takes on the EPA and wins consistently. Liars typically do not win arguments.

Recently, the group obtained through the Freedom of Information Act, a number of documents describing human clinical experiments involving high exposures to particulate matter conducted by the University of Rochester with EPA funding. The end result was they found that the EPA was reporting data falsely to justify its continued existence long after the clean air problem in the USA had been solved.

Without putting you through the EPA rhetoric justifying its findings, the EPA falsified the risk of inhaling airborne fine particulate matter (PM), i.e., soot or dust much smaller in diameter than the width of a human hair in its December 2012 **Federal Register** notice tightening the PM ambient air quality standards. In the document, they note that short-term exposure to PM. in outdoor air can cause a fatal heart attack. At the University of Rochester, human study subjects up to age 60 were exposed to much-more-than-normal outdoor air levels of PM.

Despite exposing human study subjects to 20 TIMES the level of PM. in outdoor air, the University of Rochester researchers told the institutional review board responsible for approving the experiment that the EPA's alleged emergency room visits and deaths related to heart attack are, in reality, "small" and "theoretical" even in those with "severe coronary artery disease"!

In other words, their report was bogus. EPA's PM rules wreak havoc on the American economy to the tune of hundreds of billions of dollars. Oddly enough, despite their erroneous methodologies and conclusions, these studies served as the primary justification for the agency's ozone standards, which had been anticipated to be the most expensive EPA regulations of all time — all built on demonstrable lies. Moving forward to 2015, the EPA claims that the tightened ozone standards would provide big health benefits, but as numerous analysts have found and have commented—the EPA's health assessment "does not withstand scrutiny." Yet, this is one of the President's favorite agencies. Why?

Chapter 6   Who Do Chemical Corporations Care About?

Corporations are built to survive!

So, now that we have defined the notion of a corporation and we looked at the general points of the clean air acts, why can't everything just be OK? Left on their own, we know that corporations are beneficent citizens and will always do what they can to make America a better place – even if it cost them a bit of bottom line profits.

Of course I am kidding. I sure wish that was the case but corporations have demonstrated for the most part only selfish motives. Their most powerful motivation is survival. Their second motive is profit.

Perhaps corporations are simply enterprises of self-interest, whose one and only goal after survival is to increase shareholder profitability. I would agree to that if the corporate moguls would agree. Corporations are surely more like greedy collectors than beneficent benefactors.

Corporations do anything to survive. When environmental regulations come their way; for the sake of survival, and no other reason, corporations will do for the public only what is needed to survive, and typically not much more. When regulations are such that they are unreasonable and unworkable, corporations as well as we the people will do our best to not comply so that we all can all survive.

Are corporations really bad for the environment?

Yes, it is true that large unincorporated entities and large corporations have been documented to be some of the worst polluters of all time. Moreover, they have been documented to have been engaged in systematic cover-ups to avoid detection. Escape and evasion are always their best avenue for survival—along with a good lawyer!

Perhaps if it were possible to have a reasonable agency, not a yes agency, but not a no agency such as the EPA, we might get better results from all our corporate entities.

Corporate chemical scams?

As human beings, we can consider that when the EPA guerillas are outside our fences, we would be most typically inclined to hide our important stuff. If you are a corporation and your only fear is the wrath of an unhinged EPA looking for environmental issues in your plant that affect Americans, would you not expect the same—even though it is not right.

The US chemical industry, in particular, intrinsically believes that it can be put out of existence with one bad report. Like Puff, you're gone! With today's McCarthy driven cutthroat EPA, they are 100% correct.

So, before a chemical company concludes that it can ever comply with regulations, as a rule, it hides from regulations and the regulators using whatever escape and evasion techniques that it can invent.

The companies in many ways are like kids that discovered they had actually eaten so many cookies that the bottom of the jar was beginning to appear. Whoops! chemical companies know when they are in trouble as soon as they get into trouble. They see the bottom of the jar immediately!

To protect themselves and to survive, chemical companies conjure plans over time to privately fund research. Their objective is not compliance but a desire to gain information needed to devise responses to any potential threat from agencies or the unforgiving environmentalists.

Perhaps if they thought the EPA was a fair and reasonable agency (not that they needed to jump in bed with them), corporations would spend their dollars incrementally improving their predicament, rather than paying tons of lawyers to make the problems they fear go away on technicalities.

Industry understands the risks of pollution better than anybody but the leaders of the companies do not trust that they can share identified risks with the EPA or the public. It would be like setting the number at one for their days would then be numbered.

"Guerillas in fatigues," which is how I would characterize the EPA do not evoke the notion that cooperation is the best strategy.

Therefore businesses, large and small, chose escape and evasion as their strategy and lawyers, are very good at such techniques.

Company tactics are typically to release just enough information to reassure people of the safe nature of the company's products, and that they work. After that, companies along with their lawyers will cover up any uncertainties or potential problems tirelessly, to stop any government regulation or intervention.

Plastics in the Food Industry

As you are sipping on your water bottle or a Gatorade right now, or drinking a nice cold cocktail in a huge plastic goblet, you may be oblivious to the possibility of toxins from the plastic seeping into your libation.

Yet, we know from published reports that certain plastics have been found to be more toxic than others. In the 1970's however, when chemical companies were all excited about the potential use of plastic in the food and beverage industry, the data was not always available that things were safe or unsafe.

Don't forget the Chemical Company's credo of escape and evasion. At this time, government was needed to save Americans from corporations that would serve us anything if it gave them larger profits.

You may remember or you may have read that in the 1970's negative data emerged from European investigators that certain plastics were linked to cancer. Can you imagine how this spooked the chemical industry? Plastics were becoming the most successful products ever produced from chemistry techniques.

Yet, there were potential health dangers. What would you do if you knew there was even a potential risk of poison from a food container? That's why chemical producers felt escape and evasion was their best tactic.

Companies were worried that the public might view all plastics as threatening to health if there was full disclosure, and so items like plastic wrap, hairsprays, floor coverings, and a ton of other consumer products would be at risk.

Feeling the heat, the US chemical industry's response was to deceive the government and mislead the public in order to hide the link between plastic and any potential for health dangers. The EPA was not a good and thoughtful partner to industry so industry chose to ignore the EPA 100% for their own survival.

By the way, if you want your business to survive, the EPA is the last organization you would call in to help you with an E-issue. The EPA, persistently and religiously follows its "love nature first" agenda. Because of this, one might think that there was an EPA war against chemical companies.

Contrary to popular belief, however, it was not the EPA agency that blew the lid on chemical company issues.

In 1973, the EPA was just a startup agency. It was the US Food and Drug Administration (FDA) that took on the chemical companies.

Today, the FDA often is forced to take orders from the EPA. Back in the early 1970's however, the FDA was the lead agency in discovering that plastic liquor and wine bottles were leaching vinyl chloride into the liquor and wine.

Ultimately the FDA banned its use for liquor bottles. Today, Boxed wines with the special plastic bag inserts are considered food safe as are specially made plastics for liquor containers.

The kind of plastic that booze comes in is called polyethylene terephthalate (PET). This leeches much less toxin than the other types of plastic bottles. Most of those of us, who consume such products, are noticeably still alive. Overall, the FDA considers these safe today but then again, there is nothing like glass.

There are some seniors of today who are thankful that the FDA found the problem a long time ago. In the 1970's many of today's oldsters were just in their late teens and early 20's. Looking back, however, the penniless college coed of that era would not have had to worry anyway as the popular beverages of the time for the *"I'm broke, how about you crowd!"* were Ripple and Swizzle and other potent "wine-like" products.

These were packaged in glass containers. The contents might kill you but the container was safe. Many swear that within the bottle nothing of consequence came from even a single grape. It was a mystery—a product of America's finest chemistry. Some might call it *"alcohol from thin air."*

Ripple and Swizzle were the lowest cost products (rotgut) that a young person with limited funds could buy. It seems the only ones whose brains were affected negatively now serve in Congress. We know it was not caused by the plastic. Perhaps it was the smoke.

One of the honest industry studies of the day, did find that vinyl chloride residues from bottles and packages had also migrated into vinegar, apple cider, vegetable oil, mineral oil and onto meats. Over time, after these variants of plastic products were withdrawn, better and safer food-grade plastic products were developed.

The FDA is continually double checking that all is OK, and for that I am grateful. I almost trust the FDA, but its being under the thumb of the EPA in today's world makes me more skeptical than I once was. The FDA has its own issues but they actually do protect the people from the corporations. Under FDA guidelines when new packaging materials are developed for food use, the FDA reviews the submitted test data and must be satisfied with the product for its intended use before it gives the OK.

The FDA checks out a lot of factors in its attempt to assure human safety. For plastics, it checks the migration potential and the substances with which they are made. The objective of course is for the packaging not to migrate into the food.

Tests are conducted to assure that there is just a minimal amount of transfer between a plastic package and the food it contains and that any transfer does not pose a risk to human health. The FDA's mission is to assure that humans are safe from factors that affect food and drugs. The rule of thumb continues to be that if you can taste the plastic, discard the container.

The EPA operates differently from the FDA. From my perspective, they work like a bunch of thugs, with their major purpose to assure that nature is not harmed by man. If it were up to the EPA, I would bet that the harmful plastic products would still be on the market as it would shorten human life, an arguable EPA goal.

In this way, each human being would have less of an impact on nature. Maybe that is too harsh a thought. Maybe not! I have no proof of this per se, just a conclusion formed by reading and observation.

In summary, the FDA is mostly good; the EPA is mostly bad. Please do not credit the EPA for anything about plastics.

Chapter 7 A Few Outrageous Environment Responses

Conservatives are on fire

There is a great group of conservatives -- **Conservatives on Fire** at http://conservativesonfire.wordpress.com. They offer a smorgasbord of conservative oriented stories on the various government agencies. So, after explaining FDA, USDA, and EPA as I have done so far, I want to say that the FDA is mostly good. I think that is the correct conclusion. But, in today's world the EPA holds the upper hand to all other agencies that purportedly try to make better the issues in people's lives.

The EPA unfortunately is downright nasty and corrupt and therefore very dangerous to the economy, and to humans in general. Yes, the other federal agencies also get carried away with their excessive power, but mostly they hold by their adopted charters. The EPA seems to chart its own course with the blessings of the Miffintiff in Chief of the Keystone Pipeline Postponement Project (KPPP).

The charters of other agencies, unlike the charter of the EPA; is to help the country with real issues, not political notions. Their charters are not to mess up the country. Moreover, they typically like to help the people at large, rather than position people as subservient to nature, as the biggest part of any problem to be addressed. They are not in concert with the opinions of the EPA as a whole. But, the EPA of today lords over them with a boot on neck demand for obedience.

Conservatives on fire (COF) is a group that is up in arms over the FDA, USDA, and EPA, who they refer to as "Obama's Storm Troopers in Action." They got many of their stories originally from the Daily Caller but their new blog posts are ripe with comments about most government agencies under Obama. A commenter at the end of a number of stories noted the TSA also needs to be on the list of bad agencies and the COF agreed. We agree.

Conservatives on fire (COF) think that the governmental agencies charged with monitoring and "helping" us are all out of control and they picked these several particular stories because they "make their blood boil."

At first, in the stories we show, you will be inclined to laugh. Please hold back the laughter because unlike some light-hearted stuff in this book, this may seem silly, but it touches those directly affected in a very hurtful way. In many ways, we are all affected when these agencies are let out on the loose, typically with a bunch of Democrats backing their every mordant action.

Outrageous Story # 1

The first story that we tell has to do with the FDA and an Amish farmer. The FDA had an agenda to destroy the farmer and the farmer had an agenda to survive government oppression.

In April 2010, federal agents raided the dairy farm of Dan Allgyers in Pennsylvania. The Amish farmer produces unpasteurized milk on his farm and, until this fiendish act was discovered, he sold it to families who prefer dairy products in their natural state.

The sale of unpasteurized milk across state borders has been illegal under federal law since 1987. States control the laws of milk within their own borders.

Clever farmers and willing customers have been able to make it all work OK for them without government interference. Some form private clubs where raw milk is a benefit of club membership. Others get into more formal relationships, and some simply do it sub-rosa. Uncle Sam does not appreciate their little tricks to get to drink the best milk available.

Selling unpasteurized milk at the retail level is legal only within ten US states and only if the seller has a permit. Seven states permit licensed sales on the farm site. Eleven additional states permit unlicensed milk sales on the farm site, but some of these states have limits on the amount of say goat's milk that can be sold.

On the "legal" side of the unpasteurized milk issue, there are also eight states that permit what are called herdshares / cowshares as long as they are registered with the state.

Finally, seventeen states have declared that unpasteurized milk is contraband and is thus illegal, period. This is quite a bit of potential legal trouble for an innocent little product like milk; don't you think?

Herdshares / Cowshares

It is not particularly intuitive what a herdshare or a cowshare actually is. So let me give you an example. Let's say Joe Milkman wants his family to be able to drink unpasteurized "natural" milk just as it comes from the cow or goat or sheep or other animal. He can join with a number of other families (often in the low hundreds) as shareholders in a dairy farm.

Let's say Joe's required investment is $225 for three shares. In some organizations, this would entitle him to a partial ownership of a farm's say with 15 cows. One or more hundred others share the cows also. To seal the deal, Joe would also agree to a maintenance fee of say $80 a month which theoretically covers the other costs and the labor.

In this scenario, it is probable, depending on the state and the share contract that Joe's three shares would entitle him to three gallons of milk each week. Depending on the arrangement with the herd / share manager, the milk might even be delivered to drop-off points in various communities as an important convenience to the milk shareholders. The bottom line is that shareholder / consumer pays a shared ownership fee and the manager of the farm assures they get their milk, even if may not be delivered.

We know from civics classes that The Constitution advances states' rights above all other rights, except the peoples' rights—and that includes the Federal Government. The people reign supreme in the US.

But, we also know from the April 2014 Cliven Bundy / Nevada story how intrusive the Federal Government can be if it aims itself against states' rights and regular Americans.

Now that we understand the milk issue itself, let's bring the story to the present. We know that back in 1987 the FDA determined that there was 'some' risk to consuming raw milk and it assured passage of a federal law prohibiting the sale of unpasteurized milk across state lines.

However, more people than the FDA could count believed that there were actual health benefits to drinking raw milk and they wanted raw milk for their families. To get around the federal law, and the laws in the states prohibiting sale of raw milk products, they worked with dairy farmers to form private clubs, which allowed club members to buy the milk they wanted.

Now, let's go back to the outrageous story from April 2010. Federal agents surrounded and entered the Amish dairy farm of Dan Allgyers in Pennsylvania. FDA "storm troopers" put a stop to Farmer Dan's illegal operation. A number of his customers were not from Pennsylvania, which gave the feds jurisdiction.

Like a chapter from the "Untouchables," FDA agents without Elliott Ness in charge, infiltrated the buyers' group by posing as customers and placing orders for delivery across state lines. Can you see a guy like Ness with a sledge hammer, smashing the contraband? Do any of us think justice was served in this case?

The storm troopers stirred-up a hornets' nest because of this action. Yet, even Ron Paul, who took an active roll in the dispute, could not force justice to be served. The farmer was able to join a group protesting the FDA's heavy-handed approach to raw dairy but eventually the effort failed.

Most of the protesters were getting their products from Farmer Dan, and were looking forward to a Ron Paul-sponsored bill to prevent the FDA from getting in theirs and Dan's business in the future.

Ron Paul was the best person on freedom and liberty in the country from whom Farmer Dan could expect help. But in this upside down world in which Edison's light bulb and sixteen ounce Bloomberg drinks can be outlawed, our judicial system voted for the nanny state over individual rights.

Doesn't it make you wonder who in the world thinks this is one of America's important issues? How many more of these costly yet worthless searches and seizures shall we pay for before Americans take back our freedoms. When a harmless Amish man is targeted by federal officials, while our embassy in Benghazi is left defenseless, and we have money to attack milk plunderers, our priorities are certainly not right.

Purists may say that selling raw milk across state lines is a federal crime. I bet the lobbyists from the huge dairies that make tons from pasteurized milk have had some input into that deal. For Dan Allgyers, all he had was his farm. It cost him his livelihood. For his customers, it took away an American choice. The Farmer shut down his farm in 2012. A progressive federal judge sided with the FDA and put Farmer Dan out of business. Bet you the judge was a Democrat!

Ron Paul is no longer in Congress but he has not given up the fight. You gotta love Ron Paul. He sees the milk matter, the light bulb matter, and the 16-oz drink issues as matters of personal freedom. The former Congressman is very pleased that Rep. Thomas Massie has picked up the torch. No action, no matter how it looks along the way is assured. Wait until the dairy lobby starts wining and dining our corrupt representatives!

Thomas Massie R-KY introduced two bills in March 2014. He got help from Congresswoman Chellie Pingree D–ME as well as from a bipartisan coalition of 18 other lawmakers. Together, they introduced legislation to improve consumer food choices and to protect local farmers from federal interference.

The two bills – the "Milk Freedom of Act of 2014" and the "Interstate Milk Freedom Act of 2014" – are the first in a series of "food freedom" bills that Rep. Massie plans to introduce in 2014. These are still not laws so let's reserve applause until the process is complete but, in the meantime to do our part, let's send our representatives some friendly messages that we are watching.

A Second Outrageous Story

This story has to do with the USDA and a few little bunny rabbits. It will make you laugh before you cry. Let's take a look at the story:

Like many businesses, this little experiment began as a hobby. The Dollarhite family in Nixa, Missouri were hoping to teach their teenage son responsibility. They saw the bunny rabbit business the same way we might view a lemonade stand.

All of a sudden, the business was successful. Not only did their customers notice what they were doing, the federal government also took notice. They had sold several hundred rabbits over a two year period, and just like the milk crime above, this bunny rabbit crime had to be dealt with by a heavy government hand.

One day the family woke up to discover they were in debt to the government to the tune of a $90,643. It was a "reduced" fine for not complying with the law. The USDA said by law the Dollarhite's had to cease and desist in the sale of bunny rabbits, and pay the fine.

Figure 7-11

Ironically and quite unfairly, the fine came more than a year after authorities insisted the business be shut down. The family complied by immediately halting their part-time business and they liquidated their equipment.

For selling a few hundred bunny rabbits, don't you think that a fine of over $90,000 is a bit steep? The family's lawyer also thought so too.

Their attorney wrote back: "My client rejects that proposal..." Attorney Richard Anderson sent a formal letter in which he noted that according to USDA's own literature, its 6,000 annual enforcement cases average 'a penalty of $333.33 per case. He asked how it was appropriate for the Dollarhite's to face a penalty of $90,643.00.'

With an average case fine of $333, anybody with half a brain would conclude that anything approaching just a thousand dollars would be overkill for the USDA storm troopers. You won't believe what a USDA spokesperson had to say:

USDA spokesman Sacks agreed that the $90,643 fine looked curious for sure. However, he defended it by insisting it was necessary for the USDA to punish violators who choose not to register their businesses.

Sacks argued that in this way, legitimate businesses that have registered and paid the government all of the associated fees may find value in their registration. He noted that this fine would make sure that businesses across the country would register. Otherwise, like the Dollarhite's, they too would find themselves on the USDA's radar screen for inspections of potential violations, and the imposition of large fines.

The crux of the problem was that almost nobody but the USDA knew about the regulations. Yet, lack of knowledge of the law is no excuse for going afoul of even an obscure federal regulation. The statute they violated was one that prohibits non pet stores from selling more than $500 worth of rabbits to a pet store without a license from the U.S. Department of Agriculture (USDA). Under the law, pet stores themselves are exempt from regulation.

It gets worse. After hearing nothing for such a long time, the Dollarhites were told that they had three months to pay the $90,643 fine or else they would face additional fines totaling nearly $4 million. We must keep in mind that this was for selling a total of $4,600 worth of rabbits that netted the family a mere $200 in profits. It was a respectable little business / hubby built solely to teach a teenager how to be a man.

Recently after a lot of bad publicity and direct Congressional intervention, the USDA backed down and offered to waive the fee provided that the Dollarhites stay out of the Rabbitry business. Additionally, they can had to agree to never apply for a license, and they had to endure one final inspection to ensure they no longer bred rabbits. The remaining rabbits on their property also needed to be counted and documented.

This story may be over but in researching it, I discovered that the Dollarhites are not the only people the thugs from the USDA have harassed.

Ironically, the EPA is the biggest thug in the US agency business. It gets its power by joining into partnerships with other agencies such as the FDA and the USDA to increase its reach.

Ask yourself a few questions about this travesty and the many more to come: Is the FDA becoming a partner with the USDA and the FDA in various undertakings not an awful lot like HAL deciding that it should control the humans in the Movie 2001. How about the EPA with its expanded powers controlling humans today? If Congress wanted its agencies to merge or form partnerships, why is that not in the law?

Chapter 8   A few More Outrageous Responses

Outrageous Story # 3

On May 24, 2011, the Texas Senate read on the floor for the first time HB 1937, which bans the TSA and any other State or Federal Government official from using a "pat-down" without probable cause as a condition for entering an airplane or a public building.

Most of us have gotten backhanded by the Transportation Safety Administration (TSA) as they prove to their satisfaction that we are not terrorists. Texas, a fully incorporated state of the US, regardless of the thinking of the thugs at the TSA, is permitted to make laws governing Texas.

Yet, the TSA, claiming to be "bigger than Texas," sent a letter to Texas noting that if the state passed this law, which would make pat-downs illegal and a felony in the state, that the TSA would impose a no-fly zone over Texas.

After State Senator Dan Patrick, one of the sponsors, delivered a very impassioned speech in support of the bill, calling it a come and take it moment for Texas, he withdrew the bill from consideration that evening, without even allowing it to come to a vote. I regret to say that the feds are bigger than Texas. Literally, the feds and their henchmen in the TSA are very grabby for power.

Their brazen, unconstitutional, illegal threats against Texas are enough to bring the founders out of their deep sleep to recast the parts of the Constitution the federal government does not understand—a.k.a. the limits of federal power.

Senator Patrick's withdrawal did not end the Texas issue. As it was again being discussed, Infowars.com described the matter quite succinctly in these words:

"Aside from all the constitutional minutia, the fact is that a police officer, an FBI agent, a park ranger, or anyone else in a position of authority cannot legally stick their hands down an individual's pants without probable cause in any situation, so why should the TSA be any different?"

Unfortunately for America, after the Texas House passed the bill that would make it a misdemeanor for TSA agents to "intentionally, knowingly, or recklessly [touch] the anus, sexual organ, buttocks, or breast of the other person, including touching through clothing, or touching the other person in a manner that would be offensive to a reasonable person," the bill did not pass the Texas Senate.

Male Texas Senators with the item in discussion had apparently detached and shipped their own personal cojones to Mexico for refurbishment. With their items safely in Mexico, they defeated the bill as passed by the Texas House. So ends the Texas No Fly Zone story

What a shame. If the US is ever going to get states' rights back, it will be through the efforts of great states like Texas. As a Texas wannabe, I think Texans should simply vote real Texans into the Senate next chance they get.

The ultimate outrageous Story – No hope in sight!

This is the ultimate outrageous story. In April 2013, the US Senate held a confirmation hearing for Gina McCarthy. She was President Obama's nominee to head the Environmental Protection Agency (EPA). She received the nomination and now she leads the agency. That is bad news for the future of America.

Figure 8-1

I thank the Heritage Foundation for always providing substantial analysis on items affecting our freedom. The EPA is a parasitic freedom stealing agency and thankfully again, they are constantly within the radar range of the Heritage Foundation. But, their chief parasite is also a predator.

This last outrageous story in this chapter has to do with how much damage President Obama's EPA plans to do now that it is a year too late to stop his progressive liberal Marxist environmental whacko nominee, Gina McCarthy.

Her tenure at the EPA has already begun the continuation of the policies that are leading our nation down a path to misery by governmental choice. President Obama sent his signal by selecting McCarthy last year.

For years, we all know and it cannot be denied that our President is not interested in economic recovery—not an iota. I speak about stifled energy and job creation, a federally micro-mismanaged economy, and restricted consumer choice, such as milk, soda, light bulbs, and even rabbits for little to zero environmental gain. With McCarthy at the helm, things have already gotten worse, and the plan is to make Americans pay for the good life we once had.

McCarthy for example agrees with Obama on extra-constitutional matters – sans Congressional approval. She said: "I didn't go to Washington to sit around and wait for Congressional action. Never done that before, and don't plan to in the future."

She believes that she is permitted to go around our elected officials to clobber the economy with unworkable regulations. The president loves expensive regulations so why shouldn't she? McCarthy knows that her regulations will cost industry $billions and cost American's jobs; but she does not care. It is her boss's plan or he would have picked somebody else.

We all know that humans blow off carbon dioxide (CO2) when we exhale yet she sees this as a harmful gas. Supposedly created to help humans and the human environment, the EPA's policies on CO2 hurt living human being while having no appreciable effect on the earth's temperature or overall global emissions. Ironically in the midst of the "warming debate," in 2014, with economic numbers for the first quarter coming in at .01%, the Obama regime blamed the especially cold winter. The truth is hard to find. Perhaps the fact that the earth is not warming is an inconvenient truth tucked inside Al Gore's private lock box.

In other words, the truth does not matter because the environmental religion is much more important than economic realism.

McCarthy has no conscience and no big concern for businesses being successful. Her actions show a lack of concern for fuel for power plants of for Americans staying warm in the winter. It seems perfectly OK in this agency if regulations bring gas prices to $20.00 a gallon. If a single mosquito or tsetse fly gets to live, their efforts are deemed worthwhile.

Like others of her ilk, McCarthy is also against fossil fuels including natural gas, the cleanest fuel—especially if gained by hydro-fracking. Consequently, she is in the process of handicapping the most productive sectors of the American economy with rules that duplicate what states are already doing to manage gas extractions, coal extractions and even wind and solar.

It is not just that dirty fossil fuels are bad. It is that energy is bad. Humans who expend too much energy, flatulate and spcw out SO_2 or H_2S or other nasty sulfur bearing gasses, are suspect. But, cows are the real culprits today. McCarthy's EPA hates cows. They may not like steak dinners either. Cows who hunt for the finest grass on places like the Bundy range eat lots of grass, expend lots of energy and their flatulence has a high concentration of methane, which is a bad-guy greenhouse gas. Ironically, to the EPA folks, cow excrement is the most valued asset from the digestive process.

In these times, Vladimir Putin has become the most famous tough guy in the world partly because he controls the energy for Europe. The US could quickly ratchet up an energy industry with our vast resources and end Putin's expansion sooner than later. However, McCarthy and Obama have shut down all opportunities to stop Putin and his energy thugs and to help Europe and our allies. See the following chart, which came to me in an email today. It will give a perspective on just one aspect – drilling permits:

Figure 8-2

DRILLING PERMITS APPROVED

58% FY1992 VS FY2000   116% FY2000 VS FY2008   36% FY2008 VS FY2011

SOURCE: BUREAU OF LAND

FOX NEWS .COM

Unfortunately, with McCarthy at the helm, there will be a relentless push to eliminate coal, reduce fracking, prevent the Keystone Pipeline, and continue to buy tankers full of oil from the world's most notorious terrorist countries.

The EPA that did its job in the 1970's is gone and this EPA should no longer be in operation. The American economy does not need the economy-stifling regulations coming from big brother EPA and its surrogate partnership agencies.

The regulatory attack of the modern era is unprecedented and it drives the cost of everything up, especially food. One can conclude and when you finish this book, you will see that the

EPA is hoping that it can reduce the footprint of humans on the planet. You may be surprised.

Although their harsh regulations provide no substantial improvement in our environmental or well-being, the EPA does have an extremely negative impact on the economy. The damage the EPA is doing with the President's blessings will last far beyond when Obama leaves office.

Summary

These last several chapters contained peripheral and background information to help us all understand how far out of the mainstream of rational thought the EPA has drifted. From the Silent Spring days of Rachel Carson, Americans have been blessed by an attentive Congress and the Office of the President in keeping the air and the water safe for all humankind in the United States.

As we move further on in this book, however, you will see that Silent Spring was way too loud in its prescription for overkill on the protection front. The EPA will not be happy until it controls or eliminates humanity.

Nobody thinks that America is not better off for the environmental protection that we have received over the years since the big smog episodes in LA in the 1960's. Some of the help came from the EPA and lots came from the states' Departments of Environmental Resources. With the plastics issues and food issues, a lot of good help also came from the F.D.A.

As you will see in subsequent chapters, when something gets so big like the EPA; it takes on a life of its own, and when it no longer works for the people, it is time for it to go.

The EPA has long outlived its usefulness to the American people. It now appears that it is more powerful than the

Congress that once drafted the legislation creating this agency gone wild. President Obama seems to enjoy marginalizing the power of Congress through the use of his EPA. He does it all the time.

The EPA over the years has morphed into something that is dangerous for Americans. Though we are all interested in clean air and clean water, it helps to remember that the Clean Air Act and other positive laws were enacted by Congress, not the EPA.

When they came on board, the EPA was needed and they did their job well for years. The EPA, as an agency of the US government, had a job to create regulations that were in the spirit of the laws created by the Congress.

Unfortunately, as the agency grew in people and power, through its regulations it decided that it would solve all of the problems of the planet. Along the way, it decided that mankind was one of nature's biggest problems.

For the EPA, Mother Nature does come first. Humans have been documented for ages as being the world's biggest polluters. So, it is natural that the EPA sees the very people it was chartered to help as the biggest threat to its own survival. Why should the EPA like humans?

Chapter 9   Snake Oil & Honeybees

EPA delivers large doses of snake oil

EPA regulations are often silly but they are always hurtful. Most regular human beings, who have not overdosed on Presidential Snake Oil (OSO), see the sins of the EPA for what they are. OSO is a substance which the EPA should ban one day as a mind pollutant.

Nobody really knows what the next banned substance will be? Will it be two-ply toilet paper, outdoor dining, fireworks displays, or perhaps human flatulence? I should be careful to not give the EPA any ideas; they are already silly enough. Their latest target is antibacterial hand soaps. No kidding! Maybe they make hands too clean.

Perhaps you have heard of Triclosan. It is a chemical substance added to many common products— toothpaste, mouthwash, soap, toys, mattresses, clothes, and kitchen utensils. Triclosan is back in the news as an FDA target. Since the EPA hides its emails as does the State Department, we won't be seeing the communications between the FDA and the EPA, its big brother, anytime soon. Nonetheless, in this venture in an unholy alliance for sure, the FDA has partnered with the aggressive EPA to make sure that Americans are safe. Cough! Cough!

Triclosan was once used in products simply for its anti-bacterial and anti-mold properties. It is in general use now. It permits manufacturers to say that their products, such as soaps, are "antibacterial." Industry experts are expecting a ban. When the EPA gets you in its "gunsights," things will not be good for your business in the future.

EPA ignores the dihydrogen oxide threat

On August 9, 2011, Patrick Hedger put forth a hypothesis on a dangerous substance that he said should be regulated by the EPA because it can be harmful and it can be toxic if breathed in small quantities or ingested in large doses. The problem, according to Hedger is not being addressed. It is the chemical, Dihydrogen Oxide, which is also referred to as Hydric Acid.

Hedger laments that the substance is everywhere. He asks whether such an insidious chemical should not have more priority than others for the EPA, due to its broader availability in the environment. Hedger writes:

"Dihydrogen Oxide is everywhere and it is killing people through over exposure and the adverse weather and other environmental conditions it creates. The EPA has worked to create and implement regulations that have either banned or labeled hazardous far less lethal substances. So we must demand the EPA take action and regulate hydric acid right?

After all the spread of Dihydrogen Oxide is so great that every single human being has close to a 70% contamination level. So where is the action? The dangers are proven. Why do we allow Hydric Acid to kill so many people and destroy so much? Simple:

"Dihydrogen oxide's chemical formula is H_2O. Hydric acid is water.

"So clearly it would be silly for the EPA to take action against water. Sure it can kill you, but you can't live without it. If we safely use and recycle water, we can prevent most of the dangers it poses. Sure we can't stop the thunderstorms and floods can be a bear to prevent, but just about everyone knows how to avoid drowning or that sticking your hand in boiling water is a bad idea. So if we can safely use a chemical or substance, despite its inherent dangers, it would be silly to impose government regulations on it. Right?"

I sure hope nobody from the EPA reads the above or there will be great demand for Hydric Acid when it becomes regulated. If it cannot be obtained, I can see the vast preponderance of adults seeking out fermented grapes or distilled spirits, even if they are in those unsafe plastic bottles.

Nobody thought the EPA would ever declare CO2, a major human exhalant as a toxic greenhouse gas. Yet, they have in fact done so. After study, will they decide that the number of humans must be reduced. Then again, maybe they have already drawn such conclusions and Obamacare is the solution?

Sure this all sounds silly and I am treating it lightly but it is very serious. I believe that the EPA more than the items it has chosen to regulate is a threat to my long-term health and sustenance as a human being. Hang on, you'll get there too!

The honeybee scare

You may have heard of the decline in the honeybee population in this country and across the world. What you may not have heard is that honeybees are not indigenous to America and probably came over with the pilgrims on the Mayflower. The phenomenon is true and it has been diagnosed but the cause is not known with specificity. The name of the problem is colony collapse disorder, or CCD, and it typically manifests itself with an abandoned hive with just the queen bee as the only occupant, apparently unable to reproduce.

Hannah Nordhaus has a great new book on the topic called "The Beekeeper's Lament," which is now available in popular bookstores. She offers a great perspective on why bees may be dying and it is not necessarily that the clothianidin pesticide by Bayer, one of a number in the neonicotinoid (systemic) family is killing them.

This reasonably new pesticide now does the work that DDT once did quite well. DDT will be given its story day in a later chapter. You won't believe the non-truths in the DDT story!

This new bug killer by Bayer is taking the blame for the honeybee problem by a number of environmentalists. Can it be that since it replaced DDT it must be bad? Nordhaus knows because she is an expert in bees. She is taken back by "the pathetic rush to judgment" on the subject as she observed just how quickly environmentalists want to blame somebody or something for any problem in nature, often without having any facts.

This is the story of the EPA that we tell throughout this book. In fact, I predict that neonicotinoids will be found to be partly culpable in the reduction in honeybees and quite frankly the reduction in an insect population once robust enough to support animal predators such as tons of birds of all kinds.

Now even the bird population is dwindling and the ornithologists are looking at the lack of insects as that problem. DDT is hardly in use at all in the world, so it is not this one time environmental fall guy that is causing the problem. The EPA would say that it is not nice to fool Mother Nature, and right now it is looking for a culprit to blame, right or wrong.

The three dirty letters DDT however, are not coming up. You see it is well known that DDT is a type of pesticide that is not harmful to bees, whereas neonicotinoids appear to be harmful to just about everything that is alive. Sometimes the cure is worse than the problem.

Ironically it may be the bad politics of possibly having to back off their DDT ban that has the EPA in a quandary currently. Like the truth of Benghazi took time to evolve as a lying administration covered it up, there is no up-side for the EPA to suggest that maybe DDT is not so bad after-all.

Scientific proof so far shows that the DDT replacement is a far more lethal substance than DDT. Can the EPA face that as a possibility? Anyway, I thought you would like a summary of Nordhaus's take on all those quickly trying to solve the problem—with or without facts. It is a great theme and it describes the EPA to a tee. The EPA is It is a fact-free agency since they have the power to divine anything for anything if it fits their agenda.

Here's Nordhaus:

"Dying bees have become symbols of environmental sin, of faceless corporations out to ransack nature. Such is the story environmental journalism tells all too often. But it's not always the story that best helps us understand how we live in this world of nearly seven billion hungry people, or how we might square our ecological concerns and commitments with that reality. By engaging in simplistic and sometimes misleading environmental narratives -- by exaggerating the stakes and brushing over the inconvenient facts that stand in the way of foregone conclusions-- -- we do our field, and our subjects, a disservice. "

Amen!

Keep nature happy

Many of the EPA regulations are not only silly but they are very hurtful to people and to business and a good part of those regulations that are hurtful are stupid also.

You can tell that Hannah Nordhaus has a sense of disgust in her words. She feels similarly to me about environmentalists as she eloquently puts the scenario in perspective. It helps for all of us to remember that the EPA, as the enforcer for the environment movement, has just one goal—to make sure nature is happy. If you can actually come to accept that major premise, then everything the EPA does makes perfect sense.

Oh, I forgot there is one other notion in life that comes before hitting the peak of Maslow's Hierarchy of Basic Needs. The peak by the way in this pyramid is self-actualization – a self nirvana if you will. The notion that comes before all other notions in the pyramid is basic survival.

Can the EPA be trying to assure its survival by creating threats to humans, so we think we need them, while in their hearts, these pinheads all believe that humans are the problem and humans must be eliminated, so that the planet can be safe for all other life.

I think that Obama would be OK with eliminating humans as long as several hundred were left to serve in his entourage. Oh, and perhaps a few more to refine gasoline for his engine-craft items such as Airforce One.

Right now, there are no constraints for Obama's EPA. Nature comes first. If life gets a little bit or even a lot uncomfortable for humans because of the EPA and Mother Nature is happy—so be it. C'est la vie. Nature wins!

A few stupid EPA regulations to ponder

Let's talk about a few really bad EPA regulations that have become well known over the agency's 40-year life. There are far too many to get more than a sampling as there are hundreds of regulations that most normal people would call stupid. Most are still on the books.

As an aside, in 2013, the Federal Register logged over 89,000 pages of new regulations, mostly written by bureaucrats. My advice therefore is not to try to keep up with it. Don't try to find the federal registry and do not try to read it. Instead, when you violate even an obscure law, know that they will eventually find you and put you out of business.

So, make sure, while things are OK, you get one of Al Gore's lockboxes to tuck your cash into while it is rolling in unfettered. It will come in handy unless somebody changes currency to say the Chinese Yuan.

By the way with a business climate such as ours, is it no wonder people cannot find jobs?

Early EPA regulations once pinpointed real problems and addressed them point on. Today's regulations are reflections of somebody's ideological agenda and they are structured such that attempts to kill, say one amoeba, would be executed with a huge bunker buster bomb. But somebody in the EPA would object to the killing anyway. More than likely EPA personnel would be lining up on the side of the one celled parasite rather than working to help humans get rid of such threats to human health.

The new EPA regulations appear designed specifically to inhibit job creation and growth by private industry at a time that we are in economic chaos? Our parents would not believe we would let this happen. In the next few chapters, let's take a look at a few of the most egregious EPA initiatives that have taken their toll!

Chapter 10   EPA Hates Farmers

Punishing Farmers for the EPA is fun!

The EPA loves life on the farm. Unfortunately, the EPA is too busy punishing farmers for tilling the soil and taking out precious minerals. The EPA also has too much time available to crack down on farmers for their fine work in feeding mankind.

Consequently, the EPA gives farmers little credit for fighting insects and fungi and all kinds of pests and diseases to bring a food crop to market that they can sell and we can use at our tables. Instead of human food, the EPA cares about the insects and the fungi. Why do we pay them? We should stop.

If we had full access to the EPA wish lists, we would find that there are more than a few insects or fungi that the EPA would like to put on the endangered species list. Perhaps that is a big reason for their angst and their dissatisfaction with American farmers.

The EPA sees things differently from those of us who go to market and enjoy the fruits of the farmers' labor. EPA and its surrogate agencies have whacked farmers but good, with a lot of costly and expensive rules and regulations. If their intention is not for farmers to give up, pack it in, and let us all eat cake, it sure seems like it is.

CO2 Emissions

As an example of the pain caused upon farmers by the EPA, those in the industry know that American farmers consider Title V of the Clean Air Act as a major threat to their survival. This is a CO_2 emissions standard which applies to small farms such as those with over 25 cows. You and I exhale CO_2 and so do cows and pigs and other animals.

To get a permit to operate under Title V, it cost farmers a mere $46,500 and the pre-construction permit to get things in order costs $84,500. That is pretty menacing don't you think? In fact, it is legalized extortion. Yet, that is how the EPA does business.

Dust Regulations

Then, of course the EPA has its so-called "Dust" regulation that the agency posted as not true in mid-September of 2011 right after Herman Cain, Godfather Pizza CEO, nailed them in a Republican Presidential debate. I bet after the debate the EPA's thoughts quickly went to banning the harmful effects of Godfather Pizza. Unfortunately for the EPA, right now at least, Godfather Pizza is under the purview of the FDA.

The EPA now says dust is not one of their priorities. They admit they are considering / studying it. Farmers are always on notice because the EPA does not need Congress to OK its regulations. So, dust is definitely on the EPA agenda. In fact, no matter what lies they tell, the EPA is looking to crack down on farm dust.

Its proposal is already well formed and it involves treating farm dust as an air pollutant. Any dust from farm equipment, dusty farm roads, or those nasty farm animals kicking up dust would therefore be regulated by the EPA, when the rules are fully formulated and in place. Don't laugh, it is true. Can you

see why more and more long-time business owners are
saying, "Enough!" and simply retiring.
You can thank our "friends" at the EPA for that.

Manure Regulations

The EPA gets its kicks from getting into other people's dung.
For example, they are into farm manure big time. They force
the farmers to measure excrement as if they are trying to
determine if the farm is large enough to warrant the big
licensing expense as noted above.

If a ton of excrement per month is the count, it may mean
that the farm has 26 head of cattle and not the 24 as reported
to the EPA. In this case, perhaps the farm needs to upgrade
to the more expensive licenses. Does this harassment help the
American food consumer?

Not only is it a burden measuring and providing exact counts
for things that we would call crap, farmers also must
complete a ton of oppressive paperwork on EPA forms to
properly account for the manure.

Unfortunately, God has not yet invented an animal that can
go a lifetime without any excretory action. To satisfy the
mounds of paper required by the EPA, there are documented
cases in which farmers have spent upwards of 15 hours a
week just filling out the forms so the EPA can track each load
of manure that their animals generated. Maybe next year,
they can add an excrement fee or perhaps ban excrement
completely? No, of course that would be silly!

Figure 10-1 Manure Happens

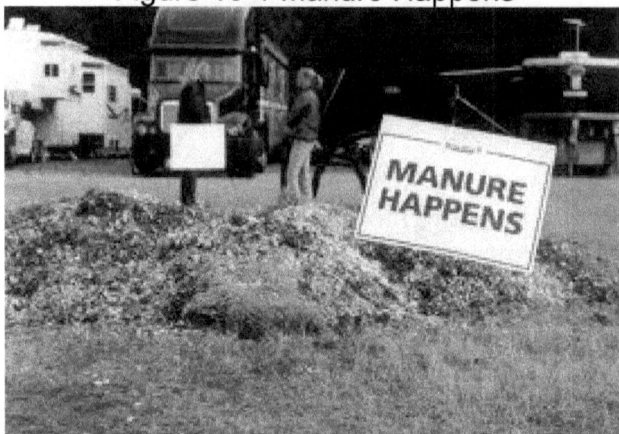

Chapter 11   EPA Hates Energy & Keystone XL Pipeline

Power Plant Regulations

In addition to farmers, The EPA hates utility (energy) companies. The EPA inflicts big pain on this industry, which then is forced to raise utility rates, paid by people who are already trying to break even in their lives. In addition to harming today's economy, the actions taken by the EPA reduce the competitiveness of US industry and negatively impact our national security.

Figure 11-2 Nasty Power Plant

More and more utilities including American Electric Power, Duke Energy, and Southern Company have announced they are not going to take it anymore. Why should they?

They are preparing to close a number of coal-fired power plants. The cost of EPA regulations for them and many others is just too high. When the plants close, there will be layoffs, higher electricity prices and the possibility of power outages. It does help to remember that it is not the EPA's responsibility to assure that humans are comfortable.

The EPA would make sure its buildings have power. They are immune to the pain of their ordinances.

Can the EPA really be anti-energy?

The EPA can and does hurt businesses in many ways and all at the same time. They are truly ambidextrous. While blocking coal as a fuel source for electric power plants, the EPA is also blocking an easy means for the same plants to use natural gas or petroleum.

This rogue agency (whoops, they do operate with presidential approval) simply does not like fossil fuels and so its intent is for Americans to pay through the nose for power produced by oil, gas, or coal. The EPA does not really understand nuclear that well. It is regarded by scientists as a clean source of energy; nonetheless, the EPA is against it.

The Keystone XL pipeline saga

The EPA is active along with their environmentalist cronies and Hollywood celebrities with the intention of blocking the building of a new pipeline known as the Keystone XL pipeline. It would bring a huge amount of oil from Canada to Texas. It would be a good thing for America and it would assure that this valuable source of energy from Canada is 1 not diverted by the Canadians to Asia—I.E China.

Every drop of oil counts when you are energy short as we are in America today. This Canadian Oil would supply start by providing 900,000 barrels of oil a day and provide billions of dollars of tax revenue. The EPA is against it and so is Obama but Obama must appear that he is undecided to please his union friends. In April 2014, on Good Friday after everybody went home, Obama issued a press release that the thought process on Keystone XL is so exhausting, that they won't be able to reach a decision until after the November 2014 elections.

When Americans stop pandering to the Obama love-fest and Obama's obvious concern for his own butt more than America, we will all be empowered to say some things for real. For example, we can say that anti-American actions by a US president are tantamount to treason. Treason should not have to go to trial with the wimp Congress we now have in place. While America and Crimea, and the rest of the Ukraine suffer, our president fiddles or worse! Meanwhile, he empowers the destructive EPA to make it even worse.

Since it is you and I who pay the 18,000 EPA employees their salaries, one would think they would work for us. Unfortunately, we do not get to evaluate their job performance regularly. However, we can elect new officials who can change their mission statement in a moment, and they can also eliminate the agency completely.

Our employment contract with the EPA says they get paid anyway, whether they help the people or hurt the people.

Since during the building process, the pipeline may hurt nature a bit, just like a new home may cause hornets to be forced to get their own new home, does not mean it should not be built. In the future, the pipeline would clearly be helping humans.

However, those of us looking at this objectively have concluded that the president's EPA is not interested in the pipeline ever being built. Apparently, this is a direct order from President Obama himself who continues to place the deal on hold for further study.

Obama may be the most corrupt president ever. He is a rich multi-millionaire who picks on millionaires and anybody else to make him look good. He has many rich and prominent political donors to his electoral war chest who raised environmental concerns. Yet, they pick up a lot of US treasury money for their pet projects. They get paid off.

There are also those who are not as grabby who are already rich. They are part of the President's heavy activist environmental group. He is not running again unless he does so well in the next year or so that they people demand him a third term. The environmentalist money people always threaten to withhold future campaign support if projects such a Keystone Pipeline XL get the go ahead.

It is no secret that Obama wants to remain and American hero and he wants all of the environmentalists who run the Democratic Party to all talk about him when he's gone. Maybe Obama will need all these people for a third term bid but it cannot happen unless … to be revealed in the third edition.

Working through the issues of the day, we know the President loves the EPA. If the EPA has identified Coal as its big target and it Is trying to get Power plants that use coal to shut down or convert to something more enviro-friendly, who do you think is in the background pulling the strings. Yet, Obama does not want to be associated with any policy decision because if he can blame George, and George, he is better off politically. The truth has certainly taken a hit in Obama Times.

Regardless, the truth is that the EPA and Obama are blocking needed oil by not permitting this direct pipeline to the refineries in Texas and Louisiana to be built. So, what does Obama's EPA want us to do, bring land-based oil in from Canada on tankers? Maybe they really want to create a heating and cooling crisis in the US? Can that be the plan? Does any of Obama magic make any sense? Do you trust the EPA?

President Obama is not very good at making any decision. We all know that not making a decision however is a decision. Obama gets away with it because the media is corrupt, and they want us all to believe that all decisions from the white house are made by Susan Rice, or Joe S, the ragman, but never Obama. He is the only President in recorded history that the people love because no bad issues are permitted to stick to him. Obama may be ebony but he is as pure as the ivory baby—99 and 44/100% pure!

Our President has no history of success so we should continue to forgive him for his misdeeds. Don't you think? He was a very ineffective US Senator and he leads from behind so that he can second-guess all results that otherwise would be directly attributable. Obama is the same Obama who voted present innumerable times in the US Senate and thus he had no real record when he ran for President. But, the people love worms better than snakes so he is still popular

Present, however was the only way Obama could vote when the unions were looking for 20,000 construction jobs and the environmentalists were pushing for magic, rather than the pipeline to deliver energy to homes in the US. A real leader would have OK'd the pipeline because it was the best thing for our country.

Obama never says never! Thus every major energy issue, upon which he has ever had to decide, remains open today. In this latest non-decision, the President delayed Keystone again. After the November 14, 2014 election or after the November 8, 2016 election, it is expected he will finally kill the planned $7 billion Keystone XL pipeline project.

Then again, he and the Democrats may keep it open until after the November 6, 2018 election, or after the one after that or the one after that. Indecisive people make decisions by not making decisions. The pipeline, if approved on Obama's first day in office, would be long built and would have already been a boost to the economy and would be a great start in lessening our dependence on terrorist oil.

Should we conclude that Obama does not care about America, though he does seem to care about wielding the most power in the free world?

The President knows that about 20,000 union jobs are likely to go elsewhere with inaction. But, following his lead, the EPA has been able to keep the US in a bankrupt energy position. Perhaps the objective is for the economy to completely collapse. The more Americans he can fool, the closer Obama's apparent wish for a permanently weak America is to coming true.

The President's decision to table the pipeline rather than go hog wild to make it happen hit a lot of trusting people right between the eyes. Which project developer or supporter can take a year off waiting to see if the temperamental President will ever say "yes?" The Keystone XL organization has already pumped $1.7 billion in to buy steel pipe as well as millions of dollars to obtain right-of-way easements to assure a proper construction path.

The project had been under study for three years before Obama became the stumbling point. The environmentalists assured that there were the requisite volumes and volumes of impact statements and justification documents produced to properly characterize the work effort. There is nothing left but an Obama "yes or no!"

It should have been a go long ago but emotion and the win at all costs mantra of environmentalists often trumps the facts. President Obama actually fears the EPA protagonists more than he fears Putin. So, putting the pipeline off forever has

been a great political move for a guy who wants to trick
people into supporting him.

Since the pipeline crosses US borders, the State Department,
called upon to investigate a long, long, time ago, had
previously determined that it would have "no significant
impacts." They had controlling jurisdiction.

Then-Secretary of State Hillary Clinton had softly deemed
Keystone XL to be in the national interest. Despite her quiet
voice on the matter, President Barack Obama shelved the
project again in January 2012. This was during the run-up to
his re-election campaign and Obama did not need the
Keystone Pipeline or Benghazi from interfering with the
politics of his reelection opportunity.

Obama of course is a big con artist and flip-flopper just like
the guy who now supposedly has control of the Pipeline
decision—John Kerry. Hillary Clinton, head of the State
Department during her four years chose to mostly stay out of
the foray and she was not seen as a major advocate.

She and her boss became the embodiment of Sergeant
Schultz. The "I know nothing" strategy has been working for
a long time for Democrats because their fawning public loves
them so much. Americans get the lousy, corrupt government
we deserve because we do not have the guts to stop such
thieves in their tracks, though we well recognize them by
their limp.

The State Department, until they realized it was a political
football, had been prepared to offer formal approval by the
end of 2011. Unfortunately, this self-imposed timetable
provoked environmental activists to push even harder for the
administration to reject it.

The White House, under control of the Environmentalist in
Chief, rejected the Pipeline by postponing it and quietly in
April 2014, they have done so again. Obama risked his

tentative relationship with Canada and went with the environmentalist whackos v America. The EPA and Obama campaign supporters had a party. America wept for itself.

Inactions such as Keystone XL and overreaching regulations by Obama's EPA have led the US from the number 1 economy in the world to number 2. Inactions and actions both have consequences. We are now in 2nd place behind China. Perhaps we can have another party when we hit # 3?

It is really tough to accept for those who expect the best from this administration. Disappointment has been the lesson to all of us who hoped for a good change in 2009. All of the agencies—EPA, FDA, USDA, DOE, etc.—are in lock-step with the President, regardless of how off the mark his leadership take them. Such unquestioned blind loyalty may help some careers but it is killing our country.

Since all agency personnel make over $100,000 per year, no government employee has had the guts to find fault with any of Obama's lame strategies. The pay checks remain for these staffers are miraculously delivered by USPS mail or by e-systems each and every payday without a miss. Who will be the first to risk financial ruin to argue truthfully about policy?

So, we citizens must all stay well awake as this President will not give up until he is clearly defeated. His surrogates, such as the EPA will not give up until there is no hope. Their life's missions appear to be aligned so closely with the President's that they move like twins in simpatico.

None of the President's agencies, especially the EPA seem to really care about the welfare of America or Americans. The sooner citizens realize that we are on our own, the sooner we all will be able to fend off the incessant volleys and move together in only one direction – the direction that helps America the most. It is always the direction opposite to which the President is heading.

It is really inconceivable that a president who blames everybody else for job losses can turn his back on 20,000 jobs plus and get away with it. The press does not challenge him. Keystone XL was a great opportunity to move several percentages towards energy independence. What motivates such a president to turn away from things that help America? More and more observers conclude that this President may not wish the best for America?

Update on Keystone Xl Pipeline

Nobody expected otherwise. President BHO on Friday November 6, 2015 denied energy company TransCanada a permit to build the Keystone XL pipeline, putting to bed a seven-year partisan push-and-pull over its construction. The president said he agreed with the State Department's recommendation to kill the project, as it "would not serve the national interests of the United States." Some like me think Obama must have missed the briefing that energy was good for the US and those of us who like to be warm in winter.

Obama said the pipeline was "too often used as a campaign cudgel" by both the right and left instead of "a serious policy matter." Those tuned into politics know that the Prez would have missed a few donations for his next post-Prez project if he said no to environmentalists. If you think the Clinton Foundation knows how to scarf up funding, watch the 2017 released master fund-master BHO. Last time anybody checked the White House, however, the T-stats were set to cold in the summer and warm in the winter. No wonder he doesn't care. It's all political.

"The rejection of the Keystone pipeline is largely symbolic," writes Maddie Stone at Gizmodo. The pipeline wouldn't have significantly stemmed the burning and extraction of fossil fuels from Canadian oil sands, but it does send a message. "The United States may finally be ready to assume a larger role when it comes to tackling climate change, coming a long way since failing to ratify the first international climate treaty, the 1997 Kyoto Protocol," writes Stone. Of course in terms of recent farces, climate change / global warming is at the top of the goofy list unless you want to be a Gore Billionaire.

Chapter 12   BP Oil Spill—Not Obama's Finest Moment

Obama comes down against American energy independence

The Keystone XL Pipeline is not the first time for Obama to vote against American energy. The US Interior Department got a piece of the action in the Gulf in 2010 after the BP spill. Wherever the government was involved, things stalled or got worse. Thanks to the Obama government, the people in the gulf suffered more than even the Katrina disaster. I bet the very idea makes George Bush smile.

Who would have expected after the southern states were hit with such drastic job losses that the President's men would increase, not decrease the time period in which these Americans would be unemployed. Is this our Jobs' President or is it just a little Obama snake oil?

You may recall in 2010 that U.S. Interior Secretary Ken Salazar declared a six-month moratorium on deep water drilling following the Deepwater Horizon oil spill. If you were working someplace else in the US, you may not have noticed. This action by Salazar from Interior, and Obama the ideologue erased access to 7.5 billion barrels of oil and nearly 60 trillion cubic feet of natural gas along with tens of thousands of job opportunities they would have created. The corrupt press chose not to report this atrocity v working Americans.

Pipeline crews do not hold in place, since these men need to work. And, so the other Gulf drilling rigs picked up and took the jobs and they went overseas. They did not sit around hoping Obama and Salazar would start playing nicey-nicey with them. They left the gulf for greener pastures. That is why no company that can do well anyplace else, wants to operate in America. It explains a lot about Obama's war on farmers as we have already discussed. Farmers have no choice but to grin and bear it.

By the time the courts told the President that he did not have the authority to terminate operations in the Gulf, the damage had already been done. However, this did not stop Obama from forcing his way—even though it was mostly moot.

To demonstrate to this lowly judge that Obama was the president of the US and judges are puny little members of a branch of government with lots of puny little judges, many of whom are appointed by the President, he chose to trick the court, rather than comply.

Obama changed a few minor things in the Salazar regulations that had been overruled by the judge, and then directed that the judicial orders be ignored since the new regulations had not been brought to court. In a move of complete lawlessness, the President ignored the court order to drop the moratorium. Obama is above the Constitution and unfortunately, the US Senate, which may include one or both of your Senators, has his back.

Unfortunately, nobody, Democrat or Republican really challenges this powerful prince as he destroys America piece by piece with his agency power.

The EPA is the worst domestically but despite the power of the oil companies, the mighty Obama humbled them and thanks to his fine work, instead of gas prices at $1.80, they have more than doubled and again are about $4.00 per gallon. How is that good for America? Does the President pay for his own gas?

Nobody has forgotten the big 2010 BP Gulf Oil spill. Rational human beings could not believe that the EPA was hurting rather than helping in the cleanup. Why was that? It was because they actually had another agenda. When people are working their hardest, regulations and red tape are not tools to get the job done. The EPA hurt the cleanup work and offered no real help. They operate under Obama's direct orders.

Obama seems to like it when those subject to his control are forced to cry "Uncle." Then, and only then, is he satisfied. If you happen to be suffering in the meantime, it is no consolation that the President and his EPA believe that there are already too many humans on the planet. Nobody from government is brassy enough to suggest that if you don't like living in America, then, why don't you check out permanently? Perhaps Obamacare, a system as effective as the response to the BP oil spill, will help you be able to check out sooner than you may have planned.

The EPA and many other "authorized" US agencies were constraints to all those trying to help the people of the Gulf to get rid of that nasty oil, and give them a better life. But, for those paying attention, it should have been expected. The mission of the EPA is not characterized as "helping man." The EPA job is to help nature and most of the time man is the guilty party. Nature, innocent in the foray, gets hurt simply because there are too many people.

Nobody would accept help!

You may recall that during the Gulf disaster, within three days the Dutch had offered to fly four huge oil skimmers that would suck up tons of the toxic water and oil per day. These were huge monstrosities and had already proven their worth in deployments in Europe. The oil would sink into the tanker's belly, and the mostly pure water would be pumped off back into the Gulf. Each ship would collect 5,000 tons of oil (36,500 barrels) each day.

This technique was not acceptable to Obama's EPA. The turned the offer down. Turning down the Dutch skimmers just shows a total lack of leadership in the oil spill.

Standing still and criticizing BP and others, using a typical Democratic Party ploy, the blame game, became their mantra of execution. They were not looking for a solution. It was as if Democrats were enjoying the spill of that nasty fossil fuel, and the more they could convince people that oil was bad, the further their left wing agenda would move.

The fact is the EPA held to a regulation that water that contained any oil could not be pumped back into the ocean, even if just 1% of the 100% collected were returned. How about that for a no win deal. Take 100% oil in and put 1% back. The EPA said "No." They had their regulations.

Rather than waive the regulation to help the US recover; the EPA stubbornly stuck by that regulation. After all, they had written it. So for 50 days nothing was permitted in the Gulf while the oil was racing in.

After much public pressure, after 50 days, the EPA relented and of course there was no problem found from the Dutch skimmers once they went into operation. After 50 days, however, the big damage was already done. The time for the skimmers to be at their most effective capacity was before the oil had spread so far.

Regulations come before humankind. It is the EPA's M.O. The EPA expressed no remorse. BTW, why does our country, which needs far more oil to survive than the Dutch, not have a fleet of such phenomenal ships? Maybe we simply do not want drilling for fossil fuels, regardless of whether it can be 100% safe or not.

Criticism of the EPA and Obama's lack of leadership came from all over the world, including the people in the gulf who were constrained from helping protect their own shoreline.. It is hard to believe that the US and English big oil companies did not have the modern technology or the ships ready for an oil spill response. Some suggest that it is far easier to buy politicians and use illegal dispersants than to invest in what is necessary to prevent a spill and then be able to clean it up with minimal impact.

There are Belgium firms, DEME, and Jan De Nul Group for example that have contended that they can clean up oil with extreme accuracy at a depth of 6,000 feet. They are prepared for a spill. Belgium is a teeny country. Why is it that the US has no such capability? What is it that we lead the world in? Oil consumption? Shame on our government and the agencies such as the EPA that care more about bad mouthing fossil fuels than permitting us to use them safely. Obama turned the European offers down.

Dinesh D'Souza is one of America's most influential conservative thinkers. He wrote a book titled, "The Roots Of Obama's Rage, and he did a few videos that were in theatres in 2012 just before the election. BTW, D'Souza is now being persecuted by the IRS, but surely not because he bugged Obama with his videos...? In this book, he explains the unexplainable about the conundrum in chief. He has choice words to say about Obama's response in the Gulf:

"Next let's consider Obama's response to the devastating oil spill in the Gulf of Mexico. As torrents of black oil gushed toward southern shores, Obama sounded lethargic, almost bored, with what was going on and what needed to be done to stop it. Even Democratic strategist James Carville expressed amazement at Obama's personal and emotional remove from the situation. 'I have no idea why they didn't seize this thing. I have no idea why their attitude was so hands off here.' Listening to Obama talk on the subject, TV host Keith Olbermann responded: "It was a great speech if you were on another planet for the last 57 days." Maybe that is why Olbermann lost his job. The salute cannot end without consequences.

"Finally, addressing the TV cameras on May 14, 2010, Obama managed to work up some enthusiasm. Time and again he condemned "British Petroleum"—an interesting term since the company long ago changed its name to BP.

"Given our anti-colonial theory, it's no surprise that Obama wanted to remind Americans of what BP used to stand for. He was equally outspoken in whacking the other oil companies for their "ridiculous spectacle" of "pointing fingers of blame." Actually these companies were not responsible for the spill, and the only blame, in addition to that of BP, belonged to the Obama administration for its Katrina-like incompetence in responding to the disaster.

"Addressing the nation on the spill on June 15, 2010, Obama stressed that Americans "consume more than 20 percent of the world's oil, but have less than 2 percent of the world's resources." Obama went on to say that 'for decades we've talked and talked about the need to end America's century-long addiction to fossil fuels.'

"Unfortunately, 'time and again the path forward has been blocked' by, among others, 'oil industry lobbyists.' Now, on the face of it, this is a perfectly reasonable statement from a liberal politician who thinks this is what the American public wants to hear.

"But ask yourself, what does any of this have to do with the oil spill? Would the oil spill have been less of a problem if America consumed a mere 10 percent of the world's resources? Of course not. The point is that for Obama the energy and environmental issues reduce to a simple proposition: America is a neocolonial giant eating up more than its share of the world's resources, and in doing so America is exploiting the scarce fuel of the globe; consequently, this gluttonous consumption must be stopped.

"This is the heart of Obama's energy and environmental agenda: not cleaning up the Gulf or saving the environment in general, but redressing the inequitable system where the neocolonial West—and neocolonial companies like BP—dominates the use of global energy resources."

Obama's tax returns where not audited in 2014, but Dinesh D'Souza's were. If the tables were reversed, would D'Souza, as President, have audited Obama? I do not think so. Doesn't that give us a clue about how ruthless this President actually is? If you don't like his environmental policies that destroy business and jobs, you can keep your opinion, and then you can go to hell. With the prevaricator in chief controlling his brown shirts in the EPA, most of us feel we are already on the journey!

By the way, Mr. President, if you are planning to audit my tax returns for offering some negatives about your leadership, please know that Brian W. Kelly is merely a pseudonym of a great author that I had barely heard about. It wasn't me. Excuses have worked so well for you that I hope this confession works for me. The real authors of this book are Patrick J. Buchanan, with help from Sean Hannity, Rush Limbaugh, Snerdley, Warren Buffett, Bill Gates, and a host of others including Sarah Palin, the bravest person in America.

Brazil Can Drill

Ironically, after the US had invested over $2 billion with Brazil's state-owned oil company, Petrobras to finance offshore exploration in their home oil fields in the Santos, which is close to Rio de Janeiro, Obama came out of Gulf hiding (the oil leak) and pledged that America would become one of Brazil's best customers. The President had just violated court orders to turn off the oil spigot for American drillers.

Could it be that Brazil had offered a Plexiglas flexible pipeline between our two countries? Why else would the President have given the OK to Brazil? Would he have approved the $2 billion if Brazil were like Alaska, a state of the US separated from the mainland. Or, was it because it could not benefit the US? Does the Brazil deal mean they have to abide by EPA rules? Does Obama say "no" only if America has a chance to gain? Who knows what the decider in chief thinks about before he makes decisions?

No pipeline, period

Considering the Keystone XL pipeline was an inland connection between Canada and the US, it is hard to understand that way back on March 19, 2010, President Obama explained his decision to give Brazil a head start against America in this way:

"At a time when we've been reminded how easily instability in other parts of the world can affect the price of oil, the United States could not be happier with the potential for a new, stable source of energy."

Doesn't that make you want to ask about Canada and Montana? Why Brazil instead of the US?

Obama's delay on the pipeline may eventually force private developers, the kind of people who hire Americans, to kill the pipeline project altogether. It must be inconceivable for a stakeholder in the pipeline to observe our lackluster ambivalent President, who resists making energy decisions favorable to his own country. Why would such a stakeholder want to trust any investment in Obama's America? And, of course in mid- 2015, we finally have an Obama decision. He is so powerful today he can actually say "No," to the Xl Pipeline without hedging; and he has done exactly that.

If there were an honest press in America, regular Americans would be outraged at the games Obama plays with the well-being of America. Americans that pay attention are not happy by Obama's pipeline put-offs, and are not happy with his big final "No," on the deal. They know there is no real reason, such as clearer facts, that a pipeline decision is better made after an election than before. The two notions are unrelated unless your motivation is purely political and selfish. Does a postponement help any of the players? Perhaps for now that Obama has finally said: "no." The corrupt press herald his decision.

Many see this as all negative. They felt that the President had already made a decision since postponing it makes no good sense for America. Either way, our energy plans must be made. They looked at the decision with no false hope for they believed the President made his decision long ago and has been playing politics. Nobody needs six years to decide about anything. Obama has made the decision. He just did not announce it as a decision. The bottom line is that there will be no Canadian / US pipeline until we have a new President.

TransCanada CEO Russ Girling, knows more about the situation than anybody. He offers these thoughts:

If crude delivery can't begin as scheduled, "those shippers will only wait so long, and then they will start looking for other markets. Similarly, the refiners can only wait so long for Canadian crude oil to come into their marketplace." A key prospective market is Asia [China]. Will this be known as the big Obama jobs loser of all time? Sure looks that way but the President remains unapologetic for the damage his indecision has caused. He just doesn't care.

If any other president were in control of the EPA, for example, nobody would expect that president to advocate courses of actions that would hurt America. With Obama, it is not the case. We expect the worst from him and we often get a lot more negatives than we have come to expect. .

Kill the EPA post haste

The government through the EPA is taking control over as much of American industry's production as possible, and as soon as possible. Their intent can be nothing less than to kill off American industry and American energy. It would be far better for Americans to insist that Congress kill the EPA monster first. Defund it tomorrow, please!

In his day in the limelight, Newt Gingrich always rooted for America. He still does. In his time of power and prestige, he pleaded on behalf of regular Americans, He repeatedly expressed deep concern about the grabby-ness of the EPA. Unlike Ron Paul who is all for shutting the monster down without a trace, Gingrish suggested that there should be a replacement agency for the current biased and out-of-control EPA. He suggested calling the new agency the "Environmental Solutions Agency."

I fear such an announcement would reward a bad apple for going rotten. I like Newt Gingrich immensely but I worry about giving progressive Marxists an inch into America as I know and understand America. They have no right to any of America.

I fear that any concession such as Gingrich's attempt at amelioration would be a failure and the same bums would simply be located in new offices. Let's do it right. Start by ridding ourselves of this scourge. Kill the agency and let the EPA employees get real jobs on farms or oil rigs—or collect unemployment for a while. Maybe they should find that they are under-qualified for most jobs. Their work at the EPA surely has been substandard, if not sub-human.

Thomas Sowell has his pulse on the heartbeat of America because he cares. Let me quote the eminently qualified Thomas Sowell, who always has a great perspective on the issues that haunt Americans. On June 15, 2010, writing a timeless article for the National Review Online, Sowell titled his piece: "Obama's Snake-Oil Spill." Sowell has Obama pegged pretty well. Here it is:

"Nothing will keep a man or an institution determined to continue on a failing policy course like past success with that policy. Obama's political success in the 2008 election campaign was a spectacular triumph of creating images and impressions.

"But creating political impressions and images is not the same thing as governing. Yet Obama in the White House keeps on saying and doing things to impress people, instead of governing."

Thank you Thomas Sowell! Stay well sir! Keep your guiding light in the "ON" position.

Expanding on Sowell's thoughts; have any of us seen any grandstanding in this administration while governing might have been the better option? Have any of us seen outright lying in this administration when facing the facts would have been the nobler proposition?

Does the truth even matter to this White House team as long as their guy survives? Are popularity and electability the only "gods" or at least the only "virtues" that matter today? Can we ever expect the Obama team to tell the truth if it hurts their "beloved" boss? Why do we pay them if they do not work for us?

Does the founders' original thinking about maintaining freedom over hundreds of years mean anything in the current environment? Does it matter that the country is failing; we are failing; our friends are failing; our families are failing; and nothing is going right? Does it mean anything to those who would give up their freedom for the approval of the President?

Maybe it actually means a hell of a lot. Maybe it is why it is as it is. Are too many Americans too timid or too nonchalant to tie our own shoes? Can we last if we choose to not honor common sense? Let's find our mettle and rid ourselves of the EPA and get on the road to a real recovery—for real!

Ben Franklin knew our President Obama way back in the eighteenth century. He saw him in his foresight. He knew Obama was very powerful and he had very dangerous pied piper tendencies, even though his leadership was poor. He could ask people to follow him for any purpose and his devoted following would give it all up for this one of a kind false prophet. Did Franklin see him as a Messiah?

To those not enamored by his magic, our President presents himself as a liar that Ben Franklin and all honest men can immediately recognize. Franklin was a god-fearing man who would recognize a false prophet in an instant.

This President has lied officially while carrying out the duties of his office so often that Ben Franklin surely wishes he could come back and make it all right for us. But, that is our job. We are not dummies. Will Ben Franklin, if he returns, be proud of how we handle our problem? Would a man who pledged his life, his fortune, and his sacred honor be happy with a man who desecrates that pledge with a smile and a shrug?

Franklin in his day often stated forms of the following: "People willing to trade their freedom for temporary enrichment from a leader they admire, even if that enrichment is simply a smile, deserve neither freedom nor enrichment and they will eventually lose both."

OK, Franklin did not say that but he almost did: "People willing to trade their freedom for temporary security deserve neither and will lose both."

When America smartens up, we will all be able to again become the America of our forefathers. The message is that we must smarten up or lose what we seemingly do not value – our freedom.

There are no messiahs or gods in America in government positions. There are none such as these who control us. We are a free people and yet freedom has a cost. Once freedom is gone, it is almost impossible to regain.

On our way to recapturing our freedom, we must take control back from our tyrannical government. One of the first actions we must take when we regain the power is to dissolve the EPA, the major subject of this book.

It even feels good to say!

As a great chapter closer, no sooner did I finish this chapter when I received one of those unattributed cartoons and it hit me right where I have been hitting you...at least I hope regarding me. So, I promise to remove this from future printings of the book if the artist tells me to do so. I received it off the Internet in an email as most good thoughts come today. Here it is as the closeout to this chapter:

Figure 12-1

SNOW WHITE , SUPERMAN , AND PINOCCHIO ARE WALKING ALONG. THEY SEE A SIGN. IT READS "CONTEST FOR THE WORLD'S MOST BEAUTIFUL WOMAN." SNOW WHITE GOES IN, LATER COMES OUT SMILING AND IS WEARING A CROWN. THEY WALK ALONG AND SEE ANOTHER SIGN THAT SAYS "CONTEST FOR WORLD'S STRONGEST MAN" SUPERMAN GOES IN, LATER COMES OUT SMILING AND IS WEARING A BELT. THEY WALK ALONG AND SEE A THIRD SIGN "CONTEST FOR WORLD'S GREATEST LIAR". PINOCCHIO GOES IN AND LATER COMES OUT WITH HIS HEAD DOWN CRYING AND ASKS "WHO THE HELL IS BARACK OBAMA?"

SHARE IF YOU LAUGHED

Chapter 13   The Infamous Delta Smelt

Central Valley California Farmland?

Let's look at one or two more egregious issues with the EPA and its surrogate agencies. This one is both heartbreaking and as most EPA adventures, it is also silly. But, again, please remember, the EPA is not about making humans happy or comfortable. It self-ordained purpose is to protect nature regardless of the cost to humankind. If you noticed that I have said that before, you are getting the overriding message of the book.

Until 2009, California's Central Valley was once considered by many to be the richest and most productive farmland in the nation. Add their rich soil to a long growing season and California's Central Valley was tough to beat, and so for years it was the most productive farming region in the US. The EPA stopped all that by taking away the rights of the farmers to irrigate their crops.

For years, California provided a substantial percentage of the produce for America. Because of the EPA, this land is still being threatened by a small, harmless-looking minnow called the delta smelt.

Recently, the smelt has landed on the endangered species list, causing a federal court to shut down vital irrigation pumps to farmers in the Central Valley. As the smelt, a small bait fish for Salmon Fishermen has been preserved; the Central Valley

has become a desert. Pictures courtesy of
www.biggovernment.com

Figure 13-1 The two-inch Delta Smelt

Figure 13-2 Farmers Looking for Relief

As an aside, it will be quite a while before you find California
tomatoes out East, but don't worry, Mexico has taken up the
slack and they are ready to deliver all we need. Check this
link when you have the time:
http://biggovernment.com/asparks/2011/02/18/californias-
delta-smelt-is- raising-your-food-prices/

Figure 13-3

A portion of the Sacramento-San Joaquin Delta. (CA Dept. of Water Resources)

I have been pointing out throughout this book that the EPA is not in business for humans. They are fully supported by the liberal left and the progressives and Marxists. If you know the strange things that progressives and liberals advocate then you can appreciate that it will help their agenda if the US farmers have to buy their food from other countries or they have to go on Food Stamps.

This smelt deal is fundamentally anti-human. You can now see the full EPA agenda. Animals and even inanimate objects have been given the same moral status as human beings. The EPA wants to please nature, not man. The EPA wants nature to live and in order to permit that, their posture is that less humans need to be on the planet. The less creature comforts, including food, that there are for human beings, the more humans may get the hint to go someplace else. But where? Mars? Now that the Russians are in charge of Space, maybe even that is out of the question?

The fertile Central Valley has just about turned back into desert; thousands of jobs have been lost; family farms have been lost and the list goes on. It is truly shameful what the Obama administration is doing to America with help from its whacko friends from California and the EPA.

Who will ultimately win this battle? Some with a dog in the fight believe that the progressives will have to go hungry, and find their kids dying of starvation—before anything is done in California. If it is not you that is hungry and it is not your kids that are dying, perhaps nothing will change. Like me, those in the Central Valley see the EPA as one of the worst things to ever happen to this country. For them, it has been devastation. The Clean Air Act was good but the EPA is B-A-D!

Figure 13-4 Central Valley Dust Bowl

The US government, through its regulations, has choked the life out of the Central Valley. This is Obama tyranny and it must come to an end before more and more breadbaskets in states across the Nation, become deserts. When Obama has the only grain, who will be our Moses?

Some of us believe the Obama progressive agenda has always placed government at the top of the food chain. It helps to keep in mind that a government that wants to control its citizens must control their health and their food supply. Watch for more atrocities from the EPA when the smelt finally delivers a knockout punch and wins this game.

Population control is another unspoken precept of the environmentalists and the EPA. Obama would never admit to population control yet Sarah Palin's death panels are for real. Nature is king to the EPA and man is a known polluter with too many un-redeeming qualities.

Would the EPA knowingly make it difficult for humans to be able to find food? Here are a few salient quotes from some real nature lovers. These are big names to EPA zealots.

"In order to stabilize world population we must eliminate 350,000 people per day." Jacques Cousteau, French oceanographer, United Nations Development Fund for Women 1994, page 84-85

"Phasing out the human race will solve every problem on earth, social and environmental. " -Dave Forman, Founder of Earth First!

With policies such as these, you can see why mostly all of our food, oil, and consumer products now come from outside of the US. We have been regulated and taxed almost to the point where we can no longer function independently as a country. Not only is this bad for our economy. It makes us more and more vulnerable to attack. It is time to end that. Let's kill the EPA before it kills America.

The smelt continues to win

On Friday, September 23, 2011, the federal government (Obama and Eric Holder) filed its opposition to the

Pacific Legal Fund's (PLF) petition for writ of certiorari in Stewart & Jasper Orchards v. Salazar. This is the case against the delta smelt. The Natural Resource Defense Council's (NRDC) opposition to PLF's petition had been filed in July.

What this means is that after three years of drought, the federal government is still fighting tooth and nail to assure that the smelt wins in its battle against human beings.

Just because 80,000 people are out of work in the Central Valley and California's jobs picture is in the toilet. Farmers throughout this area are now on unemployment and / or collecting food stamps. None of this human misery moves the leftist progressives on these courts.

Meanwhile, Governor Jerry "Moonbeam" Brown continues with his "Hey, what's happening man!" mantra at the Governor's mansion in Sacramento. So, nobody expects any action from him. When California comes to the rest of us in a few years for big time contributions for a bail-out, let's tell them to ask the thriving smelt for help.

Since it is California, it seems the problems have to do with the "red diaper doper babies," that Michael Savage likes to talk about. Savage defines these as the children of leftist intellectual baby boomers, raised from birth on Marxism and a drug tolerant environment, and now in places of political and intellectual influence." I think that about does it.

Add a little Obama Snake Oil (OSO) to the mix, and you have a situation that can only work if Obama moves his preferred constituents to his private island.

"Last Update on this matter—March 13, 2014
After getting some relief in the 2011 decision, the parched people of California and the farmers in the drought stricken Central Valley have lost again to the Smelt. A split decision by the U.S. Court of Appeals for the Ninth Circuit means it will be even tougher for residents of small, often disadvantaged rural communities in the San Joaquin Valley as well as 25 million Californians statewide and 3 million acres of the nation's most precious farmland to have water for survival.

The vote was 2-1; but we all know that Californians are the most liberal progressive people in the nation and humans do not matter to progressives. The Ninth Circuit overturned the 2011 ruling by U.S. District Court Judge Oliver Wanger that found the science used to establish biological opinions governing the flow of water through the Sacramento-San Joaquin Delta was 'arbitrary, capricious and unlawful.' Now, it is OK and the smelt wins another round against the people.

Dan Nelson, Executive Director of the San Luis & Delta-Mendota Water Authority is on the people's side. He writes:

"These biological opinions have harmed south of Delta water users by reducing the amount of water delivered to people, farms and businesses. And for this sacrifice, the fish agencies have yet to demonstrate that taking this water away has resulted in any benefits to the fish. People should demand results."

Chapter 14   The EPA Is Obama's Tool to Marginalize America

EPA v. mankind

Some may see the EPA as a rogue agency that seemingly began to do its own thing as the demands of environmentalists became more and more political. Over time, however, more and more are seeing it as a plan to teach America, the EPA perceived land of pollution, a big lesson.

Under the control of Obama, the agency is viewed more as an extension of Obama and it does his bidding without question. It is an Obama enforcer. I concur with that thinking and I further submit that one of the worst parts of the EPA is that, as the Obama enforcer, it has been complicit in the undermining of the separation of powers provision in the US Constitution. What does this mean?

Congress makes the laws and the president uses the executive branch of government—many, many employees, to enforce the laws. Presidents are also able to use their power for executive orders when Congress does not seem to have the time to address an issue adequately, and a decision must come out swiftly or the country will be harmed. These are called Executive Orders and are most often temporary.

When Congress has voiced its opinion on a matter by producing legislation, as the voice of the people in the US government, the President is prohibited from invoking an Executive Order contrary to the will of the Congress.

Moreover, it is the President's duty to enforce all laws put forth by the Congress. If the Executive branch begins picking and choosing laws to enforce and it uses Executive Orders in a dictatorial way, then the executive branch is engaging in tyranny, and it is up to the Congress to take action against the President.

Many people see Obama as a tyrant but nobody seems to take it as seriously as they should. I found this syllogism on http://obamalies.net/obama-the-tyrant.html. The first interesting comment from the author was that Obama the Tyrant told sixteen lies in just seven minutes in his last state of the union message. How is that for a "factoid?"

The Obamalies site believes it has the proof we all have been looking for that Obama is a tyrant. This is directly from the site:

"Here is the proof that Obama is a tyrant. Now this may seem like complex logic for some as it does use what in math we call a transitive relation. But it should be right at home with the elitist types that seek to control every aspect of the general populations' lives through big government.

A. Obama likes Big Government
B. Big Government is Tyranny
C. Obama is a Tyrant

"For those that need a little help. A (Obama) is related to B (Big Government). B (Big Government) is related to C (Tyranny). Meaning A (Obama) is related to C (Tyranny). Or in other words, Obama is a Tyrant.

Since Obama continues to support measures that seek to increase the size of government even in the midst of one of the biggest recessions in years. I think it's safe to state that point #1 is true.

"Therefore the truth of this proof lies in the strength of point #2. So, is Big Government Tyranny? Unequivocally, YES. Big Government seeks to oppress the people. It seeks to burden the people with extreme taxes. To regulate every aspect of their lives; robbing the people of their very freedoms. The peoples' right to life, liberty, and the pursuit of property!

"The Founding Fathers of this country tried to strike a balance between Tyranny and Anarchy when they framed the United States Constitution. They strove to create a system of government that wasn't weak, yet wasn't oppressive. They did a good job.

"It's time that Obama the Tyrant stopped oppressing the people, and started easing their burdens. Reduce taxes. Quit growing the size of government. Help businesses, and quit punishing people for making money. Do it now! Quit waiting! It is not evil to make money. Obama needs to quit punishing people that do, or we will never get out of this recession."

A big AMEN for the folks at Obamalies,

House chickens out on EPA showdown

Rather than kill the EPA, which they did not have the guts to do, the House introduced legislation in September of 2011 called the "Train Act." This is a bill that is designed to slow down the EPA's regulatory train wreck and determine whether the EPA should be permitted to go ahead with an onslaught of job-destroying regulations.

I say: "Why bother? The proof is already in! Just kill the EPA!" However, the elitists in the Senate, such as Pennsylvania's own Bob Casey Jr. might not approve.

There are a host of new EPA regulations that are just becoming felt and others that are in the on-deck circle for future release. Many are specifically targeted at coal-fueled power plants. One is called the "MACT Rule" and another has been dubbed the "Transport Rule." These are products of an agency gone wild with the full permission of a tyrannical president.

These rules will significantly raise energy prices, impact the reliability of America's electricity supply and destroy hundreds of thousands of high-paying American jobs. Ironically this stuff is supported by Obama at the same time he is trying to convince the public that his 'Jobs bill' is not a farce. Rest easy, the "jobs" bill is a farce.

America's mining, manufacturing, and energy producers warn that this onslaught of regulations will significantly weaken economic growth. The EPA does not care about the economy as witnessed by forty years of decrees. And so it continues to push these burdensome dictates with impunity. The 2011 House "Train" legislation was intended to slow it down.

Some say the EPA has done this all without examining the consequences they will place on America's economic and global competiveness. I disagree. The EPA knows full well that this will inconvenience Americans. The EPA simply does not care. Obama will try to make the EPA the straw man in this one, but do not be fooled. The EPA is Obama's enforcer. The President knows exactly what is going on and in fact he has ordered it.

Congress seems inept to tackle all things Obama. It is time to stop the EPA in its tracks, not by slowing action down to assess the cumulative impacts of its job-destroying rules. Any sane person knows the agency is an Obama tool and is being used to downgrade America's capabilities. Don't waste time slowing it down. It is time to defund it and shut it down for good.

MACT Update from 2013

As part of the ongoing Obama War on Energy, specifically the War on Coal, on January 31, 2013, the EPA published its final Boiler MACT rule. The National Association of Manufacturers (NAM) and business and environmental groups filed legal challenges in a federal appeals court. The NAM also petitioned the EPA to reconsider this latest rule, along with related rules involving air pollutants for area sources (Boiler GACT, or generally available control technology) and commercial and solid waste incineration (CISWI) units.

The EPA estimates that the MACT portion of the rule alone will impose capital costs of near $5 billion, plus $1.5 billion more in annual operating costs. The NAM will continue to advocate for achievable and affordable Boiler MACT regulations.

In 2011, there were well over 26 million Americans who were either unemployed or underemployed. To be underemployed means that people take small jobs to make a quick buck on a temporary basis. Good jobs are disappearing quicker than liquor over candy. It is a rare day when a good job comes along.

Our molasses slow recovery is one for the record books. It hasn't gotten better since 2011; Other than a few rays of hope, it is substantially worse, and it looks like a real recovery will never arrive.

Job growth averaged 174,000 per month in 2011; 186,000 per month in 2012; 194,000 per month in 2013; and 177,000 for the first three months of 2014. None of those figures come close to population growth which has averaged 218,000 Americans per month since the start of the Great Recession.

Because of population growth, our workforce is still increasing while the percentages are poor. For example, it grew from 153.1 million in 2007 to 155.8 million today. That is severely anemic growth. What should frighten us all are two additional facts. First, real unemployment stands at 23.8 million including those who haven't looked for a job in the last year. Second, the number of Americans not-in-the-workforce has exploded from 78.7 million in 2007 to 91.6 million today an increase of 13.1 million who are jobless.

As proof that there is some intentional distorting of the facts to make the administration look better to the people, in the first week of May 2014, the official unemployment rate was reported as 6.3 percent. This is the best since George Bush was president and it was about 4.6%.

However, when you do the math about the suffering of all the jobless in the country, the story is more clear and not as nicey-nicey as the administration would have you believe.

Real unemployment plus not-in-the-workforce equals 36.9 million Americans! How more depressing can you get? It is the fact that so few people are working that keeps depressing our economy. Subtract that many consumers and as they say, the engine of growth not only sputters; it comes to a halt eventually.

Obama knows that. The EPA knows that. They do not care. So, while speaking about a jobs plan on one side of his mouth the other side is barking out orders to the EPA to shut down the energy industry. And as a good servant, the EPA answers with many new regulatory burdens at a time of much needed economic growth.

Who cares? Not the EPA! Not Obama! Those of us, who are out of work do care but we do not count! Ironically, instead of punishing Obama by not reelecting him, the people overwhelmingly voted to reelect him. In the eleventh hour, his snake oil charm was overwhelming and he buffaloed the public into believing his economic failures were George Bush's fault. Dad but true!

The Obama and Democrat tricks are legend. First seniors get scared, then there are diversionary tactics suggesting the opposition hates blacks and Hispanics and women, and there is talk of a new minimum wage and increased unemployment benefits, or some other grab bag that the people must need to survive. All of this hurts the economy, but Obama is the best snake oil salesman in politics.

Some predict that the second four years of Obama may mean that America will no longer exist. The EPA is helping this President to get closer to that realization.

The EPA v Wood Stoves

Forget about those marshmallows. The EPA won't be allowing it for much longer. . Though it is a natural product of the environment, even wood isn't green or renewable enough anymore for the EPA. Wood has got to go.

The EPA in just the last several months has banned the production and sale of 80 percent of America's current wood-burning stoves. This is the oldest heating method known to mankind and still is a mainstay of rural homes and many of our nation's poorest residents. Sorry Charley, the EPA knows best.

As usual, the EPA's ruling is a stringent one-size-fits-all and it apply equally to heavily air-polluted cities and far cleaner plus typically colder off-grid wilderness areas such as large regions of Alaska and the American West.

Think about that romantic getaway in the cabin, trying to get the solar panel positioned so that it can find the sun between the clouds and the drifting snow. We all know that the EPA would not be making standards if they could be met.

Unfortunately for home owners and cabin owners, most of the wood stoves that warm us, all across this vast country cannot meet the new EPA standards. And, so, older stoves—those that cannot be traded in for updated types, must be rendered inoperable, destroyed, or recycled as scrap metal.

The EPA ruling affects many families. For example, the fair counting Census Bureau statistics show that 2.4 million American housing units (12 percent of all homes) burn wood as their primary heating fuel, compared with 7 percent that depend upon fuel oil. Who elected this king and this court of jesters?

EPA's fight against boilers

Let's go back a bit to the discussion of boilers as the two are somewhat related. Jim Hoft posted an article on June 26, 2011 on thegatewaypundit.com site about the controversy as it existed at the time regarding factories with boilers and the EPA's intentions to put them out of business. He titled it "Obama's EPA Sets Out to Destroy US factories with boilers; affecting millions of US jobs."

The Environmental Protection Agency is not fully immune to criticism if Big Boss Obama tells them to slow it down. So, in June, the EPA decided that it would postpone issuing final regulations aimed at cutting pollution from factory boilers until April 2012. This was again postponed until after the November 2012 elections, and it will be postponed again for sure. Bad policies that are well known do not enhance electability. Yet, this is coming.

In September 2010 when this was a big media deal, Sen. James Inhofe of Oklahoma, a people's champion against the EPA and a ranking Republican of the Committee on Environment and Public Works, issued a report titled, "EPA's Anti-Industrial Policy: Threatening Jobs and America's Manufacturing Base."

As expected, his report found that the proposed EPA rule changes to boilers and incinerators could easily kill 800,000 jobs at risk. "Inhoff acknowledged cleaner air was desirable but that the Gestapo manner in which the EPA set the standards to reduce coal emissions is impracticable and too costly for Americans to absorb.

Obama postponed the regulations to avoid political suicide before his reelection. He how has nothing to hold him back. With 26 million already unemployed, why would we force more organizations to close their doors? If these boilers can no longer be installed and run in a cost effective manner, kiss millions more jobs good-by.

By-by boilers

You and I know that boilers have been around since the 19th century. The reason boilers are being targeted by Obama and the EPA is because they are necessary for industry and commerce. The EPA, from Obama's direction wants industry and commerce to slow down so nature can recover from the devastation inflicted on it by mankind, and it might provide a comeuppance to what Obama sees as an arrogant America. The EPA does not mind at all when a factory closes because it is just one more thing that will no longer harm nature.

If you think my conclusion that the EPA wants to destroy America may be off base, rather than begging the argument, I would ask you to check out what the Canada Free press has to say about it. It makes a fitting end to our chapter on

Obama's tool to marginalize America – the EPA. A piece of it follows:
http://www.canadafreepress.com/index.php/article/39717

"Most of America understands common sense guidelines and regulations that protect our environment, food sources and water. No one of whom I am aware, wants forests to be clear cut and pollution smog to take over and darken a city. However, long ago, simple and clear protective guidelines turned into an orgy of invented paranoia and schemes, designed to fulfill the vision from the progressive left and Obama. This vision is simply to destroy the American economy, business and energy systems.

"The last few years we saw the rise of the global warming mythology, Al Gore emerged as one of the messiahs, even getting the Nobel peace prize for this fraud, then everything smelly hit the fan. Real science leaked out; the lies and lack of real data was exposed enough that the US and the world were slapped out of their drunken and 'warmed' tilt.

"You mean there was no global warming that would destroy the world if the UN didn't tax and control the US? The Polar Bears would live after all? …. instead there is global cooling and these cooling and warming cycles have been going on for thousands of years… We saw idiot speech after idiot speech and billions spent on this contrived, international looming disaster. This was led by the progressive left and Obama…

Scientists finally exposed it all…."

.

Chapter 15   Who Thinks the EPA Should Die?

EPA claims they help the sick

Let's start this chapter by giving credence to some EPA claims. For example, they claim their latest job-killing regulations will prevent thousands of heart and asthma attacks. That strikes me in my carnival loving heart. I would ask if the next line will be, "Bet I can find the pea," or "Who'll be the first to buy a bottle?" The readers of this book mostly know the snake oil presented by this administration. Nonetheless, to fully discuss the notion that the EPA helps the sick; the facts dictate the use of a word that starts with bull and ends in a synonym for manure. That should best describe everybody's reaction to that EPA statement. They are really full of it.

This caring EPA uses the notion of asthma attacks as a reason to stop providing heat for buildings while at the same time it demands that real asthmatics no longer use the best CFC inhalers ever made—that actually work. Asthmatics needing the most functional inhalers now must use less effective methods because of the "caring EPA." In other words, the EPA has hurt a large block of sick asthmatics by banning the best inhaler. It is sick for them to say they actually help the sick.

The EPA not only buys all the global warming junk science that the progressives put out as reality, they also sell it and they make bad policy from it. Along the way they hurt little children and make them gasp for air with inadequate inhalers, because of bad EPA policy.

Let's be frank here. The EPA banned the best inhalers for children. We will cover this in detail in later chapters. They have no right to claim they help the sick. The small amount of CFCs in inhalers hardly matters to the atmosphere—even if the science behind it were legitimate and not junk.

The EPA knows that. But, this is the same EPA that held up the Dutch skimmers from cleaning the gulf for 50 days because it violated one of their asinine regulations. There is no "greater good," notion for the EPA. Thus children have died gasping for asthmatic medicine that the new inhalers simply cannot provide.

Please don't get sick of me saying this. The reason the EPA takes no action on bad policy is because it is not concerned about humans and human comfort or human lives—even the lives of our precious children. The EPA is concerned about nature first and Obama is tied in with nature and the EPA is his nature agent. Why Obama never chose to step in and help asthmatic children—now that is cause for concern. What is on his mind? Once child dying, from my perspective is reason for the entire EPA to be killed. And, the children are dying.

Newt Gingrich proposes killing the EPA?

From his website, Newt Direct: "The Environmental Protection Agency (EPA) has transformed from an agency with the original animating and noble mission of protecting the environment into a job-killing, centralizing engine of ideological litigation and regulation that blocks economic progress at every turn while also frustrating the EPA's original mission of protecting the environment ...

The EPA's activities have gone well beyond protecting the environment; instead, the EPA is focused on centralizing and asserting unlimited federal power over the economy.

The EPA should be replaced with a new and improved agency dedicated to bringing together science, technology, entrepreneurs, incentives, and local creativity to create a cleaner environment through smarter regulation..."

Though this is a great purist solution recommended by a great American, the reality is that with this Gingrich notion, the same old people would be back at their same old desks simply wearing different arm bands. No, Newt, Sorry Mr. Gingrich! The EPA, like the brown shirts long before it, must be killed dead before anything positive comes from its one time existence.

Democrats & Republicans on the EPA

Of the old 112th Congress, it appears only four brave Democrats rose up to stop the EPA in its tracks and none of them want to kill it dead. Rep. Nick Rahall of West Virginia, Rep. Collin Peterson of Minnesota, Rep. Dan Boren of Oklahoma and Sen. Joe Manchin of West Virginia expressed support for a bill backed by 43 Senate Republicans that would bar the EPA from using federal law to control greenhouse gases from power plants, refineries and other industrial facilities.

In other words, only four Democrats, and Pennsylvania's Bob Casey Jr. was not on that list, care enough about Jobs to force the EPA to back off its destructive path.

How is it that the party of the working-man, traditionally the Democratic Party, no longer wants anybody to work and doesn't care how many jobs the EPA steals from this dismal economy.

Newt Gingrich is not the only Republican who is fed up with the EPA. Democrats for the most part love the EPA. Michele Bachmann wants to padlock the EPA's doors, and Rick Perry thinks an immediate moratorium on EPA regulations is in order. Ron Paul has wanted the EPA eliminated along with a number of other do-nothing good agencies. Herman Cain, wanted the EPA eliminated at least 999 times.

Cain thinks a private commission should determine the validity of regulations and he wants the committee to include oil and gas executives. The fact is the environment should be a states' issue except when the states have disputes. Lots of dollars are being spent by states and the EPA is not necessary in 99.9% of the issues they solve.

Mitt Romney is an oddball for a "conservative. He somehow likes the EPA, believes in global warming, thinks ethanol is good and ethanol subsidies are good. So, Mitt is not our guy moving forward for sure. John McCain loves Democrats so he is out too!

My favorite candidate from the 2012 Republican Primary was Michelle Bachman, a real conservative. She had to drop out and eventually two other good conservatives, Herman Cain and even Ron Paul made their exits. If they had prevailed there would be no EPA today and life would be better.

What can be worse than Ozone?

Because there is no evidence that typical ambient ozone levels have affected actual public health, the EPA resorts to dubious laboratory tests to provide a rationale for its claim that there is no safe threshold of exposure to ozone. They don't know what they are talking about but it does not stop them from talking.

To put this in perspective, we should consider that starvation, exposure to the cold (no heat) and/or stress from loss of income are probably greater threats to human health than any reasonable amount of Ozone or other flutter proposed by the EPA.

Many bloggers on the Internet offer thoughts about the negative impact of the EPA on US civilization. With the corrupt national press providing Obama cover-up news relentlessly, one must find news in different spots today.

For example, one particular blogger on the Internet suggested that EPA regulations would change substantially if Congress modified the Clean Air Act with some repercussions. Suppose for every 10 private sector jobs lost due to an EPA regulation, one EPA employee who worked on writing the regulation would lose their job. Right now the EPA can throw smoke bombs into crowded amphitheaters and they pay no price for their actions.

His thoughts were that the EPA would suddenly find that maybe this or that supposed pollutant wasn't really that bad for humans after all. Of course this is another good idea from somebody sick of the EPA. My plan to kill the EPA completely will work even better.

Summary: Who thinks the EPA should die?

The chapter title hoped to suck all of the readers into considering the EPA as a disposable item in much the same way as it considers human beings that live in America. That would be us!

So, I can certainly say that if by the Lord's graces, a good Congress comes into being and a good President in 2016, there is a fine chance the EPA can be and will be eliminated, and no more court cases will be required to give the people back our country.

I sure hope after this chapter or as many more as you need to read, you too feel the same.

Chapter 16

Our President is the EPA!

A President—stronger than Terminator II

Obama is the EPA energizer bunny. He is full of unlimited energy no matter where he gets it. I cannot forget when at the 2008 RNC Convention Sarah Palin dealt candidate Obama a death blow from the podium, and Obama was irreparably harmed.

However, instead of rolling over, Obama melded into a highly advanced Terminator II-like being. He appeared to be built of liquid metal and he used shape shifting and attitude adjustments to regain his composure as the Energizer Bunny. He was rebuilt, back alive, and stronger than ever. He simply would not "die." Pain "killed" him in her speech but he would not die.

Soon in a bad trick played on America, Sarah Palin became the victim rather than the perpetrator. The corrupt press in a series of "gotcha" "take-down" interviews had convinced the simplest Americans that Palin, not Obama would be bad for the country.

Too bad there are so many simpletons, aka—low information voters, in the country and too bad the Democratic Party knows exactly what specific lies are needed to motivate them for the Party. Meanwhile, the ever resilient, energetic, and entirely corrupt Barack Obama is good at fooling everybody.

Though there may be some times like when Pail "killed" him that he may need time to collect himself, he is very dangerous. His liquid metal shape-shifting prevarication engine is always in the ON position.

To help his 2012 election chances recently, while winding down his first term, Obama issued an executive order postponing a plan by the EPA to tighten ozone standards. What a great guy! He was not interested in those paying attention, to think he was the bad guy so instead he got credit for a postponement of his own policies. That is a clever trick. But, it is a trick, nonetheless.

As much as Obama really does want to stop progress in the US, and he has done quite well in this regard, he does not wish to be blamed for stopping it.

The President cannot afford to tell the truth about his inner feelings about America. However, Dinesh D'Souza captured them quite well in his hit movie "2016." Americans learning that their president has true disdain for their country would not be inclined to vote for him for dog catcher. Obama has just one goal and it is to be reelected as often as possible. He would love a third term if he can get it. In the Obama reelection scheme, real Americans count only because they each have a vote.

Obama thinks America takes too much of the world's resources for itself. His presidency is based on taking as much as he can from some Americans and giving it to other Americans. He also likes taking from America, as he did with the Petrobas $2 Billion dollar investment, and giving it to other countries.

His "fair share" notion also extends to taking the hard earned money from regular Americans and so he can give it to illegal aliens and then when he makes them citizens, perhaps they will make him President for life. By now, though I am a

Democrat, as a conservative first, the President knows that he cannot count on my vote for anything other than an early retirement.

The President loves to use class warfare to assure his personal victories and now he is campaigning for the Democratic Party using the same techniques. We are now seeing the beginning of the program. The President and Democrats in Congress are trying to distract voters by highlighting a series of issues that will do almost nothing to improve economic opportunity, but they will make the most gullible Americans more dependent on Democrat largesse.

We've seen it all before and unless Americans wise up, we'll be duped again. The faux issues are the votes in the U.S. Senate to raise the minimum wage to $10.10 an hour; the elimination of the so-called pay gap between men and women and an even more deliberate redistribution policy in the name of fighting income inequality. None of these are designed to help America. But, if they don't work, the next page of the playbook says to scare seniors, and nobody is as good at this as the Democrats.

If Americans were not so capable of being taken by lies from Obama, Democrats, and the corrupt national press, it surely would help. Each of the faux issues is designed to hurt the idea of Republican brand as much a possible ahead of the 2014 midterm elections.

The objective is not economic recovery in any way. It is to make it seem that the Democrats are the only party that cares about promoting economic opportunity. If there was going to be economic recovery based on their plans, we would at least be seeing a little bit of it by now.

Obama's real objectives are to siphon as much as possible from the economy to feed the huge government machine that he has created. Additionally, as a "1%er" himself, he has a deep desire to confiscate the wealth of the other rich. He wants to make them substantially less rich.

The President also wants to give to the non-producers / non-workers the bounty produced by the labor of working Americans. He is ready to use the tax system to accomplish this and he will use the EPA to suck the blood out of all US industry. The bottom line on Obama and the economy is to not be disappointed. Do not expect any jobs any time soon, regardless of the last Obama lie you may have heard.

Ironically, Obama sucks in a lot of Americans into his web of deceit. He prospers on the misfortune of others as they depend more on his "benevolence," especially now that things are not going so well for many families. His lies are very believable and when he tells the downtrodden—who caused to be downtrodden—that the government can take care of all their needs, to those riding on hard times, t is an easy sell. Just like his EPA, Obama is a plague on America. He brings out the worst in otherwise good people.

Americans love America for many reasons. One of the reasons is the notion of the American Dream. Every one of us can be rich if we devise a notion that impresses the world or we become the best at what we do. Obama has no use for American exceptionalism and he would be pleased to fully eliminate the American dream for such dreaming gives people hope and it may cause them to question their government.

This President would have no problem if he could get away with it to never permit anybody ever again to achieve or get rich or to take their proceeds if they happen to succeed. What fun would that be? It would be like communist Russia, the USSR! Yet, it is the natural landing point for creeping socialism.

Even those folks down on their luck would not want to hit the jackpot and have somebody from the Obama regime show up and snag 99% of it? So, to prevent the dream from ending, Americans all have to watch the class warfare games this President likes to play. Remember he uses the same effective weapon as Satan—the lie.

He is very good at the game for sure. He plays the game because he does not care about America or Americans. He cares only about Obama. Notice that the Obama's have not given up any of their vacations, which they take on the taxpayer dime. They have given up nothing while they ask everybody else to put in a "fair share." Obama paid about $100,000 in taxes this year, and it was just 20% of his income. He has had much better years. For a guy who wants the "rich" to pay 99% in taxes, the President sure is not teaching by example.

Is Barack Hussein Obama the real deal or is he a fraud and a charlatan? Will he one day be the only one left living the American Dream? Can he talk us all out of our own dreams?

Obama of course thinks he can talk to Americans in their neighborhoods and in their living rooms because he has that special "gift of gab." He thinks we will feel differently about him simply because, as a narcissist, he knows he is the one and only true Obama.

I am surely not denying that our President is the real Obama. I am not denying that he is convinced that all Americans will therefore love him and vote for him in his try for a third term if we permit it. Unfortunately for the country, we have learned that there seems to be nothing more important to many Americans than Obama and all other Democrats getting reelected? I might suggest an alternative—how about having a nice life for starters?

Is anybody really concerned about Obama and his presidentially appointed czars? The conservative base is enraged about how he is using America for his own benefit. Any postponement of doom for taxpayers or industry is simply temporary and it is because there is always an election two years hence. Obama is the smartest politician who ever lived. Did our parents ever teach us to be cautious around politicians? Obama is why!

Postponing regulations is something the Obama can do and will do simply because he wants to get reelected, and he wants there to be only Democrats in the Congress. I would love to deny him both. Such denial is something he deserves after delivering to America the worst economy since we were colonies of England.

You may recall that Obama backed off Obamacare temporarily, until the right political climate emerged. Then, he and Pelosi pushed it to passage. Since then, he has issued over 40 illegal changes and thousands of exemptions to his friends for signature legislation simply because he wants to keep the power over your health. Short of that he wants all remaining power to be held by Democrats.

The coming EPA regulations, nasty as they are, will be out there to plop in whenever Obama believes he has an opening. Now that he is in his second term, he is ready indeed, but he has acceded to Democrat demands to hold off until after the election. They know when this boom falls it will be devastating and will take at least two years for even gullible Americans to forget.

They want the chance to get reelected before Obama permits this big shoe fall on the necks of Americans. One thing for sure—it is all coming faster than any of us want.

Any postponement of bad medicine gives the prevaricator in chief the opportunity for some identity protection for any election. One of the Obama goals has recently been achieved.

It happened quietly with no fanfare. China is now the # 1 country in the world. This happened on Obama's watch.

He is not apologizing for the China thing or the bad economy. If he were called on it, he would blame Bush and most Americans in the simpleton class, would believe him. He is that good at lying.

Getting the US to #2, and then #3, etc. has been his plan all along. Obama's mission has always been to deny America its # 1 rating in the world. It has now been accomplished. But, don't expect to hear that from the corrupt media any time soon. Secretly there are big parties at the White house with big progressive liberal rock bands performing with all the guests sipping lemonade and getting stoned on the taxpayers.

The annual cost of these new EPA regulations is staggering. We're looking at from $19 billion to $90 billion. Private sector analysts estimate they would also result in the loss of 7.3 million additional U.S. jobs. That would bring the total officially unemployed to 33.3 million from 26 million. No wonder Obama postponed the start date. He is not politically suicidal but again, this will happen only after Obama Democrats win in 2014.

Chapter 17

Is Obama's EPA a Rogue Agency?

Obama's real energy policy?

Mackubin Thomas Owens wrote a great article in mid
September 2011 for the Boston Herald titled, "Obama's EPA
not a 'rogue' agency at all." It is a perfect and a compelling
read:

http://www.bostonherald.com/news/opinion/op_ed/view.
bg?articleid=1365720

Owens notes that Obama really does have an energy policy
though it is not one that is helpful to America. It is simple
and it has one objective—to reduce access to fossil fuels by
raising their price, thereby making "alternate" or "green"
energy sources more attractive. If the economy collapses
along the way since the second term is well under way, who
is there that would really care?

It is too bad for this fine campaigner that the words he uses to
solidify his base cannot be used for the rest of Americans.
You see, Obama's base is really that far left. I'll say it. Those
who love him the most are Marxists. Regular Americans
have a problem differentiating left from right politically so
Obama begs the argument with euphemisms like "war on
women," and "Republicans are evil."

With these simple phrases, like a serpent that can speak, he
convinces the bulk of Americans, having a tough time in life,

that he is their savior. He is not. We know it. But, those suffering do not know that the one making the promises is also the one making life miserable for them all.

The drivel he delivers to them, he hopes will never reach his base of progressives, Marxists, and socialists. They are so far left that even the cliffs of the US West Coast cannot stop them. They are half way to China. Perhaps that is why they like the Chinese so much that they keep giving American businesses reason to build their facilities and operate them in the People's Republic.

Ask GE, Obama's pet corporation, why they moved so many operations to China. Ask Obama how it is that when Bush was president America was the # 1 economy and now that distinction goes to the new #1 Communist Chinese.

You see when he was speaking to the liberal press in San Francisco while campaigning in 2008, Barack Obama promised to bankrupt anyone foolish enough to build coal-fired power plants. How would these bankruptcies have helped the sluggish American economy? That line could have been delivered by an EPA spokesman as Obama and the EPA are almost 100% in synch.

Candidate Obama also discussed his "energy plan." He said that his policies would intentionally make energy prices 'skyrocket' as the energy industry passed along the exorbitant costs of his cap-and-trade (energy) policy. Now, as another mid-term election has passed, Obama had been postponing as much as he could of his aggressive anti-American agenda, but not for the good of the nation. It was so he can dupe Americans into thinking he is not the radical anti-American leader that he actually is. Now that the 2014 mid-terms are behind us, Obama can resume being the messiah in chief.

There are those who think the EPA does its own thing and when Obama finds out about it, he gets upset and then reins them in. Not so! This liquid, shape changing president, just like Terminator II can use government policy to raise oil and gas prices, subsidize alternative energy sources, and he can then mandate the use of the latter for his cronies in that industry. They pre-rewarded him with the cash to cover extravagant inaugural displays and large campaign warchests, and they paid for his elections. Why should he not favor them over America?.

If Solyndra, an Obama crony capitalism reward for political donors, had not gone out of business, we would all be mandated to use solar power, even if we could not get it and even if it were unaffordable. The good ole good partying Solyndra gang, were always heavy Obama campaign contributors.

Obama wins each way. None of his uncultured followers in the neighborhoods of America understand this President's erudite leanings. He does not want them to know that he lives like the 1% he campaigns against. It may be distorted but clearly crony capitalism is a win-win for Obama. The people unfortunately are on neither of the winning sides. Somebody has to lose, and it is always John Q. Public.

Owens writes: "The EPA is not rogue. It is a very important tool for implementing Obama policy."

 Another blogger chimed in saying that the progressives "are using our dependence on energy to regulate and control Americans. The EPA is Obama's brownshirts, who have long since moved on from clean air and water and now tell us what appliances to buy, siding, roofing, massive regulations on pickup trucks, increased energy bill taxes, and how to build our houses. It's easy to see what is going on in America, with Obama's use of the EPA..."

And it is not good.

Owens has listed a number of other items that Obama has in store for us in addition to the postponed Ozone plan:

"First, the agency recently issued final regulations curbing power plant emissions of sulfur and nitrogen oxides in 28 states and the District of Columbia. The so-called Cross-State Air Pollution Rule,[which was supposed to take effect in 2012, [but did not because of litigation,] aims to slash power plant emissions that drift across state borders.

"The new rule comes only six years after the EPA ordered a 70 percent reduction in the same emissions by 2025. The new rules have the potential to severely impact nearly 20 percent [more] of the nation's coal-fueled power plants. Financial analysts estimate that the cost of this rule will be $130 billion by 2015.

"In March of this year, the EPA proposed new standards for coal-fired plants that would establish a "maximum achievable control technology" standard for mercury and other hazardous air emissions, requiring utilities to install equipment that is prohibitively expensive or, in some cases, doesn't yet exist. The resulting closures of coal plants due to the ruling would reduce the output of electricity by 30,000 to 70,000 megawatts.

"The EPA is considering regulating coal ash as a hazardous waste, based on the claim that it contains toxic metals.

"But coal ash contains only trace quantities of such metals. Since coal ash is used in many beneficial applications, e.g. road construction, its regulation as hazardous waste will result in the loss of as many as 316,000 jobs and a cost to the American economy of $110 billion over two decades, according to financial analysts."

Mackubin Thomas Owens is professor of National Security Affairs at the U.S. Naval War College in Newport, R.I. The quoted areas above are his views but they do make a lot of sense and they explain a lot. Job loss in America is intentional. It is the Obama plan as executed by his protégés in the EPA!

At the very end of April 2014, the EPA scored a major victory, according to their own press releases. The mostly progressive liberal Supreme Court of the US, SCOTUS, almost gave the full go ahead for the EPA's program for harmful coal plant emissions that cross state lines. But, it held back intelligently.

Admittedly, and I might add thankfully, the EPA still faces important policy questions -- as well as litigation -- as it moves to implement this nasty policy aimed at killing coal.

Euphemistically, the EPA seemingly has been trying to implement a "good neighbor" rule for two decades, but its previous efforts have been thrown out in federal court. This ruling by the Supreme Court does not give the EPA carte blanche, and so the EPA still has a lot of explaining to the American public for making life harder for regular Americans. Let's hope that Americans blame the President, who is the real perpetrator, rather than his personal surrogate agency, the EPA, for the President's affront against the American people. Removing the EPA as an agency would be the same as taking a weapon from the hand of a madman.

The bottom line on where this stuff stands is that the SCOTUS gave the EPA a plus in certain area and a big minus in others. For example, it noted big time that costs needed to be considered in deciding which states and which pollution sources must cut emissions.

So, the EPA idea that they could bankrupt a state that is forced to comply with their silly little regulations just because they say so—that part of the regulation is gone. The EPA at this point must start over in order to hurt America on this account. Vote for any representative that promises to rid the US of the EPA!

Obviously, the compliance dates that have already come and gone leave many legal issues unanswered. Litigation puts a hold on bad things, and when the litigation ends, the dates in the original regulations hold no real water and must be redone.

"There are a whole host of issues that still remain at the D.C. Circuit," said Joshua Frank of Baker Botts LLP, who represented utilities in the case. He characterized the current status of the EPA industry choking program as a legal "quagmire."

For example, there are three states -- Ohio, Kansas and Georgia—each of which separately challenged the EPA's implementation plans in their states. Those cases were put on hold pending the Supreme Court decision and now, they can move forward.

The notion of Obama ruling the USA by dictate through the EPA has been pushed backwards but the effort will continue. For this small victory, we should all have our own secret little party without lemonade for the good of America. Perhaps the service area of the White House can be made available for its hosting?

Much more importantly, the Supreme Court decision did not technically lift a federal appellate court's stay on the EPA program, which had put it on hold. The EPA must decide whether and when to ask the U.S. Court of Appeals for the District of Columbia Circuit to take such action.

In this day and age, a court win is not really a court win and thankfully, a court loss is not a court loss. If the EPA were eliminated, however, we Americans could gain a better economy and save a lot of wasteful spending.

Chapter 18

The End of Incandescent Light Part I

The EPA is nuts!

It is daylight as I write but there are still lights on in most homes in most cities in Pennsylvania. That really drives the EPA nuts. More than likely they are incandescent light bulbs. That too drives the EPA nuts. By now, the EPA is plenty nuts.

Over the years, the people have grown accustomed to the warm glow of the incandescent light bulb invented by Thomas Alva Edison. You may know that Edison was born in Ohio, a neighboring state to Pennsylvania and he grew up in Michigan. Edison invented so many things that were useful in his day and ours, that he received 1093 patents. The EPA stance on Edison is: "What does he know?

Edison lived the spirit of Americanism at a time when even Presidents enjoyed being American. Such exceptionalism was the order of the day in Edison's time. There was much to be invented, and America was a welcoming place for inventors.

Today Edison would need so many EPA permits to conduct his experiments, that he would be lucky to invent much of anything. In fact, there is probably an agency today that would find his efforts to be anti-government and they would shut him down post haste. Who does he think he is?

The Obama EPA for example, as you may know, orders everybody around, including simple homeowners like you and I. The thinking around the EPA is that homeowners are culprits and are to blame for bad air, bad water, and a host of other maladies. One of our big sins is that we burn light bulbs. And, so by order of the EPA, in December 2011, all of us were to learn the depth of the disdain the EPA has for home-town America. But, we got a short reprieve.

Figure 18-1 Thomas Edison – Source Internet Unknown

No 100 watt incandescent light bulbs were available for purchase after 2012. The EPA won this battle unchallenged while American homes at night were just a bit dimmer.

Over the next few years afterwards, all incandescent light bulbs, including harmless 40 and 60 watt bulbs were taken off the market. Selling and buying all incandescent light bulbs is now against the law.

After December 31, 2013, no incandescent light bulb was able to be sold legally in America. Perhaps the incandescent light hoarders will have the EPA make a storm trooper run

on their homes sometime soon. And, you thought the EPA
was just a puff agency. Nope, our Congress actually
permitted the slow demise of Thomas Edison's magic
creation even before replacements in America were available.
America is now out of the light bulb business it created.

To repeat, the final phase of the ban on incandescent light
bulbs went into effect in 2014, leaving consumers with pricier
energy-efficient options that are expected to save people
money over time. But is not that a violation of freedom of
electricity. Why should government get to be the final arbiter?
Don't they work for us?

Can you imagine the light bulb luminaries who get arrested
and find themselves doing time in the big house on a light-
bulb rap? After over 100 years, the EPA found out that light
bulbs were bad for the health of Mother Nature. They are, by
the way, OK for human nature. So, how did this happen?

Congress did it and Obama likes it

Obama's EPA does not get the full whack on the notion that
the incandescent light bulb has become illegal. Politicians in
Washington, including our own from Pennsylvania voted for
a goofy law in 2007 that banned cheap incandescent bulbs in
favor of the more expensive and carcinogenic compact
florescent bulbs (CFCs). How is that an EPA winner?
Answer: the agenda matters and all wins matter for the
agenda.

Obviously the people we elect think we cannot make good
marketplace decisions in our day-to-day lives. So, Congress
proposed and passed legislation to protect all of us dummies
from ourselves. In mid-2011, Congress began to rethink the
ban and brought it up again, even after the TEA party had
cleansed the house of all of the supposed florescent lovers.

Yet, the bill to revoke this asinine law constraining Americans on light bulbs did not pass because of some unknown reason. Perhaps even the freshmen in Congress need to be extricated from our towns and cities in the next election. Who do they think they represent: morons? The elections brought with them a slew of representatives who do not trust their constituents. It's time to repay the favor.

What is wrong with consumer choice and soft yellow lighting or less expensive incandescent light bulbs? Why every home should instead be subjected to the unnatural, office-like white light of Chinese-made pricey mini fluorescents confounds the logical mind.

One might objectively ask if even Republicans have given in to the nanny state after the 2012 and then the 2014 elections. It seems that today, we already know the Republicans have caved completely to the whims and wishes of their seemingly more powerful adversaries across the aisle. We conservatives know them as the "Democrats." What is wrong with this picture?

The most annoying proponent of the light-bulb ban by the EPA for my money, had been the Secretary of Energy Steven Chu. This guy is not with most Americans on the notion of needing government to make decisions in our every-day lives. Chu loves the notion that all Americans get to buy their lightbulbs from China instead of America. Imagine him saying these words as he did, and you will have his speech verbatim:

"We are taking away a choice that continues to let people waste their own money."

Obviously, Chu liked the notion of Big Brother as the government could preselect everything for the dumb US citizens and of course illegals...also so that there is no guesswork for the feeble brained population. Government will do the selecting and it will be perfect.

For those rooting for America, the good news is that On February 1, 2013, Chu announced he would not serve for the President's second term and he resigned on April 22, 2013. It was not chu soon! Sorry about that! It was not too soon!

One time Senator John Warner (R–VA) thinks Chu was spot on and he offered his thoughts on the one time potentiality of repealing the 2007 law. : "We'll be dropping backwards in America's need to become more energy-efficient."

Jim Presswood, who is with the environmental activist group, Natural Resources Defense Council, has his own perspective: "Clearly, consumers, the economy and the environment will suffer if these standards are repealed."

His organization claims that the ban would save consumers $85 per year. So, let me ask, what is the real cost of freedom if a piece of it can be purchased for less than $100.00 per year? Is freedom worth the price-tag in dollars or must it be in blood?

Let me ask you this one question: Do you think our forefathers came to America so that some bureaucrat someplace could make all of their decisions for them? Do you think that either government is much better today or do you think that people are more incompetent than in the founding era?

What is the rationale for government being the sole arbiter as to what is good and what is bad for the public? What does the public get to say? Will government actually punish those who break their illegal rules?

So, now that the stores have run out of incandescent bulbs, and since the US is not making them anymore, must we all switch from these simple and cheap light-bulbs that we now use to expensive, dangerous halogen or fluorescent bulbs? Is this an order from the government? Who told them they had the power of coercion over the people?

The EPA says these new expensive Chinese-built bulbs are OK but incandescent bulbs are bad. OK, they did not say that exactly but is surely the way it sounded. What they said was that the 100 watt bulb cannot be sold any more as of January 1, 2012. So, shop for all you can while you can. Over the next two years, 75, 60, and 40 watt bulbs will no longer be able to be sold. That time has also come. There are no more incandescent legal bulbs in the USA!

The law was being phased in over three years. Here are the dates when Americans had to be prepared to change their bulbs if they burned out. Thank the EPA or kill them as I suggest! Incandescent is dead! Long live incandescent!

Today's Bulbs	After the Standard	Standard Effective Date
100 watt	≤ 72 watts	January 1, 2012
75 watt	≤ 53 watts	January 1, 2013
60 watt	≤ 43 watts	January 1, 2014
40 watt	**≤ 29 watts**	**January 1, 2014**

According to the EPA, the second part of the law requires that most light bulbs be 60-70% more efficient than the standard incandescent today; this will go into effect in 2020. Many compact fluorescent light bulbs (CFLs) and many Light Emitting Diodes (LEDs) can meet this requirement today, shaving energy usage compared to standard incandescent bulbs by 75%.

What the EPA doesn't tell you is that these new bulbs are very expensive and there are special procedures to assure your family is safe if one of them breaks. So, don't break one.

Why is this law needed and how does it benefit consumers?

This is direct from the EPA site: "EISA is eliminating unnecessarily wasteful products from the market."

Should we be pleased? EISA is the name of the congressional act but we know that the 2007 act is a brain child of the EPA. I have a question for you. Did you ask for the EISA or the EPA or Congress or anybody to unilaterally eliminate unnecessarily wasteful products? I did not ask them either. I think both the iPad and the iPhone are unnecessary. Will they be banned eventually? If not, Why not?

The banning of consumer items is just another big intrusion of big Obama government into the lives of regular people. If you don't see enough of Obama on TV, wait until Obama is in your doctor's office! He is already in your light fixtures. He wants to be wherever you go and he wants control of your every movement.

The Obama intrusions are not fully appreciated, but when all the pictures in your Doctor's office, including the Saturday Evening Post picture of the little doll being examined by a physician, are replaced with pictures of Obama helping Americans in need, you will know what Obamacare really means. It will be a lot more Obama than care... but that may be another book. No man can exact that much control on a set of people and have us accept it!

Perhaps the EPA guerrillas will take the time to visit your neighborhood and mine to see if there are any other issues. Maybe you are an energy perpetrator and you keep certain of your lights on too long? Maybe you use too many garbage bags? Maybe your dog excretes amounts that are dangerously over the farm manure limit?

What's next? Don't worry! Obama has a few surprises in store and you'll see them when the thousands of regulations that are being held for campaign reasons are released now that this 2014 big election is over and the campaigner in chief feels safe to emerge again as our president.

Chapter 19

The End of Incandescent Light Part II

GE; Thomas Edison; Jeffrey Immelt

By now, many Americans have heard of Jeffrey Immelt, the former head of General Electric, the company originally created by Thomas Edison. Founded in 1890 as the Edison General Electric Company, the company merged with the Thomson-Houston Company, its major competitor, in 1892. The name of the new company became the General Electric Company.

Jeffrey Immelt is no Thomas Edison. He couldn't tie Edison's shoes. Yet, over the last few years, Immelt served as Obama's Jobs Czar. Despite all the tax credits gained by GE for its green jobs program and its friendship with Obama, in all the years since Edison, the mighty GE has been unable to figure out how to make a better incandescent light bulb in America—one that meets the Obama EPA standards displayed above. That's almost as hard to believe as the EPA telling us we can't use these light bulbs anymore.

So, since GE could not meet the government standard, it is taking its light bulb manufacturing business overseas along with a lot of other jobs, even some that may be giving a few defense secrets to the Chinese. But, hey, Obama wants all countries to compete equally so for him, helping the Chinese develop better weaponry may be a good idea. It is hard to tell.

It is also possible that President Obama did not tell Mr. Immelt that the jobs he created as the "Jobs Czar" were supposed to be US-based. Perhaps Obama forgot to tell his buddy Immelt that as President, he was looking for net gains- - not net losses in jobs. But, then again maybe Obama thinks Immelt is doing fine. Who knows? Obama is not talking about it!

Despite Americans not really wanting to give up any rights to any US agencies, in the fall of 2010, the EPA agency's regulations forced the last major GE factory (run by Immelt) that was making ordinary incandescent light bulbs in the United States to close.

This factory was around for most of the time from the 1870's when Edison first shed light on all subjects. GE admitted that a lot of the jobs at the facility were already gone when the remaining 200 workers at the plant lost their jobs way back in 2010.

In 2011, most Americans knew that GE had some good fortune. It got some extra funding from taxpayers—about $7 billion dollars in tax credits, rebates, and in gifts.

One would think, with $7 billion in cash from Obama, GE would have been grateful. Why were they not motivated to set off a boom of industrial activity and job growth in the U.S. by taking the $7 billion tax refund bonanza and using it to create a better light bulb? They should have been able to design and then manufacture whatever the EPA required as the replacement for the incandescent light bulb. They chose not to do so.

Hey even if they sold bulbs for a slight loss, GE would still be way ahead. Why did they not do that? Did Obama tell them to go to China to make the world a fairer place in which to compete?

Since over 50% of Americans agree that the President does not hate America, or surely they would not have elected him, it a fair question to ask if Obama really wants America to win? If so, why send all this work and all these jobs for light bulbs to China? Maybe it does not help to recall that almost 50% of Americans think the President actually hates us all.

Let me go through this again one more time to make my point. No matter what it happened to be, since $7 billion came from taxpayer pockets, why would the Jobs Czar, an American official and a CEO of the largest tech company in the world, Jeffrey Immelt, the head of GE, the guy gifted with $7 Billion from the pockets of US taxpayers, not build the replacement bulb, if it is really needed to be built in the first place, in America? Why did his buddy our President, not demand as much?

A lot of American plants could have been built for the $7 billion. A corollary to that question is "Why did Obama not fire him as the Jobs czar?" Is it possible that our President, does not like manufacturing jobs in America?

Regardless, GE supposedly makes its own decisions and having the inside track on light bulbs, it chose not to invest in America. Thank you GE from all Americans! I know I will remember this when considering your products in the future.

 I know I will buy any product, including light-bulbs, from any company other than GE. Actions have consequences. Don't bother stamping GE on anything anymore for it will not motivate me and perhaps other Americans to buy it.

CFL bulbs are dangerous

Many of us are learning that the class of light-bulb favored by the EPA is known as a compact florescent or CFL. Unfortunately, the EPA is not in the Jobs business and they have been rightfully accused of killing a lot of jobs. It doesn't seem to bother them. In this case, the leading replacement bulbs for incandescent bulbs are made entirely overseas, mostly in China. How can our President claim he is for American jobs in his jobs bill when he eliminates real jobs in real businesses?

So, all of America's light-bulbs now come from China, the # 1 country in the world, or other countries, and the bulbs are not incandescent. They will mostly be CFL's. Maybe this is good news for the White House and the EPA, but not for me. The bulbs made by GE will also be made in GE's many China plants.

To be cynical about it, and we should be, the brainiacs in Congress, the White-House, and the inglorious EPA have no problem forcing Americans to stop using US products, forcing purchases of products made in foreign countries, by foreigners. Pat Doyle, 54, a former GE worker, who put in 26 years working at this plant, summed it up. "First, we were sold out by the government. Then we were sold out by GE."

Figure 18-3 GE Plant Once Operating Test the bulbs

Lights out for ordinary bulbs made in the U.S.

We can blame this on the cronyism and the corruption of the Obama regime and the worst Senates of all time--the 111th, 112th, to the 114th. Add the fact that the EPA learned well how to be Obama's chief enforcer and you have enough reasons for why there are no jobs in America.

Back when Edison was innovating in the 1800's, he had the freedom to invent and manufacture because the government back then respected the Constitution. Many jobs were created from Edison's inventions. Today, the Obama EPA has the power to inhibit liberty and freedom and invention even if their intervention destroys jobs.

And it has the power to ship jobs overseas. It is ridiculous but it is true. Regulations are just one of the ways the Obama regime, is dismantling America, and assuring we have high unemployment for a long time.

You see, the Obama EPA and most regulators do not like inventions because most require power. Power requires burning fossil fuels. Case closed.

Regulators do not like anything powered by anything. They don't even like humans from Pennsylvania or Ohio or Montana needing to burn anything just to be warm in the winter or to be able to see to read. They would prefer huge coats worn all winter long and of course a ban on reading for six months in the winter. What could would smart citizens do for the state?

In its experimentation, the inglorious EPA has found that human breath, stinky for sure at times, contains a noxious gas that also needs to be banned. No! It is not garlic. It is CO_2. Yes, it is Carbon Dioxide. I surely wish that I were kidding. The EPA is nuts!

There are elements in the EPA, who because of their zeal for a nature-first, human-last environment, are also for population control. They believe that, because of his very existence on the planet, man is a major polluter. They would love to reduce the footprint of mankind on this planet so it can be safe for animals, insects, and even some nasty flora and fauna.

Blaming people for exhaling gives those in the population control circles more reasons for wanting less and less people on earth. Some suggest the EPA won't be happy until 90% of humans disappear from the planet. Knowing that, it makes me question the EPA's motivations for any of their often silly regulations.

What if humans have no breath? Don't worry! They're not going to take us off the planet that easy. I don't think the "Ban Breath Act" would pass Congress. Even the most corrupt politicians still have to breathe.

That's not all that the "blame America first crowd" of far left progressives find fault with today. They find people, especially American people to be major polluters and therefore responsible for most of the earth's global warming problems. They worship Al Gore as if his bad breath and his bad medicine is from a prophet. For returning their love, Al Gore has picked up over a hundred million dollars in net worth since leaving the vice presidency and speculation is he will soon be the first green billionaire.

As much as the environmentalists love Al Gore, they must have a great disdain for the legacy of Thomas Edison and of course for Philadelphia's own Ben Franklin. Considering that Franklin is one of those credited with discovering electricity through his lightening & kite experiments, he would not be in the favor of the EPA.

With the work of some other scientists, who helped to perfect electricity for major uses, Thomas Edison never could have invented the incandescent light bulb in the first place without Franklin's electricity. The ban on incandescent light bulbs would be unnecessary if there were no electricity.

Of course that also means that Americans would not have to begin to buy light-bulbs from China next year—again if there were no electricity. How far back to nature does the EPA want us to go? We know that teepees are out because paintings of early America show smoke coming out of the teepees—again because humans occupied these dwellings. Smoke is not something that is OK with the EPA.

Concluding thoughts

Let's end this chapter about the end of incandescent light with some thoughts from Jack Cafferty of CNN, a certifiable liberal / progressive. Cafferty is often going after the wrong causes but he is right on in his analysis of this one about GE and Jeffrey Immelt.

Remember, Jeffrey Immelt is the CEO of GE, the onetime maker of Edison's incandescent light bulbs. It is also the company that moved its light bulb business from the US to china in 2010 because of the EPA's banning of incandescent light.

Once companies find they can offshore with impunity—moving jobs to China and they still make a big buck and still get big tax breaks from Obama, they have a tendency to keep doing it. Corporations are not in business to please presidents or any other American.

Let's say the EPA forced them to learn how to get by without Americans and they learned so well, they can do it well on their own now without any help from EPA bans.

.

Hold on to your hats. GE just moved its X-ray business to China, and that is driving CNN's Jack Cafferty nuts. In Cafferty's words:

"Here is more evidence of the suicide mission this country is on: General Electric announced it's moving its 115-year-old X-ray business from Waukesha, Wisconsin to Beijing, China. The X-ray business is part of General Electric's GE Healthcare unit, and this move is just part of a broader plan by GE to invest $2 billion in China.

This will become the first GE business to be headquartered there. A handful of the unit's top executives will be transferred to China but otherwise, the company says, none of the 150 staffers in the Milwaukee-area facility will lose jobs or be transferred. However, GE plans to hire more than 65 engineers and a support staff at a new facility in China."

Cafferty can't get over that General Electric's Chief Executive, Jeffrey Immelt, is one of President Obama's advisers on U.S. job creation! Obama picked Immelt, a self-described Republican, hoping to have a man in the Jobs seat that could help in negotiating with the Republican-controlled House on a number of important items such as deficit reduction, jobs programs, and health care.

Overall, it has been a bad PR move for Obama but the President has stuck with it for some reason. On top of moving much of its business to China, and of course no trade secrets will go with the move, GE paid no income taxes last year and it qualified for a huge $3 billion tax credit. In other words, taxpayers paid GE for operating its business.

Because he was so irate on this, Cafferty opened it up for comments from the public. Since GE has basically turned off the lights and closed the door on America, I will close this section of the final thoughts with some of the comments from Americans, which Cafferty accepted when he asked this question about GE:

"Here's my question to you: General Electric is moving its X-ray business to China. What message does this send Americans?" Some of the ones that made it on the air include the following:

"Brad in Portland, Oregon: It tells the U.S. that free trade is a scam, and we need to have fair trade instead. It's too easy for companies to outsource to China and bring the goods and services back to the U.S. with few restrictions. We need to have tariffs on imports to account for the difference in labor costs between the two countries, and then China can compete with American manufacturers on the basis of quality instead of cheap labor."

"Donna: Does anyone see a conflict of interest here? Why would a corporate chief executive move an arm of his business to China when he is responsible for jobs in America? I find it outrageous!"

"Lori in Pennsylvania: It says that U.S. company executives and stock holders are greedy, and want to share as little of the profits they make as possible. I guess the national debt crisis hasn't opened their eyes as to what happens when millions of average citizens don't have a paying job."

"D.W. in St. Louis, Missouri: Thanks for all the tax breaks, Suckers!"

Chapter 20

Humans are EPA Enemy # 1

Humans are polluters by nature

As bad as it can be when regulators go wild, under the current president it is actually worse. The more people you have in a regulatory agency, the more regulations they will produce. The 2013 Federal Register, grew by over 80,000 pages of new rules, regulations, and notices all of which were written and passed by unelected bureaucrats. That's a lot of regulations.

Can you imagine the personal pride of a bureaucrat in framing a new regulation—especially one that really whacks the taxpayer, who typically is already, by EPA definition, a human polluter?

Americans who do not pay attention think that the price of everything being so high is just inflation. It is a lot more than inflation. The cost you pay for products is continuing to increase because the companies that make the products pass on the cost of the EPA regulations to the consumers. Besides paying over 10,000 unneeded EPA salaries we pay dearly for the unneeded regulations these bureaucrats produce.

It may not affect you if you die prematurely, though that premature death thing would not make the EPA one bit unhappy. If you are here to stay for a while, or you have children, expect your family to pay big time for the EPA.

As we have discussed many times in this book, unlike the FDA, the mission of the EPA is not to make human lives better. Besides, only those who heat their homes; who buy and cook food; who turn lights on; who watch TV; who use the Internet; who cool their homes; who store food in a refrigerator; etc. will be paying excessive prices for their necessities and services thanks to the EPA.

The nation's fleet of over 100 coal plants is responsible for about 40% of the electricity generated in the U.S., more than any other single electricity fuel source. The EPA hates coal and it would like coal plants to cease operating.

The proposed Obama regulations as postponed from 2012 until after the 2014 elections, target a number of coal plants that make electricity. Since most of the plants won't be able to comply with the regulations, without the regulations being substantially altered, power plants will have to close. Will the EPA and Obama push to have all plants in full compliance to avoid involuntary shuttering?

If all coal fired electric plants close, and it is highly unlikely they will; the loss will be substantial. Theoretically, there would be 40% less electric power available to the grid. Less power would create a happier EPA. However, their happiness would be our chagrin.

What do you think would happen to the cost of electricity? Will there be brownouts and involuntary periods in which no power comes through the line? You already pay for all the EPA's regulations in the cost of everything you buy. I pay the same price but the price will be going way up because of Obama's EPA. It won't just be electricity. It will be everything.

The EPA is in your house and my house and they are already commanding how you need to live. Their "work" is not free and unfortunately, they are still at work. Every product imaginable costs more because of EPA regulations.

Though the notion itself is not funny, I have an item to share with you that if I did not offer proof, you would not believe me. The EPA is made of many eco—religionists that live and breathe for the opportunity to help Mother Nature, even if it hurts people. Try this rant from an environmentalist and don't stop laughing. I found it on belch.com and the scribe had found it on the Guardian:

"The tenderness of the delicate American buttock is causing more environmental devastation than the country's love of gas-guzzling cars, fast food or McMansions, according to green campaigners. At fault, they say, is the US public's insistence on extra-soft, quilted and multi-ply products when they use the bathroom.

"This is a product that we use for less than three seconds and the ecological consequences of manufacturing it from trees is enormous,' said Allen Hershkowitz, a senior scientist at the Natural Resources Defense Council (NRDC)."

By the way, these guys (NRDC) will defend the EPA to a fault. I would say they are even more nuts than the zealots in the EPA.

Higher prices will continue for everything, including toilet paper, and your choices will be more limited. The EPA wants things its way, not your way. Everything from couches to cupboards, to radios to TV sets, to dryers and washers, to ovens, refrigerators and freezers, toilets, showerheads, and even bicycles—everything will go up in price to absorb the cost of regulations.

Yes, the EPA has gone wild under Obama and it is not just with Obama's full blessing; it is because of his direct orders.

Their job killing regulations are set to limit the energy you can use even if you can afford it. Their decrees go well beyond safety. Paying homage to the EPA way is the only way for businesses to be permitted to operate. So, many businesses will simply close shop rather than comply.

The EPA, as the only agency whose mission it is to please Mother Nature, will be pleased when businesses close and when mortuaries have unexpected upturns in their business outlook. As an environmental agency first, the EPA is interested in keeping the number of people down and the number of businesses down.

They view businesses of all kinds as polluters, and therefore harmful to the ecosystem. They actually do feel the same about people, especially those who create backside methane, a noxious "rotten-egg-like" smelly greenhouse gas that is often mixed with sulfur dioxide upon expulsion. Since CO_2 is now a greenhouse gas, all of us are in the EPA's sights. Even if your breath is fresh, your personal exhaled CO_2 and the flatulence gases—that you and the cows you eat produce are typically not welcome in the EPA's perfect atmosphere.

The one area that I did not discuss much yet is EPA paperwork. Even if you fully comply physically as a business, you must comply in the paperwork area to keep your license. This is often the most time consuming and most costly area. Lots and lots of new EPA documentation sets are now necessary to run a company.

The paperwork load is already onerous and is becoming even more onerous. Its very nature will force large businesses to use their legal and computer teams to get that work done easily while small businesses will choke on the excessive work. Many will simply say, "Enough! It is not worth it!"

According to the Small Business Administration (SBA), 'The smallest firms (fewer than 20 employees) spend 36 percent more per employee than larger firms to comply with federal regulations' – or roughly $10,585 per employee for all federal regulations. Can the country afford that? Can you imagine how many more jobs could be offered if this business cost did not exist?

Since small businesses, especially startups have always been the nation's job engine; with the EPA preparing to steal all the ignition keys, there will be few jobs started.

And so, reasonably prudent American males and females would conclude that the EPA is the great jobs snatcher! Where have all the good jobs gone? Gone to the EPA every one! When will they ever learn? Additionally, the regulations impair our lives, livelihoods, liberties, living standards, life styles and life spans.

 The EPA is far more harmful to the American economy than anything you could ever have imagined. To prove the point, we have some statistics that show the number of regulations imposed by the Obama administration up to April 2011.

During this time, Obama and his coterie have created 75 new major regulations with reported costs to the private sector exceeding $40 billion. Because businesses were complaining about this burden, in 2011, Obama offered a few rollbacks. In fact, there were six major rulemaking proceedings that reduced the regulatory burdens by an estimated $1.5 billion.

That still leaves a net increase of more than $38 billion in additional costs for businesses to absorb. This is a direct result of the EPA being on the playing field while companies are trying to conduct business.

By the way, in March 2014, the EPA added even more burdens and costs. As long as they work, Americans must pay. Not only will gasoline prices increase to potentially nine cent per gallon but that the new rule requires producers and sellers to pony up more than $10 billion in capital costs along with an annual compliance cost of $2.4 billion. Get your wallet out. Despite all the cost, you won't notice the difference.

What if those dollars could be used to employ a few more people? Of course the government workforce has expanded to handle all of the new regulatory requirements but more government is more of a problem than a solution to anything. Perhaps the worst news is that instead of easing off and giving businesses a chance to be successful, the number of regulations continues to grow. There were over 2,785 new unissued rules in the pipeline, yet to be announced, when these statistics were captured.

Can / will Congress help to stop the EPA?

Yes it can. Dear Congress, please kill the EPA quickly! But, does Congress, also known to be on the take to environmentalist whackos, have the guts to kill the EPA?

Unfortunately no! And, so we need replacement players. The Congress, for its own reasons are like scared rats when it comes to doing something without lobbyist approval. They have forgotten already the lesson of November 2010 that the people have taken back the power of the vote.

If this Congress cannot undo the incandescent light bulb law to show they have any say in government, or at least scream and scream about it individually so we hear them loud and clear, there cannot be a bright light among them and all of them need to be thrown out into the new darkness that they have created.

There are other things a real American Congress can do to protect Americans and the economy against too many rules and regulations. One is to require congressional approval of new major rules put forth by formerly autocratic agencies. Another helpful act would be to create a Congressional Office of Regulatory Analysis that would examine proposed and even existing rules independently.

Additionally, many rules of the past were put forth, supposedly at least, for one or two years but they never ended. So, a sunset date for federal regulations would also be helpful so that laws and regulations can automatically expire.

In October, 2011, a few years before this version of this book and just a few months before the first version was going to press, The House passed the EPA Regulatory Relief Act. The intent of the act was to slow down the EPA's impact on the economy and energy. The bill never made it in the Senate as Harry Reid and the Democrats chose to let the people continue to suffer under the shadow of the EPA. My suggestion is to replace all Democratic Senators because Harry Reid is their guy

The U.S. House of Representatives' passed the proposed EPA Regulatory Relief Act of 2011 (H.R. 2250) by a bipartisan vote of 275-142, Pennsylvania Chamber members urged the U.S. Senate to follow suit. Pennsylvania's own Bob Casey Jr. votes with the party 95% of the time so there was little chance he would vote with the people.

Eighty Four percent of constituents that offered their opinions were in favor of the Senate passing its version of the bill. The US Senate chose not to hear the voice of the people.

In summary, the legislation was authored in response to costly and potentially economically damaging rules developed last year by the Environmental Protection Agency under the Clean Air Act to regulate emissions from commercial, industrial and institutional boilers (Boiler MACT). Harry Reid, the Senate majority leader typically chooses to keep legislation favorable to the country from the Senate floor. The only way to change this is to replace Reid as Senate Leader by making the Democrats a minority party.

It is confusing watching Congress work. In April, 2011, for example, a measure to limit EPA power came up and 64 senators agreed that the EPA must be stopped from ruining America, but then they voted along Party lines and the April bill failed. Just 50 senators voted for the bill while the other 50, including the fourteen who believe the EPA should be stopped voted for the EPA to remain strong.

They sat on their duffs and purposely allowed the EPA to usurp their legislative responsibility with which voters had entrusted them. Though the house bravely passed new legislation in the fall, it passed but again failed in the Senate. Harry Reid and Barack Obama will not let the bill pass. Please vote in the next election to eliminate the many bad apples in this Congress. If you are wondering who is hurting the country, as a Democrat myself, I have no problem informing you if you don't know already that it is my Party—the Democratic Party— much more socialist than for Americans.

Independence Hall TEA Party endorsed my US Senate candidacy

On a beautiful Tuesday morning in October 2011 along with my sister Nancy, and my best friend, Dennis, we enjoyed a fine breakfast at the historic Thomas Bond Bed and Breakfast in Philadelphia. We had stayed the prior night at the Inn and were preparing for an 11:00 A.M. speech.

On October 18, the TEA Party PAC and the TEA Party from the tristate Independence Hall TEA Party were to announce their endorsement of my candidacy for the US Senate against Robert P. Casey, Jr. of my home state of Pennsylvania. It was a wonderful event and the TEA Party people loved my speech and I received their endorsement.

A fine couple from Seattle Washington was seated at the same breakfast table with us. Eventually, I told them why I was in Philadelphia but even before that we discussed national affairs. Their biggest complaint was that there was no courageous and effective leadership in Congress "just petty bickering." for no apparent purpose.

"Why can't somebody just stand up and do something that is right because it is right." Their perspective is that there are a bunch of wimps in Congress who know how to help America but choose, by default, not to help out. Time passes and the bad guys win because the bad guys have tireless energy and the system on their side, while good guys, if there really are any, sit idly by. Don't you feel the same way? I sure do!

My campaign manager Martin L. Devaney, one of the most honest and wonderful people who ever occupied God's earth, got very sick during this period, and though Marty encouraged me, the 2000 signatures required to be a bona fide candidate became an impossibility. Marty subsequently passed on to the Lord. Please pray that God gives him a fine seat at the table for Marty will speak well for all of us.

I withdrew my formal candidacy during this period but came back as a write-in. Since the Tea party does not recognize write-ins, I lost my endorsement, yet I persevered. Ironically, it is easy to run as a write-in candidate in Pennsylvania but real ballot access and an accurate count is extremely difficult. I spent a few dollars—not much admittedly—of my own money to advertise across the whole state of 14 million people. It's tough out there!

I asked voters to write me in. Others asked others to write me in. Unfortunately in Pennsylvania, the legislature does not enforce the counting of the ballots. So, though people were permitted to write me in, the individual counties in PA decide whether to count and/or turn in a count of write-ins. Bob Casey Jr. won in a landslide. But, to this day I have no idea how many votes I received and from what counties. Letters to the counties and Governor Corbett did not help. In Pennsylvania, ballot access is about the worst in the world, and the politicians love every minute of it.

Chapter 21

A Master Game Player Uses the EPA to Make His Moves

Congress does not know how to win!

Congress is the source of our problems—not the solution— especially when the President is a winner-takes-all player and he plays the voter sales game so well. He is so adept at winning conversations, speeches, and debates that most Americans know Congress will lose each time he is in the game. In between skirmishes, Congress chooses not to gain the skills to beat him. Our President is the best gamesman at the finest caliber. No Congress and no constituency have ever seen the likes of this President.

Unfortunately, Obama has no substance and the conservatives do not know how to even suggest that he is a shill in debate, without appearing to beg the argument. Think of Terminator II who could become liquid if need be to avoid blame. That is Obama. Since the President does have this inglorious power of persuasion, if only he cared about Americans, we might not be having this conversation.

The fact is Obama cares nothing about real Americans or real life. He lives in a Rod Serling twilight zone of perceptions. He is not concerned about being a real president, and he proves it every day.

But, at the end of the day, this President has the uncanny talent to convince many Americans that despite his not looking out for them that day, he is their only hope for tomorrow. He is just so well practiced at it that many, especially the low information voters, buy it 100%. His essence in fact depends on the people buying his game.

So, when he engages with his kindergarten ideology, which no one in Congress is willing to take-on effectively, inevitably Obama wins the day because his energy is superior, and his fervor to win is unmatched. Obama never runs out of the juices he needs to continue campaigning even when he should be governing.

Americans see him battling every day and they admire him for that simply because we are all taught to stick with it— don't give up. Obama never gives up and he has more lives than the strongest cat. Too bad he uses all that energy against US!

Sticking with it and not giving up is the Obama way. It is extremely effective. The first time Americans hear his nonsense, it sounded like nonsense. After a hundred more times it sounded like facts that they had heard before. This makes Obama very dangerous and very difficult to materialize in his true state. People may get sick of seeing him on TV but somehow, he keeps at it incessantly and somehow, it is very effective for him. He wins at all costs.

Conservatives ought to find out why this is so and create an effective strategy to stop Obama baloney from becoming the accepted standard for purity. For there will always be another election, God willing. Knowing this strategy, no matter if it is Barack Obama or Michelle Obama running for President, none of the tactics will be a surprise, and they can be repelled properly.

In each appearance, there is no improvement. He is armed with the same foolish and illogical stuff but he actually transcends the asininity of his message. Normal Americans cannot fully analyze all of his empty rhetoric. Nobody in history has ever been able to lie so well. All together the package most often sounds good. So, many buy it without analysis.

Those who pay attention hate his message, but even these Americans admire his tenacity. Obama takes fire and he is still standing. It is the only thing Americans like about Barack Hussein Obama. He is not willing to give up on Barack Hussein Obama. He believes 100% in Barack Hussein Obama. He is obviously narcissistic but he is very effective at the same time.

That certainly does not mean he is a good president, but it shows that Obama is the most important thing Obama has ever encountered. Somehow, that form of confident delivery is the message structure for which conservatives have no answer. An answer must be found or I fear Obama drivel will be able to conquer reason for all time..

Earth to conservatives: You are losing and nothing substantial is on the table because gamesmanship is beating you. Figure out what you need to do to get ordinary Americans to demand the gamesman in chief to put something real on the table to discuss.

One additional suggestion: Obama and his surrogate the EPA would be pleased to place anything on the table after he has won the battle. Watch out, the fight will be very unfair. The only thing conservatives have on their side is the truth, which by itself is unconvincing. When Obama lies, most believe he is telling the truth. That is a big problem for conservatives. Somebody out there in the conservative world is smart enough to build a strategy to defeat Obama rhetoric, and it needs to be done quickly.

This President has great political resiliency. Even when he is
buried, I have seen him rise again to destroy conservatives
with his rhetoric. Eric Holder and the EPA are his enforcer
units so they stay no matter what and it is Congress—even
with the fall 2011 EPA legislation, who will begin to doubt
themselves and I fear that the fervor of Obama will again win
the day. No wonder America is disappointed with Congress.
Obama slaps them around every day and they do not know
how to combat his poignant jabs.

In Pennsylvania, my home state, Obama gets lots of help and
it really assists him with the regular people. I suspect he has
surrogates in all states who are supposed to be members of
Congress but like the children, they too are mesmerized by
the Pied Piper of Chicago.

Each time he is needed for an extra boost, for example, our
Senator from Pennsylvania, Bob Casey Jr. has risen to the
occasion to assure the people of Pennsylvania that Obama is
the real deal and it is circumstances, not substance that make
the President appear to be failing. For those of us really tuned
in, we know Obama has no substance and he is failing
without doubt.

If you are not paying attention, it is easy to buy the Casey
balderdash!

Each time Obama wins, the EPA wins and the people lose.
Obama, as he is losing appears to many to be a winner while
the conservatives, who really are winning appear to many to
be losing. It is a matter of energy, consistency, and an
overwhelming desire to win. The Obama people are trained
more than likely by football coaches to never die until the
biggest game is well over and it is tucked away in the "W"
column.

Obama looks at each of the little issues as some coaches'
view the unimportant games before the big games. But, their

training says that they cannot afford to lose even a scintilla because each little piece adds up cumulatively to become something substantial. Conservatives need to go to the same trainers as the Obama team.

The Obama regime never accepts anything other than positive press from any media, anywhere. The media is on notice that Obama takes no negative press. The liberal press loves him anyway and they hardly ever report the truth, because the truth would hurt their guy.

Republicans seem to evaluate the value of the loss when the media slanders them, and if it is small, they don't argue with the press, even when they are right. Conservatives want to battle on but that puts them at odds with elite Republicans.

Like conservatives, who unfortunately must defer to Republican wimps, Obama never accepts a loss. He argues as forcibly when he is wrong and he argues immediately, and thoroughly, and he is unrelenting until he wins. Right or wrong does not matter to Obama. Winning matters! Winning is all important to Obama.

His compulsion to win is so strong, I'll bet he beats Malia and Sasha in Parcheesi and Checkers. All other things being equal, regardless of the facts, Obama's persistence wins. Conservatives need to find a solution to such persistence to ever win national office again.

That is the only reason why a guy with such a miserable record as president can stand in front of the American people and brag about how well he is doing. He tells lies so well because he believes them. Potential next election voters, in the midterm and in 2016, many of whom are asleep, think the great prevaricator, is the man with the truth. All he has to do is endorse somebody, and unless his message is muted, they will win. Conservatives bearing the truth have little chance against such a master liar.

That makes Obama tough to touch when there is no substance in the debate or when he has the last word. He and his team are the most formidable campaign opponents who anybody on the side of righteousness and justice could ever conceive of having to compete against.

After campaigning successfully for election in 2008, from day one of his first term in 2009, Obama has continued campaigning. He never began to govern, and the economy shows it. Everything he does is spelled out in campaign-eeze so that the simplest Americans, aka, the low-information voters, can understand that Obama is their man, and that is that. Any questions?

Eventually, you get pretty good at what you do when you do it all the time. A lousy president, he is for sure, but he is the greatest campaigner of all time. He can make the EPA seem as a savior agency and he has. Forget about the issues for a while. On the issues, conservatives win. The Obama rhetoric is really the problem. It is tough to defeat the master of rhetoric but it is still vitally important. There must be somebody smarter than Obama out there someplace who can guide the TEA Party people into the proper way of guiding the no-win Republican elite.

By the time he is finished, Obama, with his split tongue and his excellent team of liars, without regard for the people they affect, will defeat all Americans as that is their goal. Even the Obama worshippers will fall into hard times when Obama does not need them anymore.

Unfortunately, because conservatives see the Obama game as reality, they are not as prepared to compete and thus, the unprepared conservatives, as expected, inevitably lose each game. And, when inevitably that happens, America also loses.

Can Americans be persuaded again in 2014 and 2016, by snake oil and snake charm to forget about all the times they said the "guy is a jerk" and "bad for America?" It is dangerous to say "no" as the answer to that question.

Obama ordered the EPA to hold off on the light bulb regulations but look, on the QT, they are in effect, and the little piggy looking bulb is all across America. Remember, Obama promises a little something for everybody— something everybody thinks they need.

In 2012, there were many who feared Romney would take away their weekly case of beer, and they knew Obama would be giving them a post-election gift. In 2014 and 2016, will these same people who got nothing when Obama won, be sucked in again and say: Bravo, Obama is the man? The answer is yes, unless there is a believable countervailing message and it must be delivered continually.

People are not necessarily dumb but then a guy lies over 1000 times. Even when he is proven a liar, as in Obamacare, nobody wants to admit it. They still believe it wasn't him in his own words with his own face and voice who had lied to them. They think maybe he will give them something to make up for the lies if they were lies..

It is amazing but it is the way the Democratic Party keeps the low information crowd from ever jumping camp and going out and buying their own beer. Whoever the psychologists are that give advice to the Democrats, they are very smart and they are very un-American. Democrats love the rest of us out in the hinterlands. They call us the taxpayers.

Without us there would be nobody else to buy the low information crowd's votes with free beers. Yes, it is that simple. It is time for Krauthammer and Will, the two biggest brains on the conservative side, to look at the emotional side of logic and get out of the syllogism business.

Obama had a masterful strategy in 2012 and it continues. He is more a Teflon Don than the Teflon Don. It is a masterful strategy to "lead from behind," and take credit for all the gains and complain about all the losses, when you are the leader causing the losses.

Having the EPA run the bad messages through the press so the White House can remain aloof is also a great strategy. It makes Obama appear presidential and not like the puppet master we really know he is—the master behind the EPA.

So, conservatives who really agree that the "EPA must be killed," need to understand they are dealing with the master of persuasion, Barack Hussein Obama. They must be well armed intellectually and strategy-wise to engage, in order to have a chance at success. If Obama wins all the little battles, the conservatives will lose the big battles and the EPA will survive and therefore, America will not survive.

Of course there is always the hope that the people of the United States, who love the country, are greater in number than it appeared they were when the Obama vote count was tallied in 2008 and 2012. The people, when united for a cause, can stop anything when the people pay attention. But, if the message comes only from the media, there may be a big problem in 2014 and 2016 as the country tries to pull itself out of this Obama-caused "recession."

Obama did what he had to do to get reelected in 2012 because real Americans thought it was OK to sleep when boring politicians were speaking. If we want America to stay America and not become something a lot less, we all have to stand up and be counted.

I know I said this once but let me say it again, please. Might there be a psychologist somewhere who can train conservatives to win when faced with a talking blank page of paper—BHO, a handsome head with no substance? So far, I agree with the fine couple from Seattle. I have yet to see a person in Congress ready to face and beat the campaigner in chief. It takes an awful lot of energy.

I would suggest to Congress that it add the kind of staff that the President has for its outside communication efforts. This should include multiple press secretaries and strategy analysts so that Congress has people working full time just like the President has in Jay Carney and whoever his predecessor was and whoever his successor will be. Have a 3:00 briefing every day done by a bureaucrat not the head of the House or Senate. Respond to the nasty's that come from the Presidential briefing as needed. Such a briefing would have to be carried by news agencies.

Having the Speaker or other ranking conservative members of the House or Senate do all the talking may help at times, but Obama's message needs to be defeated every single day. The Congress cannot govern the nation from Congress (a huge committee) every day and also have an answer to the Obama senseless snipe of the day. It is a full time job for a full time staff.

As a point of fact, when I informed the folks at breakfast from Seattle that I was running for the Senate, they repeated the same charge for my benefit. I am unproven and so far at least, unelected. Regular people do not trust regular people who decide to run for office. It is tough to find a person worthy to run in such an environment but I for one can surely appreciate the frustration of not being able to trust government, period.

I clearly understood that this sample of America wants a Congress that is not concerned about their inept leadership but instead care about the courage of their own convictions. I think when an elected member of Congress takes their seat for the first time, they must be ready for the big fight, and they must stay honest. But, I too, especially after my personal breakfast tongue lashing, understand full well why nobody in America thinks Congress-- House and Senate-- are worth two cents.

Think about how hard it is for a good person to come forward and actually go through the crap needed to be president. Still, none of us have a choice when the man in charge is inept to write him and ask him to do nothing more to harm our nation. At the same time, we must expect our representatives, Democrat or Republican, to solve that problem. So far Congress is absent.

Sources:

http://obamalies.net/obama-the-tyrant.html

Chapter 22

We're Broke!   Part I of IV

Is financial help from Mars our last hope?

In this chapter we take a slight break from the EPA per se. As we know, the EPA is part of a much larger entity called the federal government. This government of ours is broke. When we are broke, we have no money. When the federal government is broke, it too has no money.

We all know it but we pretend all is well most of the time. The EPA is one of the major reasons why we cannot recover from being broke and from this terrible recession from which we still suffer regardless of the Obama book cooking that we are experiencing. The fact is the US treasury is empty.

So, let's sit back for this chapter, and take a spoofy look at the dire straits our financial house is in. Then, in subsequent chapters, we will resume our look at the impact of the EPA, and how it's being out of the picture for the next twenty years would improve our prospects for economic success.

Earth to Mars: send cash!

Sometimes I get thoughts that the citizens of my country, mostly on the left, believe that we live on planet earth but our funding comes from planet Mars. In other words, as a nation we have somehow been lulled into thinking that we do not have to pay for our stuff.

We think it is OK that we can incur huge deficits (loans) to the tune of over 70% of our total income. In other words, if the country makes $100 a week, we think it can spend over $170 per week. Nobody can do that; not even the government of the USA. To get the 100% clear picture about where we really are in terms of total income, total spending, and total debt, I looked up the statistics today at www.usgovernmentrevenue.com/#usgs302a and they are very alarming. It is not a secret, feel free to check them out.

This is the deal. The U.S. spends 70% more than we bring in. Though we sit in 2014 almost 2015, the stats for 2011 are very solid and they paint the same picture as the stats for 2013.

The revenue for 2011 came in about 2200 billion and we spent about 3850 billion leaving a loan of 1650 billion as the deficit. Neither Gorge Soros,; nor Bill Gates; nor Warren Buffet agreed to pick up that debt and render all of US harmless, because much to their collective chagrin, even they do not have that much money.

Do we expect to ever have to pay this loan back? If we do not pay it back, rather than one day expecting our creditors to forgive our debt, we can expect that the United States will dissolve as a nation and any money based securities, such as guaranteed pensions and IRAs will be used behind the scenes to pay off as much debt as possible and then our country will have no debt. It will no longer be the United States of America either and chaos will reign supreme. You and I and the rest of the country will all be broke. Not a penny in the account!

Nobody can spend 70% more than they bring in for too long without going bankrupt. I hope I am not the first to tell you this but if we don't do something fast; we will no longer have a chance. The end of the US will not be very pleasant. Even the EPA will not matter.

Figure 21-1 The Urkelization of America

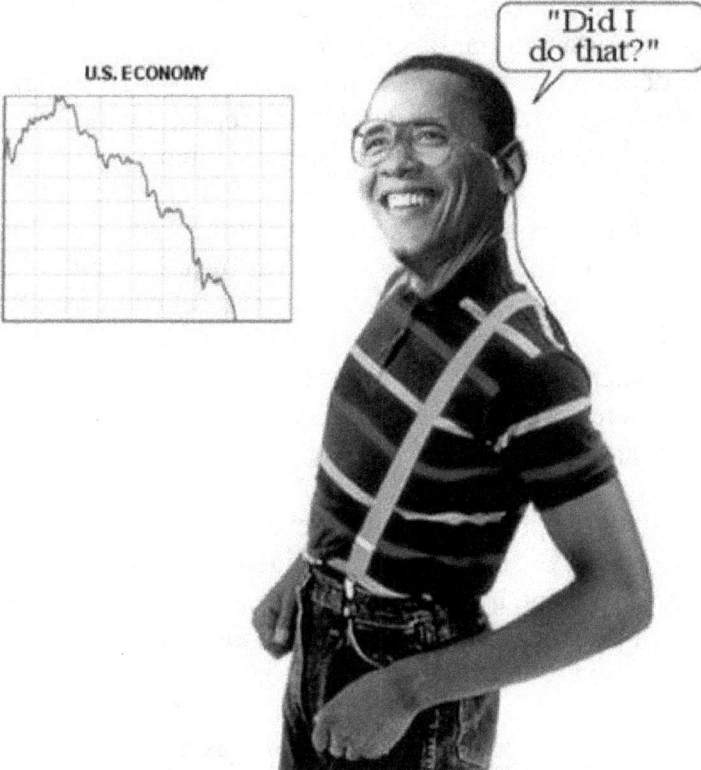

http://michellemalkin.com/2009/03/05/
the-steve-urkel-ization-of-the-economy/

As a final statistic that shows that overspending is not a recent trend, the national debt at the end of 2011 was well over $15000 billion. Now it is over $17000 billion heading for eighteen in a big rush. This is the total of all our loans.

More than 1/3 and approaching ½ of this debt occurred in the years of the Obama presidency. Nobody has hurt the prospects of an American economic recovery worse than President Barack Hussein Obama. Yet, he still smiles in a Steve Urkel sorta way as he continues to destroy things. Does he know what he has done? Does he know what he is doing? You bet he does!

The deficit began to be uncontrollable in 2007 and 2008 in the last two years of the Bush Administration when there was a huge democratic / progressive majority in Congress—in both the House and the Senate. Let me repeat it was OK until the Democrats took over both houses of Congress.

The deficit numbers seem like pennies compared to the 1650 billion for 2011. In 2007, the deficit was over $200 billion and in $2008, the Pelosi Congress doubled the deficit to over $400 billion. As good as Pelosi was by herself on spending, she had George Bush available to veto extremely large expenditures so there were no trillion dollar deficits, but the deficits were huge, nonetheless.

Progressives simply love to spend, even when the piggy bank is empty. After Bush was gone, President Obama and his administration and a complicit Congress have made an art of the deficit process. They have made an art of stealing from the progeny of today's patriotic Americans.

That is why the experts say the economy is unsustainable at such high levels of debt and deficit. Only somebody living on Mars would not be able to believe that the system is going to crash unless the debt and the deficit are addressed. The worst news that many Americans on the left want to hear is, "stop spending more than you bring in." Yet, nothing else will save us.

If you want to know how awful it really is; consider this: If all we did was pay our national debt and there was zero interest on the debt (loans), it would take us about seven years to pay it all back. 15,400 / 2200. Can you imagine in your households, if you were no longer permitted to buy anything until you first paid back seven years' worth of loans?

Now you know how bad it really is.

If you are reading this chapter, you are no dummy. You already know that we are going bankrupt. Nobody could ever pay back such a debt. I cannot believe that there is anybody out there who would loan the US another penny. I know I would not. Anybody who does make the smallest loans is going to lose it eventually.

And, I thought the Chinese were smart. What is up their sleeves? .Do they think they can steal our EPA from us just to make their environment cleaner.

Maybe they would be happy enough to make the US a minor possession of China.

Figure 21-2 Will cash come from the angry red planet?

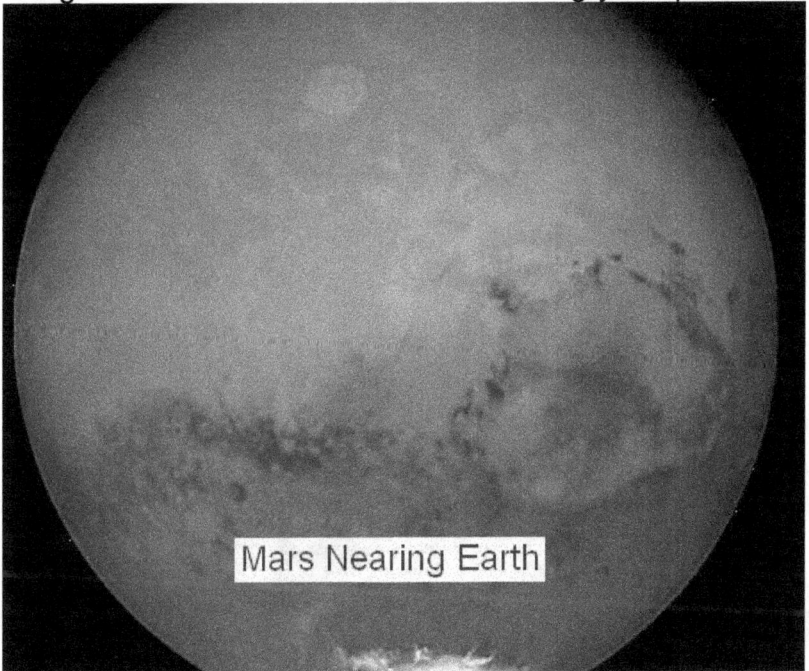

Mars Nearing Earth

Chapter 23

We're Broke!   Part II of IV

Where's the Fund?

On top of the huge and mounting debt and the massive deficits, government accounting puts Social Security and Medicare off the official financial records so their "trust funds" are not counted. Question: Why? Answer: There is nothing to count. They are bankrupt already.

Social Security is easier to talk about, and the record of the fund's caretakers, the Congress, has been abysmal. Congress has stolen every nickel from Social Security for the last 40 years. They cleverly replaced real dollars in Social Security with IOU's payable by guess who? You!

Figure 21-3 Madoff & Social Security & Ponzi

Surely President Obama is not the fault of all this? Yet, from his vacation roost in Martha's Vineyard, in late summer 2011, the same President Obama said he would not be able to send checks out to retirees if the debt-ceiling were not increased. Confused by the conflict and the apparent misinformation, Fox's Charles Krauthammer did his own analysis and wrote a column about it in damning detail about the Administration's chicanery.

Krauthammer's point is that if there are all these liquid assets in the fund, then how could failure to reach a debt-ceiling agreement threaten Senior's checks? Either there are no assets and it is a "Madoff-like" Ponzi scheme or Obama was using seniors as a ploy? But, we all know Obama does not lie.

Krauthammer may think otherwise as he is not ruling our malfeasance in office by the president. There is no cash. The federal government has borrowed all of that SS trust fund money and it has spent it. The IOU's are there in the Gore lockbox; but try collecting money from yourself. Just like you—when you spend all you have—you have to borrow. You can't borrow from yourself.

Therefore, the only possible truth about the reason the debt-ceiling prevented the checks flowing from the liquid assets is as follows:

1. There are no liquid assets
2. Government could not borrow the money for the social security checks because of the debt ceiling.

It isn't the first time we have been lied to by the Treasury Secretary and the President and it won't be the last.

Near the end of the summer of 2011, there was a big trifecta of disasters that slammed Washington DC—an earthquake, Hurricane Irene, and then Hurricane Lee. Times were surely trying.

Despite all the facts available to all Americans about the debt and the deficit, in September 2011 legislators were getting hammered by many who chose not to understand our bleak financial picture. The liberal media actually tried to nail Congress for doing something right for a change.

You may be aware that Congress had no budget for 2011 as the progressives (the 100% Obama lovers) in the Senate would not pass a budget. They though perhaps Alexander Hamilton should be brought back in a séance and let him put forth a budget. But, Hamilton has been dead for 200 years.

Not passing a budget was very intentional because it would give Congress cover from the people they represent. It would prevent the people from knowing what they (nasty dishonest politicians) were doing. Therefore, they funded government with tricks called continuing resolutions with a bill needing passage. All swine in Congress who voted for this crap should not be permitted to run again for any office—even dog catcher.

In this latest round of tricks in September 2011, the Congress asked for a lot more than what would be needed. A number of experts weighed in that they were trying to pull a fast one on the public but this never made it to the mainstream media. OK, it made it but the media is so corrupt they chose not to report it!

So, prudence reigned this time in Congress and the bill got shot down. Along with it, the disaster relief bill for flood victims without spending offsets also got shut down. The gamesmanship of our Congress is not why we elect honest representatives. But, there clearly is an expiration date on honest representatives until they actually begin to stink worse than stale fish.

The media and the progressives, who are in lockstep for uncontrolled spending, began a verbal onslaught against the Conservatives. The non-progressives, who think God not government should help us through our lives, got the usual labels such as "heartless" for not rubber stamping the disaster relief money without any offsets.

It is good that this avaricious bill for partisans, not for regular American citizens was shot down. It is not good that the Congress played games including the blame game with the public.

"Offsets" mean that somebody in Congress has to give up a few billion dollars for things like bridges to nowhere. Those holding the earmarks and the legislation that is of the pork variety must agree that it is OK to divert those funds to disaster relief. What a shameful mass.

Without the offsets, this would be a huge wad of spending authorization to a Congress that spends like it has money in the bank, and like it does not matter. It is our Congress that is killing us so we should not damn them when they do not spend uncontrollably; we should praise them.

Thankfully this bill did not pass as proposed. But something that helped those who are helpless in the afflicted disaster areas and paid for by offsets needed to pass. It just should not have been added to our national debt.

As noted, the demand was far in excess of the total apparent needs so even with disaster relief, the Congress was prepared to use chicanery as its master tactic. "Don't ever let a major crisis go to waste."

My thinking is that those with pet pork projects should pony them up so that instead of a library in Waukegone, or a study on the effects of the tsetse fly on homemade bread, the money could be used for the needed disaster relief. If not from existing allocations, where do we think any funding would come from? More taxation, of course! Those who held onto their pet pork projects were the perpetrators, not those looking to keep America solvent.

Hurricane Lee affected many of us. My basement was flooded from Hurricane Lee. I was lucky. I have flood insurance. I am not making a claim. Other than infrastructure costs this should not have been a big financial burden for the country because almost all of us have flood insurance.

Just because citizens like me get hurt does not mean that the government needs to liquefy hundred dollar bills and provide us with an ointment to ease our pain. That's what charities do! Government has no hundred dollar bills left to liquefy. But, government officials love to buy off the public with a few checks.

During the Hurricane Agnes disaster of 1972, the government solved the problem of people with no flood insurance by granting a 1% loan to those who were devastated. Then, the government made cheap flood insurance available for all the people, even renters.

For example, for $50,000 renters' (contents only) flood insurance costs $134.00 from FEMA per year. For a $250,000 pad with $100,000 contents, the fee from FEMA is $365.00 per year. It is very affordable and it is simply dumb for anybody in the flood plain to be without it. I would not mind funding a 1% loan for these people but to pay for the fact that they chose no flood insurance -- I don't think so. The government is not Catholic Social Services and taxpayers should not be on the hook people's poor choices. Besides, there really is no money.

Through this and other irresponsible spending tricks, government hoped to come up with a bunch of billions of dollars that we simply do not have, so they could continue to buy votes? There is no money left with which Congress can buy votes. Who would want to be the first to contribute to this Congressional slush fund?

The big problem for lawmakers in September 2011, you may recall was that FEMA was moaning that it would run out of money early in the last week of the month when all the action was taking place. The reason that a settlement was able to be brokered was that the budget director called FEMA's bluff and found they actually did have enough money to get beyond the crisis period. Can you imagine that they were only kidding about being broke? They simply wanted more money for more tricks.

This fact was not lost on Minority Leader Mitch McConnell, who realized the whole thing was an exercise to extort more unnecessary spending from the Republicans. It was a ruse that went unreported by CBS, FOX, MSNBC, CNBC, ABC, CBS, NPR, and anybody with a big name. The people therefore did not know the Democrats were only kidding around.

McConnell could not help but give the majority leader a slam after taking all that time on a hoax. "The majority leader has found a path forward," said, a Kentucky Republican. "In my view this entire fire drill was completely and totally unnecessary, but I'm glad a resolution appears to be at hand."

So, the Democrats in the Senate were willing to take the FEMA "crisis" and make good use of it to get more spending approved. How bad can it get? Who can you believe?

So, now that we are living on after that "close one;" what do this irascible media expect the country to do about the debt and deficit?

Have you heard a major media report about this in terms of a solution from the corrupt mainstream press? Don't expect one. They should be paid by the dictatorial Democratic Party because today's media cares nothing about any of US, unless we are registered Democrats or we are potential low information voters. Ain't that a shame? How does that hep our country?

The only possible explanation to all the dumbness we see is that there is an intelligent master plan in a lockbox someplace that will make us all right-- if they can only find it. We would all be happy about that if there were such a plan.

Stop hoping. There is no such plan. Now that gold is so high in price and rising further, perhaps someone might find some Revolutionary or Civil War era coins in the archives of the US Mint. Perhaps enough can be found to cover the debt? Chances are that will not happen. Where else could we get the funds to pay it off? If we took all the wealth of all the billionaires, we would not even touch the debt. It is that huge.

Chapter 24

We're Broke!   Part III of IV

Debt ceiling & the super committee

Our Congress is simply incompetent and deceitful. They always hope we don't catch on when they knowingly lie about how things really are. You may recall that in August, 2011 as part of the much ballyhooed deal to raise the debt ceiling and avoid a U.S. default on our obligations, the Congress appointed a super committee.

In essence the Congress admitted they could not get the job done so they subcontracted it to 12 of their members—six Democrats and six Republicans. Their job was to reduce the deficit by $1.5 trillion over the next 10 years. They had to present their bipartisan plan to the full Congress by Thanksgiving. They failed.

Therefore, the penalty phase began in 2013—yes 2013, and when it happened Congress appeared to be shocked at their own ineptitude. So, Congress through inaction had to figure out how to endure $984 billion in automatic cuts, which includes interest payments. When the boom hit, the spin machines got into high gear.

Even though the Democrats, in fact Obama himself had proposed this notion, Republicans were blamed by the mainstream press. And, so there are those wanting again t have a White House Tour know that if Republicans are still alive, this can never happen. Despite the fact that Democrats chose who got hurt, their spin doctors are so good that Republicans got blamed. Nobody can trust the Obama Regime for anything.

None of the cuts were draconian but Congress, which apparently does not want any cuts, were boohooing the deal as if the country was going to explode. The country was theoretically going to explode because these boneheads could not get anything right, and even when they lied about how much they were cutting, they could not come close to those cuts.

The debt and the deficits are real but Congress is pulling a tiny Tim and they chose to tip toe through the tulips rather than getting out a big pair of scissors and making real cuts. Worse than that; they continue to lie to us about the substance of the reductions in the first place.

They ought to be put in jail for such a prevarication. Obama, the prevaricator in chief could not have told as big a whopper as the Congress did and continues to do.

Let's look at the facts. Federal expenditures for 2011 were about 3.5 trillion. Since then there has not been much change in spending due to some real cuts. The deficit is still huge and the national debt is now over $17 trillion. We're broke and we are going bankrupt.

In 2013, the latest year with full numbers available, federal spending was again about $3.5 trillion and the deficit dropped to what Democrats say is "only" $642 billion. Progressive liberal spending nuts are using this small improvement in the nation's fiscal situation to avoid further budget tightening. They do not care about our fiscal stability if they ace get reelected. We owe it tothem all to give them a big surprise.

A new spending thrust is the wrong conclusion to draw. Following four years of Obama's trillion-dollar deficits, this is a break but remember the national debt is still going up as it approaches $18 trillion. It has already exceed 100 percent of gross domestic product (GDP) at the end of the year. In other words, we owe more than the gross business we do each year. That can't be good.

There is this big lie, like the elephant or the gorilla in the room that Congress likes to ignore. The Congress does not tell the people the real budget numbers. They have a built in system that dupes the American public.

They use a trick called baseline budgeting. With this process, the spending for each subsequent year is forecast at the prior year's amount plus some arbitrary number of let's say 5.5 percent. In other words, they first plan to increase the spending by 5.5% and any reduction they can squeeze out would come from this increase, not from the real budget.

If they simply left the budget as is, they would save this 5.5% increase each year. Congress does not want you to know that. It wants to spend to make us happy so we will reelect them. But, will we do that again this time? I sure hope not.

They like to budget over a ten year period. So, with the 5.5 percent compounded increase over the next 10 years, total expenditures will total about $45 trillion. That is an average of $4.5 trillion per year if it were straight-line. Already you see it starts off at $1 trillion per year more than it is right now.

My conclusion is that they either do not see $18 trillion in debt as a problem, or they do not care that it is a problem. Again the only solution for Americans to get our financial; house in order is to fire our Congress and our President. t

Sean Hannity, a conservative talk show host has a plan that he calls the "Penny Plan." It is really The Connie Mack (R-FL) Penny Plan and it is the only good idea out there. It does away completely with baseline budgeting. In fact, it is designed to balance the federal budget in eight years by cutting one penny out of every federal dollar spent for six years and finally capping spending at 18% of GDP beginning in the seventh year.

If Congress fails to make the necessary cuts, the plan triggers automatic, across-the-board cuts to meet the yearly caps. All told, The Mack Penny Plan would save taxpayers $7.5 trillion over the next decade, and it would ensure that our children inherit America's promise of freedom, security, prosperity and the American dream.

It has a lot of sponsors. Ask your Representatives and Senators if it has their support. So far, it has co-sponsorship from 70 Members of Congress, 11 U.S. Senators, and it is supported by leading conservative groups such as Freedom Works and the National Taxpayer Union.

Who does it serve to have no jobs and a lousy economy? Why bother going to college when companies cannot afford to pay college graduate wages? We must act to get America's fiscal house in order or our economy is on a path to be crippled indefinitely. Surely this will our way lives and our way of life.

I congratulate Congressman Mack for working to bring accountability to Washington and to give our children and grandchildren economic freedom and a brighter future. Check out the penny plan on the Internet and insist your representatives are on board for a brighter America.

Do you remember the Super Committee?

The misnamed Super Committee had a real simple job. They were to cut just $1.5 trillion out of the $45 trillion. To meet their mandate, all they had to do was cut 2.6 percent of all future federal expenditures. In other words, the 2.6 percent would not come from $3.5 trillion current level, but from the projected total of $45 trillion. They were able to use the base line budgeting charade and they could not do it—or chose not to do it.

That means that if they met their goal, the total expenditures would have had to "decline" from $45 trillion to $43.5 trillion over the next decade. Most importantly, had they met this goal, the feds would still be spending an average of $4.35 trillion per year over the next 10 years. That average is almost 25 percent more per year than the government now spends.

Government solutions are always a joke. Why would anybody want to provide this group of incompetents any additional funding through increased taxes? They would blow it on excessive spending. Democrats and Republicans are not willing to cut enough to make it matter to save the country but the Democrats actually want even more tax revenue so they can spend even more.

This notion of baseline budgeting is a trick to make taxpayers think Congress is doing an OK job. It is the second biggest government lie of all time. The lie about social security having anything left in its fund is the biggest government lie. Then again there is the one about keeping your doctor, your insurance policy, and saving $2500.00 per year. That one is a real gasser.

Chapter 25

We're Broke!   Part IV of IV

Geithner & Obama on Mars (Martha's)

Enough about the really serious stuff; maybe there is a high-tech way out of this jam if we give it a chance? Try this on as a possibility as long as we are still permitted to think out of the box.

What if Timothy Geithner (now Jack Lew is the Treasury Secretary but the analogy still applies) and Barack Obama did not really go to Martha's Vineyard together for vacation back in the summer (2011) when the country was going through the debt ceiling crisis? Suppose they actually went to MARthaS Vineyard, which may now be a regime code word for MARS.

Suppose Mars is really years behind the Earth in development as in US retro. Suppose the year on Mars is really 1977.

And, suppose Geithner and Obama made lots of progress in their trip to Mars as if Mars is in many ways an alternate Universe. Suppose again that they got to Mars using the last Russian Soyez Mars Special spacecraft. Under all of those suppositions, let's say the following happened on the trip.

First of all, they met with Jimmy Carter the President of Mars. Because Carter is reliving his US years with a few desirable (for Carter) future alterations in place, and because he is an honest man, he admits again his faults to the esteemed emissaries from earth.

You may remember the Carter confessions from back in the 1970's: "I've looked on a lot of women with lust. I've committed adultery in my heart many times." How truthful could he possibly be? Obama and Geithner then use that warm up to talk Carter into sending us about $1650 billion from the Mars treasury, which at the time was enough to cover our entire 2011 deficit. Today, we can do it for closer to $700 billion.

Carter, who on Mars is permitted to behave as an avowed socialist, has dictatorial powers there—something he and Billy always wanted for the US when they had the power. The 1977 Mars that Geithner and Obama found has two major industries -- Billy Beer and Peanuts! One of the industries is doing well.

Anyway, Carter promised the US emissaries that we would not ever have to pay back the loan and there would be no interest. Carter noted the Martians would up their standard workday in the socialist collective from 10 hours per day to 18 to make up the difference. He mentioned how important it was in the future for Mars to be a net peanut exporter and he thought this overture would help.

No beer will be exported. After Billy has his way with the beer, there is not enough to export so beer was not involved in the Inter-Solar System trade talks.

Of course none of the Mars story is true. But, the facts of our financial mess still stand.

Unless we really can get financing from a kinder and gentler Mars, and not the good ole angry planet, perhaps we really have no right to exist as a country—especially if progressives keep piling on more and more debt.

Maybe China is on to something.

When your deficit is already 1650 billion, you simply cannot continue to spend and spend and spend when there is nothing left to spend. Moreover, in our universe, as nice as it is to dream, there is really nobody willing anymore to loan US a thin dime.

Perhaps Jimmy Carter from Mars or Obi Wan Kenobi from deep space are our only hopes but then again, even as slight a chance as we have on that one, it is even dimmer because of recent Obama actions.

You may recall that there was a big disturbance in The Force in Summer 2011. Obama defunded NASA and the space program is now caput. The space shuttles are now museums in towns other than Chicago. Shucks! We depend on Russia at about $90 million a shot to get our astronauts (those that are left) to the International Space Station.

Before we get back to the dream, it seems that Obama fired the wrong agency. He fired NASA, our most successful agency instead of the clowns at the EPA.

NASA Now Tasked with Building Muslim self-esteem

NASA's new task is building Muslim Self-esteem. I think this would be a fine job for the EPA, and we can let the brilliant NASA team continue to fly productive space missions.

But, unfortunately, I kid you not. You read my words correctly. In fact, back in 2010 around the time Obama has the dismantlers working full time at NASA, he got this great idea to put Muslims on a fast-track to esteem by making it NASA's mission. I give Obama credit for this one since of course, it will be a tough job, and NASA has been doing America's tough work since JFK got us to the moon.

The head of NASA Charles Bolden, offered these comments at the time of the change when he was in Egypt:

"I am here in the [Mideast] region – its sort of the first anniversary of President Barack Obama's visit to Cairo – and his speech there when he gave what has now become known as Obama's "Cairo Initiative" where he announced that he wanted this to become a new beginning of the relationship between the United States and the Muslim world. When I became the NASA Administrator – before I became the NASA Administrator -he charged me with three things: One was that he wanted me to re-inspire children to want to get into science and math, that he wanted me to expand our international relationships, and third, and perhaps foremost, he wanted me to find a way to reach out to the Muslim world and engage much more with predominantly Muslim nations to help them feel good about their historic contribution to science, math, and engineering." End of Bolden Quote…

The reaction from a number of scholars and cynics in the US was predictable. Some felt it was like divining that the Irish had discovered the New World and not the Italians, or that Lichtenstein was the most powerful country in the world, or perhaps that the Swiss Franc had become the world's reserve currency and not the dollar, nor the Euro.

In other words, the reaction was that the Muslim world rightfully would feel left out because for the most part, they had not played a major part in science or the arts, and engineering since maybe the 17th century. Well, President Obama is still the President and four years later, all space shuttles are gone and the Agency's mission is now Muslim outreach.

I would not have predicted that. But, since it has happened and there is not much publicity about it, I hope there may be time to change NASA's mission back and take a small force of leftover EPA zealots and give them the Muslim Outreach mission, of course not until we quietly kill the rest of the EPA.

So, real events, such as no Space Program, actually have made this big dream for a debt solution that we began to discuss at the beginning of this chapter, even less likely.

If the dream (other than the reality of no Space Program) can somehow be made into a reality and Mars really is in the late 1970s, perhaps Jupiter is in the mid-1920s and just maybe Al Capone, a good guy from Chicago can give the US even more loot than Jimmy Carter or Obi Wan Kenobi.

Cross your fingers. Maybe Jupiter also has a space program.

OK, that is yet another daydream. The fact is all we can do is dream about a fix because Congress and the liberal media will not address the reality of impending doom from debt. We could vote out all elected officials and turn off the TV to get some truth, and maybe that too is a good idea.

Is it possible that nobody will help us? Is it possible that nobody can help us? Can we save ourselves by spending? Is it time to learn Chinese?

One thing on which we can all agree is that the secret to a solution when all else fails is not to keep doing the same thing (Spend, Spend, Spend) and expect different results.

While I was writing and editing this section of the first edition of this book, hoping to give ordinary Americans a better perspective on the bleak financial outlook we face, and why we must take action immediately, ironically, the following email crossed my desk:

Why S&P Downgraded the US credit worthiness

Why S&P downgraded - this puts it in perspective...

- U.S. Tax revenue: $2,170,000,000,000
- Federal budget: $3,820,000,000,000
- New debt: $1,650,000,000,000
- National debt: $14,271,000,000,000

Recent federal budget cut: $38,500,000,000

Let's remove 8 zeros and pretend it's a household budget:

- Annual family income: $21,700
- Money the family spent this year: $38,200
- New debt on the credit card: $16,500
- Outstanding bal. on the credit card: $142,710

Total household budget cuts: $385

Does somebody actually think such a pittance can make a difference? If it seems futile with chicanery men in charge of our government, remember the last hope may be to fire Congress and the President, and start a government with honest representation.

Now, this has become a very good dream; but a dream nonetheless.

And, of course we can save a lot of money by completely eliminating the EPA from its parasitic position on our backs. I have not forgotten the real topic of this book! In the first edition of this book, "We're Broke" was a big hit after reviewing all of the bad things brought forth from the EPA. Sometimes a little humour makes points better than putting it all right in your face.

Chapter 26

Turn EPA Role Over to States Part I

The EPA is against the 10th Amendment

Getting to the point quickly, this chapter again is about the EPA. Knowing that we now have no money (from Chapter 21), it makes even more sense that we stop wasting $10.5 Billion on the EPA each year.

In this chapter we spend more time evaluating whether the EPA deserves to exist at all in this modern era when state's rights have reappeared as a very real issue in American politics and more importantly in American government. If a state wants the EPA in its state then I would suggest "go for it"... Just don't make any state be forced to pay homage to a Washington entity that usurps the control of the people's buying decisions and the laws of the states.

As we learned in the last chapter, the EPA is just one part of a real sick country. If a corporation were in the sick condition of our country, the officers would be fired and thrown into prison, and a search for competent leadership would ensue.

We have five hundred forty five (545) officials at the top of our government, not counting the vice president. That is larger than most committees in any business of which I am aware.

I have a good friend from my IBM days, Jack Lammers, who likes to opine that "a committee invented the giraffe." There is another saying that means the same thing—"a camel is a horse designed by a committee."

In both cases, the committee structure, as a form of getting things done, is being attacked. And so we get the idea that the imperfect looks of both giraffes and camels are in this instance visible expressions that are critical of committees. By analogy, this applies to group decision-making.

Both notions emphasize the ineffectiveness of incorporating too many conflicting opinions into a single project. In this figure of speech, the distinguishing features of a camel, such as its humps and poor temperament, and a giraffe with a neck so large that keeps it outdoors, are taken to be deformities that resulted from poor design. Committees and/or Congresses design few things that are perfect. They design even fewer when they are corrupted by greed and special interests.

The good news about government is that it does not have to make or sell anything so the job of running it ought to be easier than being a corporate CEO. It brings in just so much money and it is supposed to spend just that much and not a dime more. In many ways the government parallels us in that it should not spend any more than it brings in. But, it does. Lots more!

What corporation or what person for that matter would hire a politician to manage its affairs? For years and years, the US was in good shape and all of a sudden, we now have a major leadership gap because it seems the "me" generation is OK having poor leadership as long as they are taking care of "me." When there was a ton of money in the treasury it appeared to be OK, but not anymore.

As noted in last chapter, we are more than broke. We owe more as a country than we can ever pay back. So, each of us needs to understand more about this behemoth country we have and what are its good parts and what are its bad parts. Nobody wants to go back to the smog filled roads of the 1960's and we won't; but we should not be making public policy on unproven science either.

We have constraints on our fiscal resources but our friends in the environmental movement do not care. Since they work for us, it is time that they must care or we must get them out of the way for about twenty-years or more until we can get this country running OK again.

If I wanted to be unkind, I would have said we have 545 punchinellos, who we elect or appoint regularly to run the biggest country in the world. I would also add that they have no idea how to run a business. They may be great politicians but they have messed up in running our country.

When our leaders see a problem, they go to the medicine cabinet and they find a band-aid because band-aids are easy to deal with for untrained leaders and untrained financial and operations planners. Richard Nixon did this in the late 1960's when he basically christened the EPA.

After Rachel Carson scared the heck out of everybody with Silent Spring, Nixon's band-aid was to create a small agency called the Environmental Protection Agency (EPA) to assure that Americans are not blowing car smoke in people's faces. He was not so concerned that after being outside for hours, the first time one's finger entered one's nasal cavity (accidentally of course), it would come out pristine with no tell tale signs of dirty air. Even Nixon did not think the air needed to be that clean.

The nature of man is to increase things that do not need to be increased and enlarge things that do not need to grow. Some businesses ought to stay the same size and provide the same services rather than switch from say—building car engines to running convenience stores. Sometimes largeness and diversity bring unintended consequences. Besides, nobody ever accused the government of being the best in anything.

So, what do we really expect when we simply send these people off without real instructions and then no matter how poorly they do; we make war heroes out of them when they come home from Washington for the holidays? Oh! And this claptrap about the "honorable so and so from such and such…" Come on already! It's time we the people got serious and our "politicians" perhaps would become leaders. We have to stop putting our hands out and they have to stop trying to put stuff into them.

So, as expected the EPA like everything else in life grew, not because it was successful but because it just grew. The Nixon band-aid took on a life of its own and here we are 40 years later and the skeleton EPA staff now is puffed up with 18,000 people on board giving orders to each other and anybody else who will listen to them.

The EPA thinks it works for Mother Nature, not the US government or the people. Therefore, it follows that its job now is to regulate man for the good of nature, and that man, the human being that through its government pays all the EPA staffers, does not matter as much in the scheme of things. Die Natur uber alles (nature over everything)

The EPA also has its own mind about how to do things. Working for itself, and in this administration, the EPA and all of the radicals in its horde are completely aligned with the wishes of the President in over-controlling the country. Their joint plan is to run roughshod over Congress and the people, and rule by the autocratic dictate of regulations. It's time the EPA realizes it really does not work for Mother Nature.

My plan suggests shrinking the EPA function to 100 or 200 employees who have no decision authority at all. With all of the job losses and the misery the EPA has caused humans in

America, the staff that loses their jobs when the agency is eliminated-- 17,800 of the most radical and uncaring people in existence, should be retrained to replace migrant workers to do the jobs that Americans won't do. By the way, I am not promising that we can salvage even one or two hundred from their lot for a shell "EPA." That's how bad they have become.

If we eliminated most of the EPA, it would still not save us from ourselves fiscally. As seen in the last chapter, we need to do lots more, but it would be a great start. It would return almost the entire $10.5 billion to the treasury each year and it would give businesses and the states a chance to get strong again.

Since the Congress likes to do cost estimates and revenue estimates in ten year chunks, that means eliminating the out-of-control EPA would return over $100 billion to the treasury. This organization has lost its focus, concentrates on nature over man, has a track record of hurting the very people it is supposed to help, and therefore it has outlived its usefulness.

On March 15, 2010, Byron Moore wrote a piece titled "An argument for killing the EPA." It is available at http://www.dcbureau.org/20100315951/bulldog-blog/an-argument-for-killing-the-epa.html

In the March 15, 2010 article, Moore singled out Senate Candidate Bill Johnson from Kentucky as a fanatic who wants to disband the EPA. Moore presents Johnson's arguments for disbanding the EPA and then he shoots holes in them, but he has poor focus and misses even when he thinks his arguments are sound.

The hallmark of his piece is that he highlights the role of the EPA in instituting the ban on DDT and then the ban on CFCs and also managing those two processes as the biggest triumphs of the EPA and he then concludes that because of the DDT and CFC bans, the EPA is indispensible and thus the United States needs the EPA.

In the next several chapters we examine some of Byron Moore's generic points about the EPA, plus and minus. In the process, we specifically examine DDT and CFCs, and I am sure you will not be surprised that Byron Moore and I do not agree. I see the DDT ban as one of the worst overall decisions the EPA has ever made and the CFC ban seems to be based on corporate corruption more than a problem with the Ozone layer.

http://capitalismmagazine.com/2008/09/epa-fascism-versus-america-the-epa-plans-are-immoral-2-of-7/

In September 2008, John Lewis Paul Saunders, writing for Capitalism Magazine, penned a seven part article titled, EPA Fascism versus America. The link for part 2 is above. His thesis is that the rationale behind most of the "work" of the EPA, including the global warming scare—and the resultant political proposals—has nothing to do with actually trying to identify a real problem. Instead it is rooted in idealism and the notion that nature is more important than both God and man. Have I said that yet?

In fact, it presupposes that man is the problem, and a logical solution of course would be that there should be fewer humans on the planet because, according to the zealots at the EPA, we are mucking it all up. Sanders notes that it is these erroneous moral ideas that are leading us to political disaster.

He writes:

"...environmentalists and advocates of socialist planning alike presume the right to assert what is good and right for others, and to impose this right by force--to the point of taking their property in the name of animals, and denying to the victims even the right to protest--as Greenpeace claims that merely to discuss the EPA plans is immoral.

"Given this moral premise, the man-made global warming claim meshes easily with other programs intended to destroy individual rights: economic redistribution of all kinds, control or confiscation of private property by the government, denial of technology and industry to non-industrialized nations, ever-increasing taxation, and most of all the establishment of a self-appointed environmentalist elite to tell us what the proper values are, and to enforce the sacrifices needed to 'Save the Earth' " from us.

"The claims to scientific legitimacy made for the hypothesis of man-made global warming have been harnessed in service to a political agenda. Politics, not science, is driving the advocates of these political proposals. Lust for a dictatorship under the EPA permeates this movement—because it is the EPA who is to enforce the alleged interests of nature over man's interests."

There are only two solutions when a strong enemy appears on the scene and is ready to eliminate you. The EPA is such an enemy. Option 1 is to convince the enemy that you can coexist. Ronald Reagan took this approach with the Soviet Union with "trust but verify." Option 2 is to fight the enemy to the point of its elimination as a threat and achieve a major victory which keeps the enemy down for a long time.

The EPA is the enemy of the people of the United States. Therefore, we need to shut it down and stop funding it. In so doing, we must get rid of all its entrails—harmful legislation and regulations. The responsibility for the environment is the responsibility of the states and the individuals through the courts system.

The federal government has no place in the environmental regulations business. Individual states are more informed about their own environment than any biased artificial arbiter in Washington. The mere existence of such an agency is an affront to the rights of states. In no place in the Constitution will you find reference to the EPA, and according to the 10th Amendment, it is clearly unconstitutional for the EPA to conduct business.

There may be a minimal need for an umbrella agency with a small staff to serve the advice and research function originally intended by President Nixon. But we must be very careful not to seed a chaotic future by putting the same ideologues into the EPA that set it on its radical course after the Nixon years. Minimal regulations could be handled somewhere else in the federal government as part of some other agency's duties. The bottom line is that this is a state's issue and the polluters are in the states, and the potential danger is in the states, and thus the best solutions will come from the states.

Trying to find actual environmental budget numbers in states is quite difficult because dollars are scattered in many different budgets from the general fund to those with names that include "conservation," "environment," "oil, gas, cleanup," etc. Though difficult to find the exact numbers, the state environmental budgets are huge, regardless.

For example in our state, Pennsylvania, just the environment budget along with the conservation lands budget comes in close to $400 million dollars per year. With all the other set asides in the budget, such as hazardous cleanup funds and underground storage cleanup funds, oil and gas funds, etc., it looks like the Pennsylvania budget comes in well over a billion dollars.

If we assumed that Pennsylvania was the largest spender on the environment in the country, which it surely is not, and that other states are just half of Pennsylvania's outlay on the average, the total of the state numbers is still huge.

We can extrapolate that the total of the state budgets would be anywhere from $25 billion to $50 billion dollars per year. This number dwarfs the huge federal expenditure of $10.5 billion. Clearly, based on their budgets, the states are already doing the job and so there is no need for the federal government duplication or attempt to preempt the states with federal one-size fits all solutions that take away states' rights.

Everybody wants clean air and clean water but that does not mean the federal government needs 17,000 or 18,000 bureaucrats to wreak havoc on every business in every state with excessive regulations, especially in this time of a poor economy. The EPA has taken its toll on an already weak economy by scaring small businesses from expanding and hiring, and by picking winners and losers in large manufacturing, such as giving its friends like GE excessive tax breaks. The states should be the final authority on environmental policy, period.

There are no environmental issues in the lands (ceded by Maryland and Virginia on December 23, 1788) encompassed by Washington D.C. other than the odor of corrupt politicians. If there were something more onerous or odiferous in Washington for which dollars needed to be spent, Minnesotans and Pennsylvanians should not have to pay the freight for Washington D.C., a locale occupied by some of the richest residents of the Union.

In fact, the public outside of D.C. should not be paying at all. Get the money from the polluters who cause the issues. If a state has certain industries that pollute that state, those industries have to be made responsible for cleaning it up to the satisfaction of the state.

Citizens should elect officials at the local level who are accountable for protecting the environment in which they live. I do like the idea of a lot of FBI officials continually overseeing the actions of the local officials so the temptation of big money does not over-influence the decisions of the locals.

A more effective response than an out-of control autocratic agency can be brought about by honest elected officials who are inherently closer to the people affected by environmental issues. This of course is in contrast to the bloated EPA system in which biased, faceless Washington bureaucrats dictate regulations to the states.

Chapter 27

Turn EPA Over to States Part II

Mountaintop Mining

As an example of federal interference, The EPA is currently looking into the practice of mountaintop mining in places such as Kentucky. Why is Washington D.C. messing with Kentucky? This type of mining is a practice that most Kentuckians passionately support. The EPA from Washington D.C. is against it. Kentucky is for it. It happens in Kentucky. Who should have the authority?

The EPA thinks mountaintop mining is just terrible because the surface look of the mountain often changes. Ironically, sometimes it changes for the better. The mine operators do build back from what they take and often create marvelously great mountain parks in the process. Yet, that is not enough for the green team. They don't like coal, period. Yet, none of them have committed to do without heat next winter to prove their point.

Perhaps the EPA would like Kentuckians to become helpless so they could get their livelihood from Obama's stash in Washington. Kentuckians would like Kentucky to stay free from Obama's regulations. Kentuckians should decide what happens in Kentucky. Pennsylvanians should decide what happens in Pennsylvania.

When states are concerned about major environmental matters, they can do their own studies. States are less affected by radical ideas such as the ones that suggest that nature is more important than man. States will do what is best for the people in the states whereas the EPA wants what is best for radical environmental extremists who care little about human life.

While we shift the onus back to the states from the central bureaucracy (EPA), a small part of the $10.5 billion that the Feds gobble up in the EPA budget can be kept for helping the states coordinate interstate work. Ideally, states that make the money from an environmentally sensitive industry such as coal should also pay the full price of reclamation. Build it into the price of the product.

The federal government should not be in the business of subsidizing any industries. The fruit growing states don't ask Kentucky or Pennsylvania to pay for their winter frosts and so they should not be forced to pay for any reclamation projects in Kentucky or Pennsylvania. In other words, keep the feds out of it. It is a states' issue.

What about interstate pollution? The state DEP offices can solve that problem quite simply. Each state is responsible for the cost of its own pollution in whatever form, period. In the few cases where you have DEPs that cannot cooperate, certain things might be an issue for the courts. The bottom line is that there is no need for a huge $10.5 billion power-hungry, job killing agency while the country is at 20% or better unemployment.

The EPA has gone too far placing the lives of aphids and white flies above the ability to grow healthy tomatoes and to sustain healthy businesses of all kinds. There should be less, not more government. In Pennsylvania, even big spenders like Ed Rendell, before Governor Corbett stepped into the Governor's mansion, have been reducing the DEP budget because environmental agencies have actually begun to make life unhealthier, not healthier for Pennsylvanians and others across the world.

Clean air is something we all want

EPA apologists sometimes cite the "air pollution episode of 1966" as another example of why the EPA is needed. This was a deadly episode in which an estimated 24 deaths occurred because of bad air during the week of Thanksgiving. Clearly this was a tragedy.

This event predates the EPA, and the implications of the EPA cheerleaders are this may not have occurred if the EPA were around to have the right regulations in place. They suggest that this is a stark example of the fallacy of waiting for politics and industry to decide the appropriate regulations. Did this occur because there was no EPA? Here's the truth:

Smog was terrible in Los Angeles in the 1960's as for the first time; almost every family had a car—some two or three, and the freeways were booming with traffic, often at a standstill. The result was smog. There was no EPA. So, Congress (not the EPA) passed a law in 1970 called the Clean Air Act, which, with or without an EPA has done wonders to clean the air.

After the Congress passed the Clean Air Act of 1970, nobody challenges that U.S. air pollution levels dropped dramatically. The problem that we have with the EPA today is that it did all its great work years ago before it picked up all of its excess and its anti-American agenda items.

Now, for this nasty un-American agency to survive, the EPA is into limiting personal freedom and liberty, and other minutia to the extent that it is having a negative impact on the economy and on the choices Americans have when shopping for home solutions. The EPA is actually the incarnation of "Big Brother," that we have feared all our lives.

Somewhere between the groundbreaking Clean Air Act and today, the EPA has decided to work on minutia to annoy human beings, which the agency believes are the world's primary polluters. The EPA does not want humans to drive or thrive. In fact, the EPA would love there to be about 90% less humans. Some go so far as suggesting the earth would be better with no human life at all. I kid you not.

Today, the states do a good job on their own of handling air quality issues. For example, California lobbied the EPA and now they set their own clean air standards that are even more stringent than the EPA's. So, how does the EPA help the states regarding clean air? It is the other way around. As noted, California writes its own regulations / standards and many other states have adopted California's standards, not the old EPA set.

Because the EPA is busy protecting tsetse flies, ringworm fungus, potato beetle larvae, etc., other states may now choose to follow either the old EPA standard (when the EPA worked for the people) or the new stricter California standards as developed by California for California.

To demonstrate that states are perfectly capable of making their own environmental decisions, it would help to know that the states adopting the California standards include Arizona (2012 model year), Connecticut, Maine, Maryland, Massachusetts, New Jersey, New Mexico, New York, Oregon, Pennsylvania, Rhode Island, Vermont, and Washington, as well as believe it or not, Washington D.C.

EPA supporters and apologists persist in defending this out-of-touch behemoth as if it were necessary for the states to survive. Instead of showing any science behind their arguments, which they cannot because it does not exist, the apologists attack people with solid arguments, as the real problem.

Americans need to join together to remove the scourge of politics from the American landscape. A goodly number of the 18,000 strong EPA personnel are politicians of the worst kind. They have not and will never be elected and so they do whatever they think is right, as wrong as it may be, regardless of whether their prescriptions may be deadly to humans. They do care a lot about nature. In fact, they care so much they do not mind hurting human beings when they believe it is for the theoretical good of the planet.

We in Pennsylvania and all other states, including California, already pay for environmental protection so let the EPA go to a suburb of Washington to show its wares. The environment is not a federal issue. I breathe Pennsylvania air. If Washington DC is suffering from a huge beer malt cloud from an Obama Beer Summit, chances are that neither Gaithersburg Maryland nor Baltimore will be affected. All environments are local. Big Government just doesn't work.

The onus for a clean environment is on elected officials and an informed public as watchdogs of the environment. Elected officials are the people's conduit to the government. Members of the EPA are not elected, yet they are the worst kind of corrupt political hacks operating in their own halogen sphere. Their political objective is to keep real people from having a clue about the proper way to handle the environment simply so they can have it heir way.

Apologists say the EPA is necessary because there is no advantage to any endeavor of getting decent environmental regulations if we have elected officials in charge. Can we conclude from this that they would prefer unelected officials?

Surely, the corrupt EPA is not America's only hope for a clean environment. Paying one-thirtieth of a percent of the U.S. budget for the EPA is simply a bad investment.

The arguments to keep the EPA intact made by agency apologists have not convinced the homeowners of Kentucky, who heat their homes with coal that is mined within their state by Kentuckians who like making a buck. Other states are likewise annoyed at the EPA.

Hopefully, the apologists will not get bit by a West Nile infected mosquito; will not need relief from asthma; and will not need to heat their homes; cool their vehicle; or consume a nice cold beer in the summer time—any time soon. Their model agency is against all creature comforts.

The EPA has got to go. They are hurting Americans by throwing a ring of bull around the great science that makes this country the pinnacle of the world.

Congressman Bill Johnson (R-Ohio) has lashed out at the environmentalists in the EPA. He writes:

"The Obama Administration's War on Coal is one more battle in their War on Jobs. With the EPA pursuing a scorched-earth campaign against job creators and the White House's denial that their misguided policies are driving our economy over the cliff, a direct assault against the coal industry will be the death knell for too many of our communities. The EPA's 'train wreck' of rules coming down the track will result in higher electric rates for working families who are already struggling to make ends meet in this fragile economy.

"As a candidate, then-Senator Obama said that he would bankrupt the coal industry. His EPA is carrying out the marching orders. The coal industry supports many communities in eastern and southeastern Ohio that would be devastated by the White House's ongoing War on Coal. With distressingly high unemployment levels throughout our state and nation and too many people giving up looking for work, it's unconscionable that the EPA would purposefully take steps that would cost jobs."

The EPA is simply an instrument with which the Obama administration can exercise more control over the people. The people get it and it is not sitting well. It is time to kill the EPA.

In all states in which the EPA makes a friendly visit, carnage to the state economy is the direct result. Some suggest the EPA ought to rethink its onslaught to avoid strangling the economy of certain states such as Kentucky and Ohio. Both are looking for economic recovery but EPA policies are driving utilities with older coal-fired plants to simply shutter many of them, thereby hurting these states directly and straining the US power grid.

If we were in a real war against a visible enemy proposing unnecessary regulations, Americans would be fighting for Americans. In this scenario, if we saw the EPA raise its ugly head, we would swat it down like a fly. The EPA is a parasitic fly which seems to help the few at the expense of the many.

The EPA makes its job to hurt everybody in every state, and they hurt Pennsylvania big time—from simple things like the Brownfield reclamations in Allentown to the new regulations that have PA companies beside themselves wondering how the EPA has such power. Unless the EPA is de-fanged, jobs will remain on the decline in Pennsylvania as the EPA is one of the biggest problem children of the federal government. If we put the EPA up for adoption, it would starve to death as it is too nasty a child to ever be adopted.

Our own Senator in Pennsylvania is not for his own people. The US Senate, including Robert P. Casey, Jr. of Pennsylvania defeated four amendments on April 7, 2011, that would have blocked the Environmental Protection

Agency (EPA) from regulating greenhouse gas (GHG) emissions. What was he thinking?

Though anthracite coal in Northeastern Pennsylvania is no longer the king, the state is currently the fourth largest coal producer in the country. Pennsylvania uses various mining techniques including underground mining and surface mining. Moreover, Pennsylvania is home to the nation's two largest underground bituminous coal mines. The EPA regulations will definitely hurt the economy of Pennsylvania.

Why is Senator Casey's voice not the loudest heard from coast to coast while defending Pennsylvania jobs? It is because Casey is a progressive liberal Marxist and devoted Obama follower first, and a Pennsylvanian second.

Pennsylvania gets nearly half of its electric power from coal-fired plants. It is estimated that Pennsylvania will lose another 59,000 jobs with these regulations. The last thing we need is EPA regulations that inflict Pennsylvania businesses with higher energy costs and eliminate even more Pennsylvania workers from good-paying jobs.

The EPA needs to be closed down, not Pennsylvania's factories. Electricity rates will rise by more than 17% under Obama's proposed EPA regulations that have already been postponed just like Obamacare, but they are looming out there ready to take effect.

Who can afford that?

The Obama administration and its regulatory toy, the EPA do not care a darn about Americans. There are so many bad EPA regulations, they are hard to count. Two particular EPA regulations that are new are viewed as quite onerous and experts suggest great damage to the US economy and the economy of Pennsylvania. These EPA proposed regulations would be among the most expensive ever imposed by the agency on coal-fueled power plants, dramatically increasing electricity rates and natural gas prices and leading to substantial job losses.

The National Economic Research Associates (NERA) organization analyzed the combined economic impacts of the EPA's proposed Transport Rule and its Maximum Achievable Control Technology (MACT) requirements for power plants. The analysis projects that the two regulations alone would cost the American electric sector nearly $18 billion per year, making them some of the most expensive EPA regulations ever imposed on power plants and as everything the EPA does, leading to higher electricity rates and lost jobs.

People in the state of Pennsylvania who are paying attention, see that instead of fighting back against the Obama Administration's job-killing regulations, Bob Casey Jr., the senior senator, for years has been jetting around raising campaign cash with President Obama. Now he just does as Obama commands.

Our Senator thinks we do not care. As some have referred to him as the "Unknown Senator," maybe he thinks Pennsylvanians do not see him. Pennsylvanians can show the Senator that we all care by making him live in his Scranton compound when his turn in the Senate comes up next.

On top of all the ineptness in the EPA and its terrible effect on our economy with its many regulations, Americans simply do not need to pay $10.5 billion or more a year for a Gestapo-like set of guerrillas that terrorize our population and the businesses that would otherwise hire the people of this great country.

Who will be the first to say, Bye, Bye, EPA!

Chapter 28   DDT & World Population Control

Malaria is not bad, unless *you* get it!

On June 1, 2003, the Senate was preparing to enact an international treaty that had been dubbed the POP's (persistent organic pollutants) treaty. Thirty some years after DDT was banned in most of the world, the purpose this time was to ban all use of DDT in all countries. How noble? This is despite the millions of people who had already died as a direct result of the U.S. EPA's "no excuses" ban on the chemical. I would have asked: "What about the millions that are still being saved every year by unauthorized use of DDT?

What about them? Do they die now?"

It was forty years on June 14, 2012 that the Environmental Protection Agency's (EPA) first administrator, William Ruckelshaus, disregarded the advice of his scientific advisors and for political reasons announced a ban on virtually all domestic uses of the pesticide DDT. This was done despite the fact that DDT had earlier been hailed as a "miracle" chemical that repelled and killed mosquitoes that carry malaria, a disease that can not only be fatal to humans, but is difficult to diagnose. The creator of DDT had received a Nobel Peace Prize.

Once bitten, the malaria parasite heads for the liver. It reproduces quickly before re-entering the bloodstream where it attacks the red blood cells. It can take from about one week to a year after being bitten for malaria to appear. Depending on where you are at the time, you live or die. About 2000 British hikers every year, who love to frequent malarial countries, come home very sick with Malaria. It takes weeks to get better. Nine of the 2000 die each year because DDT, the one sure mosquito killer is banned. In most countries— thanks to you know who—the EPA. .

You may know that a number of famous kings, emperors, popes, singers, and adventurers, either contracted malaria or died from Malaria. Al Jolson, Mahatma Gandhi, Genghis Khan, Pope Gregory V, and Davy Crockett are among those who have had serious bouts or died from malaria. At least eight US Presidents from George Washington to Lincoln, to Teddy Roosevelt to JFK were malaria victims in their lifetimes. When malaria does not kill a person, in many cases it weakens them severely, as was the case of Teddy Roosevelt's who did not live much longer. This disease has no right to still be in existence. It is a killer, and it has gained strength during the EPA's "reign of terror."

Malaria, yellow fever, hemorrhagic fevers of all kinds had killed millions and millions of humans long before DDT came along. DDT is responsible for over a centillion infectious mosquitoes being eliminated. Yet, it has been outlawed in the US by our own EPA. Additionally, the US EPA supports efforts to ban the substance in all countries. Knowing the tactics of the EPA, you can bet they demand compliance regardless of the country. Think of all the deaths this has caused when no other effective treatment has replaced DDT!

From the outset, the real scientific community was outspoken in their opposition to Ruckelshaus for imposing such a ban. Their hypothesis indicated that there was no evidence that DDT posed a hazard to human health. Yet the ban still took effect. The EPA takes no prisoners.

As expected, there has been a return of the long-gone diseases in the world. Simple diseases like malaria, which had effectively been wiped out, have come back with a vengeance. Years ago malaria had been eradicated by science. The scientific world had helped mankind. The EPA used junk science to push its secret agenda of world population control in the United States and through its surrogate agencies across the world.

So, DDT, the miracle chemical that had been permitting people to live, was banned from the globe. That's how powerful the EPA is. That is just one reason why the EPA must be eliminated. The world would be better bringing back DDT and killing the EPA.

The case for bringing back DDT is strong but so is the EPA. Four hundred quadrillion or more nasty mosquitoes— perhaps even a quintillion, had died but millions of people, who would have died in other times, lived substantially longer lives while DDT was available. Despite its miracle properties, the EPA and its dependent surrogates across the world successfully banned the mosquito / malaria killing pesticide from where it was needed the most. Since that fact is irrefutable, it comes with this fact; the EPA for years has been one of the principal agencies responsible for millions of deaths worldwide from malaria.

With DDT (dichlorodiphenyltrichloroethane) banned, in many mosquito-infested countries, there was no longer an effective way to control the disease carrying mosquitoes.

Of course the EPA would not want to take the blame for unneeded deaths for political reasons, but they are to blame, nonetheless. Malaria has killed lots and lots and lots more people than DDT ever could have. The EPA and its politically motivated surrogates across the world need to be held responsible.

History and uses of DDT

There is much information on DDT on the Internet and in libraries across the world. This short introduction to DDT has some basis in a short introductory chemistry course from Duke University.
http://www.chem.duke.edu/~jds/cruise_chem/pest/pest1.html

The formulation for the compound known as DDT was first created by a German chemist, Othmar Zeidler in 1874. Zeidler was a putterer and very bright. He had made hundreds of chemical compounds before DDT but he had not documented any purpose for them, and so his notes offered no clue about a productive use for any of them. Over sixty years later, a Swiss scientist, Dr. Paul Müller, in 1939 followed Zeidler's formulation and created his own DDT. From this, he discovered that it was very effective in killing insects. We might add, "to say the least."

Almost ten years later, in 1948, Müller won the Nobel Prize in Medicine for this work. Nothing in life is permanent and the tide of Müller's fortune turned less than half a century later, aided by pseudo-scientists with little knowledge, less intelligence, and even less nobility.

In World War II, soldiers were literally being eaten alive by bugs such as bedbugs, fleas, body lice (cooties) that were known to carry the typhus disease (Rickettsia bacteria). To combat the diseases, soldiers were dusted with Müller's compound which was DDT. It was so effective as an insect killer that some who observed the landscape before and after nicknamed it the "atomic bomb" of pesticides.

It is documented as saving the lives of thousands of soldiers in its first usage. For two weeks the soldiers were doused, and though they reported clouds of dust from the chemical compound, there are still no documented DDT deaths. However, as we have cited in this chapter, there had been lots of deaths from the pestilence caused by the bugs and the pathogens they carry.

DDT later was used on farms in the US to control some common agricultural pests that would destroy crops in short order without hesitation.

✓   various potato beetles
✓   coddling moth (which attacks apples)
✓   corn earworm
✓   cotton bollworm
✓   tobacco budworms

In addition to its use in farming, DDT was used extensively to control certain insects which carried other diseases such as encephalitis, hemorrhagic fever, malaria, yellow fever, and West Nile virus. These diseases are deadly. DDT as a weapon against the freight carrying bugs is even deadlier.

From the mid 1940's to the 1970's DDT was used extensively in the US and throughout the world. In the United States, at one point we were producing 220 million pounds of DDT a year. In other countries, where the major mosquito carried diseases had been infecting and killing many people, mostly children, DDT wiped out diseases such as malaria for many years.

In 1955, as an example of its effectiveness, the World Health Organization commenced a program to eradicate malaria worldwide, relying largely on DDT. The program was highly successful in many countries and death rates came down in some countries from several million per year to zero.

Environmentalists began their crusade the right way by trying to save human lives from the toxic effects of too many chemicals in the air. Over time, their focus warped into something unnatural. Their emphasis changed and their purpose became "saving nature," rather than saving mankind.

Their new found ideology, environmentalism, was based on their perception of nature's future decimation because of the footprint of human lives. That is a not so subtle change. It explains why more and more people are not very happy with the EPA and other environmentalists, who have abandoned logical thought and have gone "whacko."

For example, "People are expendable to save nature," is one of the major yet understandably quiet mantra's of the EPA, whereas the agency itself was formed because people needed help from excessive contaminants in nature's air.

The early EPA mantra was "Nature is expendable to save people." Nature of course had no official spokesperson so the EPA took on that role and it has been arguing against regular human beings and the needs of humans, especially for light and heat, and meat, ever since. No sane person can permit an organization that cares nothing about humans to protect humans.

Back to the history lesson... By the 1970s, some in the US began to get worried about DDT's environmental and health effects. The Environmental Protection Agency was formed in December, 1970 in the US by the Nixon administration to deal with pollution. Its creation had nothing to do with DDT; though DDT soon became a major target.

Nixon recognized the environmental activism that had become very big in the 1960's, and he saw the elitist money people backing a notion called the Environment Defense Fund. This innocent sounding group funded much of the early efforts to minimize the human footprint on the globe.

They won a huge victory in the US and the courts ordered the EPA to deregister DDT as a usable pesticide. They could not find the science necessary to ban DDT so they found activist judges to do their work for them, though the science did not support their cause.

Very shortly thereafter, in June 1972, the EPA cancelled all use of DDT on crops. For certain cases of disease control, the EPA allowed very limited use. Knowing one of their priorities is population control it is hard to trust them with the life of a common house fly.

By the way, as previously noted but to repeat for effect, the EPA and other environmental groups love to use the courts rather than the rigid scientific method to prove their opinions. With the courts, all they need is a sympathetic judge and an attorney who is a good persuader. So, there is not always exact science behind EPA decisions and court orders. There is however, a lot of emotion and opinions, and of course the environmentalism ideology.

DDT usage today – back to the present

While no longer manufactured or available in the US, DDT continues to be used in other parts of the world, wherever it is available. Despite its documented benefits and the lives it has saved and still could save, the world's environmental agencies, championed by the US EPA have substantially limited the supply and the use of DDT worldwide.

The Spokesperson for the mosquito population (MP) and the Malaria Disease Propagation Agency (MDPA), and the Hemorrhagic Disease Council (HDC), when consulted were quite pleased with the worldwide ban on DDT. There is speculation that for the interview, since the mosquitoes and the parasites are still learning English, EPA personnel had masqueraded as mosquitoes and parasites in order to make those statements appear to have been made by the affected organisms. Even the wicked will do anything to survive.

I hope you are getting my humor. The Trans Malarian Parasitic Orchestra in parasitic circles often plays in deadly spaces. For years it had labeled DDT as Malaria Enemy # 1.

These bad guys, when unwrapped from their host mosquito, come from the protozoan parasite from the genus Plasmodium.

If this were a total joke, and the underlying thoughts of this chapter's essay were not so serious, I would tell you that Captain Kirk's main man, Dr. McCoy, or "Bones," using a special tricorder app, could transvobulize the ship's dilithium crystals into a hermeticsic mélange that could reinfect the infectious plasmodium parasite with neon micro lights along with a subdural implantation of the doofus buffooni virus. I would also tell you that the only people ever infected by the doofus buffooni virus were one-time or currently are employees of the EPA.

This mélange and its effects have always proven to be deadly to creatures, from one cell in makeup to over five cells, but only in cases in which the villains have originated from the planet Plasmodium, once occupied by the Kardashian sisters. As I hope you realize, in the last three paragraphs I jest for effect. Unfortunately the EPA work is no joking matter, and it must be stopped.

This all boils down to the fact, that when DDT was no longer available for purely political reasons, malaria came back across the whole world, with a vengeance.

Over the last few years, many tropical countries, caring more about their people than EPA driven US sanctions began to thumb their noses at the environmentalists. The people in their countries started to die almost as quickly as the mosquitoes had been dying when in the past they were whacked with DDT.

So DDT, by popular demand, has made a comeback in some brave countries that either do not depend on US foreign aid, or who have somehow gained secret waivers from the EPA. Its use is simply to control malaria and other major diseases to help the people. Its use is not intended to irritate the EPA but yet it does.

From the Duke site, they suggest we all check out this graph from Ceylon, which charts malaria infections over time. Note that during the 1960's the disease was just about eradicated in Ceylon from DDT spraying, Note also that when DDT was no longer permitted, malaria made an almost instant big comeback. Who are these people that think they can play God with human beings?

DDT and Malaria in Ceylon

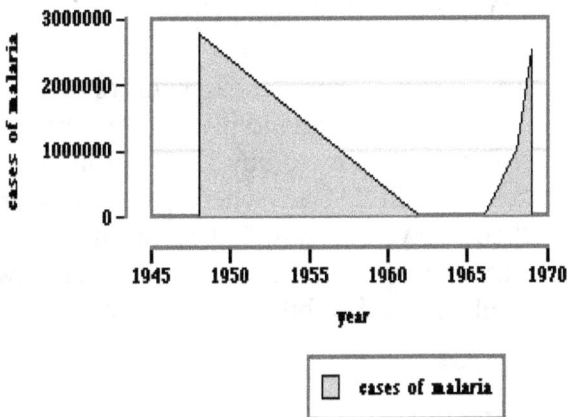

We must consider that the battle over DDT use and non-use is like a religion. The environmentalists do not care how many lives are lost as long as the environment is safe for all life—even if the mosquitoes that are saved kill humans in the process.

The environmentalists would actually be mollified if the mosquitoes live and they die. I cannot think of anything similar to this phenomenon—this death wish-than the religious zealot who places a belt of explosives on his body. Try arguing cases about religion and that is why you will find so many zealots who want DDT to continue to be banned worldwide. After all, only people die. What's so special about people?

Now, consider you wake up as the leader in a country in which the infection rate is overwhelming and people are sick all the time and many, mostly children are dying. How much do you care if the EPA tells you that you are not able to help stop the deaths of the many children in your own country by using the nasty banned substance DDT? What about your own children? Would you abide by the decrees of the US based EPA?

What would the old Pharaoh of Egypt, played by Yul Brynner do? What would Moses do? What would you do?

Suppose again that you have a cheap solution to the problem but the source of your foreign aid if you cross them will stop you from getting the money to buy DDT? Will you use your own resources to find DDT anywhere you can and pay for it yourself? Of course you would! Shame on the EPA for putting countries through that exercise, and that is why the EPA must be eliminated so humans can live.

DDT Stories

The following DDT / malaria stories from some spots in Africa show the thinking of some brave African leaders:

The use of DDT for spraying the inside walls of houses, a proven way to quickly stop the rate of malaria incidence, has made a comeback in African nations. But it not condoned by our benevolent EPA even though it has begun to save lives. The EPA would prefer that families starve to avoid getting malaria than giving them DDT.

Before DDT made its comeback, the nasty EPA permitted them to use their food money to buy an expensive pesticide soaked netting that our EPA claims is much safer for the environment than DDT. But, it is not safer for children who die of malaria.

The EPA posture would be OK maybe, if lives were secondary. Lives are now the primary motivator and saving them, especially the lives of children is a major priority for African leaders. It is not a priority in Africa for the EPA. You would be shocked at how pleased EPA zealots are that Africans have been dying because their other major goal is to eliminate humans. The term population control takes on new meaning when denying DDT to countries that need it is an invitation for infectious diseases to kill the population.

Malaria is just one of the diseases carried by parasites but it is a big enough ticket for those wishing to reduce the population – especially the young who now have substantially shorter lives in which they can pollute nature.

Saving lives now in Africa has priority for more and more brave country leaders over the fears and the lies of the environmentalists. And, as expected, for a supposed healthy environment and for population control purposes, the environmentalists are not happy about people fighting back simply because the people think they have a right to live.

At least for now, the population control notion, which had been a "given added benefit" of the DDT ban—for the whackos, is now minimized. But, remember though Americans know the EPA is bad in our own country, we cannot get rid of it. How sorry to be from a third world country fighting this human-hating group of human killers.

Logic suggests that when children are taken out by malaria or yellow fever or some other painful death, the earth and nature suffer even less over time than when an adult dies of malaria. We know by logic that the number of pollutants a human throws off into the atmosphere in a lifetime is much less when the lifetime is short. With this logic, it is surprising the EPA lets any of us live. Maybe that is why Obama wants control of healthcare.

Let's take a little trip to Uganda about a few years ago. In Uganda, caring more about people than the EPA; the Minister of Health, Brigadier Jim Muhwezi, renewed house spraying in the most "malarious" areas. He had the approval of the Ugandan Cabinet. After a while death gets sickening, but not for the sickening EPA, whose population control agenda is enhanced by death.

Muhwezi had critics including the EPA surrogates, but he dismissed them all, saying: "How many people must die of malaria while these debates continue? If DDT can save lives, why not use it as we wait for the alternatives."

His words were reported in the Kampala newspaper, New Vision.

The program has been successful, and when Uganda's story was originally written, the country of Mauritius was about to be declared malaria free because of its use of DDT.

Zambia is another example. From the time of the DDT ban, malaria incidence and deaths had been climbing. To address this, just as in Uganda, the Health Minister aggressively pursued the use of DDT to fight malaria. The theory came well tested after the great success Zambia had using DDT in the copper mining areas beginning in 2000. After just two years, there were no malaria deaths in the copper mining areas.

These are great triumphs for humanity but they are defeats for the EPA. Which side are you on?

Zimbabwe is yet another example of leaders saying "environmentalists are killing our people." Minister of Health David Parirenyatwa reintroduced DDT to save the children because, according to his words, it was, "cheap and more effective, with a longer residual killing power." He is quoted in the Bulawayo Chronicle in October 2003:

"So many people have died of malaria since January and we are doing our best to control it... DDT is very effective, because it sticks for a long time on the walls and kills a lot of mosquitoes with a single spray... South Africa and Swaziland are using it, and I don't see why we should not use it."

Why should DDT not be used until something can be made that is safer?

The US government has no business in environmental regulation for the states or for the rest of the world, especially when their scientific premise is wrong—dead wrong. In the US as we have said many times, there should be no federal regulations at all, since we have the individual states to do that work. The tenth amendment of the Constitution demands that anything like an EPA should be run by the states.

The biggest stain on America is a government that has grown so large that it has in many ways turned against its own citizens. The EPA is an agent of such a government, and it spreads its wings into less powerful countries commanding, for the sake of population control, not environment protection, that children die of major diseases and the earlier the better.

Before we close this chapter on DDT, let's review the two big items that the EPA says will kill us while it advocates the deaths of little children to complete its sordid green agenda—an agenda which clearly embraces world population control. Let's answer these two questions though we have been discussing DDT for a while already in this chapter.

What is DDT and what is the other major chemical that the EPA does not like?

250 Kill the EPA

DDT: Dichlorodiphenyltrichloroethane, CCl3CH(C6H4Cl)2, a synthetic organic compound introduced in the 1940s and used as an insecticide.

CFC: Chlorofluorocarbon: a fluorocarbon with chlorine; formerly used as a refrigerant and as a propellant in aerosol cans.

We have already given a brief picture of the DDT issues but we will look at its ban in a little more detail as a sordid means of population control in Part II (Chapter 29) before we move to Chapter 30. In Chapter 30, we examine the CFC ban in detail so you can get a full picture of what the EPA really is, and why it cannot be trusted to act on our behalf even in a matter in which nobody has to die.

Whereas EPA apologists identify just these two EPA actions (DDT and CFC bans) as the defining items in the EPA's legacy of greatness, I submit that the EPA response to the perceived issues with DDT and CFCs is exactly the reason why the EPA must go.

EPA apologists, thinking rational human beings will believe they cannot do without the nasty and corrupt EPA, ask how the banning of DDT and CFCs would have been managed in a world in which there was no EPA-devised national standard. To be honest, answering that presumption makes me feel like throwing up. Sorry!

Of course they are referring to the assertion that the EPA should be eliminated. Then what would we do? Hah? Then what? Then humans can live!

My answer is that if there were no ban on either of these products, life would be better and safer for all people, and more people would be living with less government harassment.

To help the EPA apologists remember that the people are tuned into their agenda, let's go back and review some facts about malaria in Chapter 29, Part II, and add to the fact list, and then close out and go on to Chapter 30 The truth about CFCs.

Chapter 29

DDT & World Population Control Part II

DDT Fact Check: Mosquitos or People? Who Dies?

A quick check of the facts shows that well over a million people continue to die worldwide each year because of the EPA supported ban on DDT and the rise of malaria and other such mosquito borne diseases. And, just as sure as Global Warming, and the possibility of Al Gore donating all his money to charity are both big hoaxes, the DDT ban and in fact, the CFC ban are also big hoaxes perpetrated by an EPA agency gone wild.

There is also a sinister side to the EPA DDT ban that is difficult to swallow—population control. I have hinted at it but have not really hammered it home. It is so sinister it is actually unbelievable that civilized people might advocate the deaths of children from a horrible disease so Mother Nature would be pleased.

I don't think Mother Nature is pleased one bit. Since deaths are black children, I am even further amazed that the powerful minority lobby in the US does not insist this practice be stopped with no delays. Instead, blacks and other minorities are silent while their children die.

I can see how you might not even believe me, so I came here ready to explain why. Now that we have first examined where we are worldwide with DDT, there is a lot more to say by a lot more people, Let's review what the distinguished Walter Williams has to say about this notion of population control being waged on poor blacks in other countries.

Dr. Williams is an American economist, commentator, and academic. He is the John M. Olin Distinguished Professor of Economics at George Mason University, as well as a syndicated columnist and author known for his libertarian views. If you've got the time, Williams is worth a listen, no matter what the topic.

Writing for the Jewish World Review in July 2004, Dr. Walter Williams, highlights the demagoguery and the ideological agenda of the EPA. Besides being an economist and all the credits above, Williams is also a teaching faculty member at George Mason University in Fairfax, Virginia. Like you, Dr. Williams is not a dummy!

http://www.eco-imperialism.com/content/article.php3?id=68

His work rips big holes in any notion that the EPA uses real science for its conclusions. Millions have paid with their lives for the EPA's idealism, and thirst for power. Instead of Americans and other world citizens leading miserable lives and even being killed off by bad regulations, let's get together and kill the EPA!

Williams writes:

"Ever since Rachel Carson's 1962 book "Silent Spring," environmental extremists have sought to ban all DDT use. Using phony studies from the Environmental Defense Fund and the Natural Resources Defense Council, the environmental activist-controlled Environmental Protection

Agency banned DDT in 1972. The extremists convinced the nation that DDT was not only unsafe for humans but unsafe to birds and other creatures as well. Their arguments have since been scientifically refuted."

Despite this, EPA zealots and apologists from around the world, armed with little to no supporting science, take on honest overtures to close down this killer agency. They use arguments that have long since been proven to be falsehoods, and pure lies.

I have lifted a few additional paragraphs from William's piece to show the really sinister, downright sick rationale for the banning of DDT. Does it matter whether Williams is black or white? He is human. When you read this you may find yourself muttering Williams' words:

"Maybe somebody did not like poor people. Maybe somebody did not like black people. Maybe somebody did not like the high birthrate in poor black countries, and just maybe somebody is actually using malaria as a form of population control." Why? Because they are powerful enough; that they can do so.

Williams continues:

"While DDT saved crops, forests and livestock, it also saved humans. In 1970, the U.S. National Academy of Sciences estimated that DDT saved more than 500 million lives during the time it was widely used. [That is a larger number than the current US population. We are not alone.]

"A scientific review board of the EPA showed that DDT is not harmful to the environment and showed it to be a beneficial substance that 'should not be banned.' According to the World Health Organization, worldwide malaria infects 300 million people. About 1 million die of malaria each year. Most of the victims are in Africa, and most are children.

"In Sri Lanka, in 1948, there were 2.8 million malaria cases and 7,300 malaria deaths. With widespread DDT use, malaria cases fell to 17 and no deaths in 1963. After DDT use was discontinued, Sri Lankan malaria cases rose to 2.5 million in the years 1968 and 1969, and the disease remains a killer in Sri Lanka today. More than 100,000 people died during malaria epidemics in Swaziland and Madagascar in the mid-1980s, following the suspension of DDT house spraying. After South Africa stopped using DDT in 1996, the number of malaria cases in KwaZulu-Natal province skyrocketed from 8,000 to 42,000. By 2000, there had been an approximate 400 percent increase in malaria deaths. Now that DDT is being used again, [shhhh!!!! – don't tell Byron Moore] the number of deaths from malaria in the region has dropped from 340 in 2000 to none at the last reporting in February 2003.

"In South America, where malaria is endemic, malaria rates soared in countries that halted house spraying with DDT after 1993 -- Guyana, Bolivia, Paraguay, Peru, Brazil, Colombia and Venezuela. In Ecuador, DDT spraying was increased after 1993, and the malaria rate of infection was reduced by 60 percent. In a 2001 study published by the London-based Institute for Economic Affairs, "Malaria and the DDT Story," Richard Tren and Roger Bate say that "Malaria is a human tragedy," adding, "Over 1 million people, mostly children, die from the disease each year, and over 300 million fall sick."

--Temporary End of Williams quote---

By now, you all know how I feel about the heartless EPA. This agency should be disbanded for lots of reasons but none greater than the politically corrupt / incorrect ban on the pesticide known to help people live by wiping out many diseases. For example, check out this quote from The National Academy of Sciences made in 1970, just two years before the political murderers in the EPA imposed their will on the world.

"To only a few chemicals does man owe as great a debt as to DDT. In only some two decades, DDT has prevented 500 million human deaths due to malaria that would otherwise have been inevitable."

A reasonably prudent person would conclude that on balance, DDT is a very helpful product. So, why does the EPA think otherwise? Answer – their mission is not to save lives.

Williams Quote continues:

"The fact that DDT saves lives might account for part of the hostility toward it. Alexander King, founder of the Malthusian Club of Rome, wrote in a biographical essay in 1990:

'My own doubts came when DDT was introduced. In Guyana, within two years, it had almost eliminated malaria. So my chief quarrel with DDT, in hindsight, is that it has greatly added to the population problem.'

"Dr. Charles Wurster, one of the major opponents of DDT, is reported to have said,"

'People are the cause of all the problems. We have too many of them. We need to get rid of some of them, and this [referring to malaria deaths] is as good a way as any.'

Let me translate. These people in the environmental community and the EPA have another agenda going on and saving human lives is not part of their agenda. It is called world population control and when DDT was banned, people began to die again and that was not an accident. It was a plan. And the EPA staff was able to smile.

258 Kill the EPA

The apologists / zealots will tell you that there are many other "safer" ways to solve the malaria problem. For example, there are these nets discussed earlier that are sprayed heavily with insecticide that offer protection. But, they cost a zillion dollars and in undeveloped countries that is enough for parents to make a decision as to whether their children die either of malaria or of starvation. Those into population control would be happy to simply euthanize those folks at birth or before. Oh, they already do—abortion.

Think about your requiring netting as a way of life. Is this not like having the people in the undeveloped countries live their lives with a dog-like Elizabethan collar around them to prevent them from getting in trouble and ultimately getting killed by malaria. Can the iPhone fit under the netting? Forget about stickball or even dancing while wearing the insect net. No wonder people die. People want to be free.

DDT simply kills the perpetrator and the person defended by DDT gets to live a normal life. No net boys or bubble boys are necessary when the country is armed with DDT. Just spray a house with small amounts of DDT and it costs a measly $1.44 per year. For $1.44 nobody is going to die, and there is no net needed that offers protection to just one person at a time. The net and other alternatives are five to 10 times more costly, making them effectively unaffordable in poor countries.

Poor countries often have leaders, who have a great understanding of the rest of the world, and that is why they are the leaders. Unfortunately, the "greater than thou" rich country emissaries, such as those elitists from the US-EPA that once used DDT themselves to eliminate the problem; threaten reprisals against poor countries if they use DDT. Brave leaders find DDT rather than permitting their people to be killed by diseases as powerful as a biological population control WMD.

It seems to me that many black and brown people, more than white people are being affected by these major diseases due to the warm nature of their native climates. I think this is outrageous.

I do not understand why black and brown religious groups, perhaps the Congressional Black Caucus, Jesse Jackson, Al Sharpton, and Latino leaders in the US and elsewhere, government and non-government organizations, politicians and others who profess concern over the plight of poor people around the world do not join together to stop the killing of young children, who simply want to have fun. Children do not want to live under nets or in bubbles. But, they surely want to live and their parents want them to live.

The fact is that most of those who die are black or brown children. These young people should be enabled to live long and productive lives. Nobody, including the EPA should be gunning for them. Somebody should step up and become a face to this huge problem. Yet, there is no face, and the corrupt Democrat-loving EPA-loving press in the US will not rock the boat to help anybody not living in their own homes.

A little investigation would tell them that because the killer mosquito a.k.a. the mosquito borne parasite cannot be killed by ordinary means, something extraordinary is necessary. Lots of washing and looking good in the mirror does not help.

Tell me it is not possible that what I would call mostly comfortable Americans, in the Hamptons, (who work for the EPA?) or perhaps EPA people who live in other comfortable places, while making a good buck for the EPA, have determined that poor people, especially those in other countries are expendable?

The EPA prescribed and promoted DDT bans, which created needless suffering and death. Was population control an expressed or implied goal of the EPA? The population control aficionados know that mosquito-borne malaria not only has devastating health effects but stifles economic growth as well, and thus more and more deaths can occur in poor countries and their populations can thus be controlled!

Amen, Dr. Williams!

I admit that the topic of population control is way beyond my pay grade. I am, however, very sympathetic to those needlessly killed when solutions, such as DDT, a miracle drug, are available.

Greg Baxter wrote what I see as a chilling article on population control and malaria for The Irish Medical Times. It is titled, Is malaria the solution to population control. I do not endorse or not endorse any of what is in his article but it surely demonstrates the point I am making and it brings in the serious notion that population control is not a topic to be taken lightly regardless of your position on population control or the means of control.

You can see this line of thought at http://www.imt.ie/opinion/guests/2010/04/is-malaria-the-solution-to-population-control.html

Those arguing for population control take the issue as seriously and perhaps even more seriously than I take the issue of interference by the EPA from keeping the world disease free.

This is one of those chilling excerpts from Baxter's article:

"Neither famine nor disease control population growth anymore. Nor does war. Professor of Molecular, Cellular and Developmental Biology at Yale University, Robert Wyman looked at nuclear war as a way to control population growth in a public lecture last year.

" 'The Hiroshima bomb killed 75,000 people, the Nagasaki bomb killed 25,000 people. That's 100,000 people dead in two quick flashes," he said. "But the population on earth grows by approximately 200,000 a day. What that means is that if we can imagine that some wars are going to balance births and deaths on earth, that means that every day you have to blow up two Nagasaki bombs and two Hiroshima bombs, killing that equivalent number of people, just to keep even.' "

"Prof Wyman argues that the eradication of malaria, as well as the development of family planning and economic stability, will decrease population growth in Africa – putting the emphasis on fertility, instead of mortality, as a solution. He points out that the demographic transition from high fertility and mortality to low, already completed in places like Europe, Tunisia and Japan, is still ongoing in much of Africa."

There are two sides to every story. In my story, the EPA does not have the right to play God. Its value as a force in the pollution debate is diminished by its apparent leanings towards world population control. Nobody in my government, of which I am aware, gave the EPA such power.

Chapter Summary

Going back in summary, we have learned from the EPA proponents that the DDT and the CFC bans are two of the EPA's actions that have supposedly made it a great agency. Obviously "decreases in the death rate" is not an EPA statistic that is measured or cared about or this legacy would have a big cross-out mark on it.

I am not suggesting that DDT and CFCs are the EPA's only sins but the DDT story shows the EPA has been a non-repenting killer of people. The economic impact of the major regulations against fossil fuels and other necessities of life demonstrate that the EPA is also a jobs killer. The CFC story, in which you can engage in detail in the next chapter, is pure corruption, and a marriage of government and industry that should warrant a quick divorce.

So, I had concluded even before I had given you any facts in this book that the EPA itself needs to be killed. It should not be credited with great acts for the well-being of mankind as zealots and apologists might slant the facts. The EPA is a killer of men—with no apologies.

The EPA at best is a pack of liars interested in its own power and self-preservation. They have no concern about a sane person's perception of the greater good, especially for we the people! The EPA is pro-nature, and thus, they are anti-people as they have concluded that nature—animals, vegetables, and minerals are more important than people.

Even though they do not use guns or knives, the EPA murders people, nonetheless. Sometimes they murder with WMDs (malaria, yellow fever, etc.) simply to suit their sordid agenda. Sometimes it is by denying the spirit of a farmer who can no longer work the land.

This agency cannot be trusted with our lives.

Tell the EPA, as Jim Reeves would say "it's time to go!"

Chapter 30

The Truth about CFCs

EPA Ban on CFCs (Chlorofluorocarbons)

We're switching gears now in this book to what EPA proponents like to claim as their second greatest triumph—their ban on CFCs. Let's see what they think when they read this chapter!

Many already know what CFCs are. But, for those that do not know, and for those who could use a reminder, and for those who want to know more; here we go:

CFC: Chlorofluorocarbon: a fluorocarbon with chlorine; formerly used as a refrigerant and as a propellant in aerosol cans. Freon is a CFC as is R-12, its generic name.

When I had Freshman English at King's College, it annoyed me that the professor kept pointing out how all of the men (King's was all male) in the class consistently begged the argument. In other words, we made it seem that what we said was fact simply because we had said it. Since those days, I have always tried to give credit to the source of the information as I hate begging anything, including the argument.

To the best of my knowledge, and after hours and hours and hours of research and analysis, I believe the facts that I present here are true. But, it is tough to believe that even the

EPA, an agency for whom I have little respect, is capable of such treachery.

Most people know the state of Oregon to be quite a liberal state and the EPA is a very liberal organization. The EPA as a proponent of nature over man is far more liberal than Oregon. Yet, as a state, though there are some hard and fast conservatives, few states if any are more liberal progressive than the Democrats in Oregon. Bear in mind, for full disclosure, other than two years as an Independent before I moved home to live with my parents in the 1970's, I have been a registered Democrat.

Today when the philosophy of the Democratic Party is liberal progressive Marxism, I differentiate myself by classifying myself as a JFK Democrat. I am more conservative than most Republicans because most Republicans have no idea what they are.

My point is that if Oregon is unhappy with the EPA and that says an awful lot. By the way, many think the honor of most liberal state falls to California. Most Californians, however, actually know their positions are wrong but they hold them anyway because, after all, they are Californians. Oregonians actually think they are right. That is a big difference.

As a side bar fact, the state bird of Oregon is the banana slug. Actually, the state bird is the Western Meadow Lark but there are so many slugs in Oregon that locals joke about the state bird being the slug. I was out of my car in Oregon for just a few minutes, when I encountered the first slug I had ever seen in my life, so I believe this rumor for sure. What separates Oregonians from EPAers is that Oregonians have a sense of humor.

Many the following facts in this chapter's essay are from the Oregon Observer at the following citation:
http://www.zianet.com/web/freon1.htm

Most normal people would think that environmentalists are pretty good people who are deeply concerned about the impact man is having on nature. Most would not believe that the EPA would ever put the profit needs of corporations or the survival need of the EPA agency itself ahead of the needs of the people of the US? In this instance, most normal people would be wrong.

Though I have a far more practical stance on most issues in life than the idealists in the environmental community championed by the EPA, I once held the view that overall, they were good people who were simply way too zealous about one topic in life. I now think they can be bought and sold like anybody else—even if it is against their raison d'etre—their root cause—their reason for existing.

DDT and the EPA's leaning towards global population control opened my eyes. Yet, this was an ideological issue about chemicals and pesticides and a "few" deaths. CFCs are more of an economic issue. Based on what we know so far at least as presented in this book, do any of us trust the EPA? Will the EPA fare better on this side of the debate?

Let's see!

We have already learned in the last chapter that the EPA clearly uses its regulations for population control, which is completely abhorrent and inhuman. So, would it be a lesser sin if we discovered that the EPA is in bed with select corporations that help this huge agency to better accomplish its corrupt agenda?

I think you already know the answer. That is the beauty of rhetorical questioning.

There is no other conclusion that can be made than that the EPA is now way too big for its britches; and it needs to be shut down completely before it inflicts more harm on Americans and others across the world.

It cannot be trusted; it cannot be repaired; it must be eliminated. Check out this piece of a telling article from the Oregon Observer about CFC's, a major problem as seen by the EPA's closest lenses:

"First of all, most of the people in the refrigeration industry know that the CFC ban is a scam and that since the article 'Idaho Man With Answer To International CFC Ban,' many people now realize that the EPA is in bed with DuPont on the CFC ban, so it can maintain the near-monopoly on refrigerants that it enjoyed in the Freon days. The whole world knows it also."

As a result of this article, printed in the May 1996 edition of The Oregon Observer (www.oregonobserver.com), a paper not likely to take the truth lightly, many people now know the truth of the DuPont / EPA relationship.

Using their pull, the huge chemical corporation has been able to maintain its near-monopoly on refrigerants in similar fashion to when it controlled its profits in the Freon hay days. If DuPont has a problem with that statement, check out the Oregon Observer or let's just say "it appears that way to me." I would be happy to publish comments from DuPont in this regard in a subsequent printing of this book and/or on my Web site. Since this is the second edition, so far at least, DuPont has by way of no comment, agreed with my findings.

When DuPont held the patent on Freon, ironically, there was no problem with CFCs. But, as you know, patents expire, and so when others could make Freon legally, and very cheaply without DuPont's permission, and without any kickbacks to the EPA or other agencies, it meant that DuPont no longer could receive all the royalties.

Out of nowhere, the best gas for refrigeration products ever, and thus the most efficient for air conditioners—industrial and automotive as well—all of a sudden, was not an acceptable choice. How did that happen? Enter the EPA!

There were big issues found by you know who—the EPA investigators—regarding ozone depletion yet these guys never seemed to care about Freon while DuPont held the exclusive patent. Perhaps it is just coincidence?

Perhaps, perhaps, just perhaps, Freon's inventor and once protected patent holder, DuPont, was worried that it might have its excessive revenue stream compromised if the EPA, the "watchdog of the people," permitted all "nobody's in the world" to compete for the refrigerant gas substitute business. How could a free country permit free enterprise by free people?

So, an argument in favor of the EPA would be that the agency saved the world from "nobody's" having an opportunity to be successful. What an argument. What a legacy. Could either the EPA or the DuPont Corporation possibly have been so crooked? Surely either or both would be pleased to give all comers complete access to their records on the matter.

If someone else found the marbles first, that would not make DuPont, the EPA's buddy for a very long time, very happy. If a competitor or a "nobody," happened to create a product that would be able to engage DuPont for this lucrative "refrigerant" business, large profits would not be as assured for the chemical giant. I can't quite figure out what was in it for the EPA other than controlling the game, but, maybe that was enough.

Of course the EPA received no such profits as its staffers were paid by our generous treasury. So some might suggest they had no dog in the race. But, did they?

If you choose to do research on the Internet for Freon and DuPont patents, you will find that information is not readily available for easy reading, but there are a host of opinions out there. Could there be a stink worse than the scent of Freon emerging from a ruptured AC unit on this topic any day soon?

After the Oregon Observer article, and after watching government agencies in operation, I am inclined to believe that Americans (that's US) were duped by DuPont (has a certain ring to it) and the EPA into believing that Freon was a real bad guy. Who did it ever kill? It is not a mosquito, and surely many who would have died from extreme heat were saved by Freon, for sure.

Who has the power to take anybody on to find the truth in this issue of importance to all Americans. Have we been duped? The agency surely is our Congress; but our Congress no longer seems to have the will to fight for the people. Let's see how they do with Benghazi, a national tragedy that Democrats have hired the best company in the world to solve for them – Shop Vac! Yes indeed. If Shop Vac can help America on Benghazi, then it can brighten the skies on the EPA and FREON also. Listen to the text sucking sound in the background and you will know Shop Vac is in the cover-up business.

Just remember this potential conclusion as we go along in this chapter. There is nothing less enjoyable in a real game than a replacement player. Wait 'til you see the Freon replacement that DuPont literally cooked up, and wait 'til you see the better player that showed up, but would not play ball for DuPont.

Thankfully for the DuPont team, the EPA declared the new player "ineligible to play." He was simply too good! Many wonder why. Could the very powerful Dupont Corporation have decided that nobody can have a better solution than

DuPont, and thus, they had to shut him down? Or was the EPA in league with DuPont so nobody other than the chosen corporation would get the next great patent on coolants? It is not for me to know!

There are a lot of citizens in Kentucky and other states with an opinion of the EPA. W. Ed Parker is one of those with a real opinion as far as how things affect Kentucky. The following long quote is taken from his article because Ed says it so well. He does like to use CAPS a bit more than some prefer, so watch your ears if you hear Ed screaming:

http://www.sweetliberty.org/issues/environment/ozonefreo n_fraud.htm

"The excuse used by the EPA for the ban on Freon was it somehow seeps into the atmosphere and depletes the Ozone in our air. There is no scientific data available, in or out of government, to describe this "claimed" process. Freon is one of the most useful substances ever created by man; and it has many uses. In refrigeration, its prime usage is as the substance inside the sealed refrigeration systems that allows cooling to take place during the evaporator operation, and heating during the high temperature condensing part of the refrigeration cycles. Without Freon or some similar substance, refrigeration cannot occur, and the best known alternate would be to return to ice boxes.

"Freon was developed and patented by the DuPont Company. Ironically, the DuPont patents on Freon ran out at about the same time the government decrees to ban the use of Freon were issued. The leading replacement substances for Freon were also developed by DuPont. The Freon (HCFC) substances are far more costly and far more complex, to the extent that DuPont stands to make untold billions of dollars on the change out of this substance, and consumers will have an inferior product.

Further, the DuPont substitutes have no supporting data to prove they meet environmental needs.

"Freon, the 'villain', is an odorless, tasteless, chemically neutral substance, which is HEAVIER THAN AIR, and by the laws of physics cannot rise into the atmosphere. If [it] is spilled on the ground, it will settle in the soil and become plant food. It meets the Biblical standard of "ashes to ashes and dust to dust." Freon can be commercially produced at a very low cost of $.50 to $1.00 per pound. Some recent news reports indicate that since the banning, it is now one of the leading items sold in the world's black markets. Some reported costs of Freon on the black market run as high as $50.00 per pound.

"With the expiration of the DuPont patents, Freon would have been readily available as an air conditioning and refrigeration substance for the entire world, including Third World Countries, at affordable rates. According to THE FACT FINDER, P.O. Box A, Scottsdale, AZ 85252, (1/16/95), DuPont owners have direct ties to the NEW AGE-ENVIRONMENTAL MOVEMENT which, in turn has ties to the EPA and such luminaries as Vice President Al Gore. Gore has ties to THE NEW WORLD ORDER of George Bush and Bill Clinton. According to THE FACT FINDER, Charles Bronfman of Seagrams, who controls the Board of Directors of DuPont, led the fight against Freon, his own product, because the DuPont patents to control Freon had run out."

That, no matter who you are, is a mouthful!

You may say that Ed Parker is a conspiracy theorist or you may say that Ed is sick of being lied to. I have found a number of scientists including the great team hosted by www.junkscience.com that do not trust the government on any issues because the government is accustomed to use lying as one of their chief tools for imposing their will on the

American people. Most honest Americans cannot believe there are such people who go to church and receive communion each week. I regret to say, there are.

When Al Gore, who is not only a non-scientist, but he may also be a non-human, (OK, too cruel perhaps, but let's check it out before we rule it out!) became a hundred millionaire because of "green," those with noses and nose hair scensed (OK I invented the word) that something stunk, and it was not the pre-Gore air. What is bad is simply bad!

There is a scientific debate about whether Freon actually makes it to the stratosphere but with major wind gusts it is certainly probable. But, how many cars over the years leaked quart after quart of Freon (R-12) on the roads and in the back yards and people are still breathing, and breathing fine.

Ozone is also heavier than oxygen and it makes it up there also. The real experts see this all as a big hoax, and lots of big shots including Al Gore, and the DuPont' company are making lots of money on scaring people. Thank God there is somebody out there telling the truth.

I admit that I have no evidence that anybody at the EPA is making money on the deal but I have no proof to the contrary otherwise. The truth and the EPA seem to have intentionally separated years ago. I would suspect that soon the "TRUTH" will be filing for divorce.

EPA and DuPont

Despite its clear connection with DuPont on CFC's, the EPA would never publicly announce that it was in bed with the chemical giant. However, when it smells like a rat, there is typically a rat on the scene, even if there is no D-Con. Once the DuPont patent ran out, the EPA declared Freon bad and thus it created the need for an alternative to Freon. It makes me want to know: "Who does the EPA serve?"

When the best solution to replace Freon was brought forward, as written up in the Oregon Observer, the EPA rejected it and chose the solution put forth by DuPont. When a story is a little fishy, there is normally a stinky dead fish someplace close by. Is the EPA that stinky fish?

Let me go through this one more time. The EPA created the dilemma when, without proper scientific evidence it declared CFCs, such as Freon as "Ozone Depleters," a bad label. To further its agenda and DuPont's agenda, the EPA then scared Americans into thinking that they needed protection from Freon.

Then, the EPA, the agency chartered by Nixon simply so that we could all breathe, set itself up as the protector for the masses from Freon, which most Americans did not even want to know how to spell.

Yet, this had been the same gas that for years made the masses comfortable in their air conditioners and by colling the beer in their refrigerators. Luckily after Freon was declared "bad," DuPont had another "fine" chemical cocktail available for EPA approval, and they got it.

And the good news for Dupont was that they held its fresh patent, unlike that nasty Freon patent which had entered public domain status, and after a zillion years of use, the EPA had found it to be substandard.

On the road to pulling off the caper for DuPont undetected, an even better solution to Freon was brought forth and demonstrated to the EPA. However, some say, simply because DuPont would not hold any rights to that "nobody" solution, it was rejected by the EPA. Can that really be true? That just about does it for a recap on the Oregon Observer story.

I haven't seen such a good protection racket since the Capone boys in Chicago in the 1920's. All the little guys—you and I—the consumers, would then be protected by the only protection racket in town – the EPA, and their new bootlegger partner, DuPont. Thank you for the protection, Mr. EPA.

Protection from what?

Should we thank the Lord that the EPA had not been eliminated when it used its junk science to protect us all? First the ever merciful and opinionated EPA determined that Freon was not a harmful gas? And so, for years it was permitted and overall Americans could afford it.

Then, mysteriously, when the patent ran out for DuPont, the EPA dutifully declared Freon to be a harmful ozone depleting gas.

This is confusing only if you trust that people, even the EPA people, will do the right thing in all cases. After all the repetition of the issue in this article so far, I would bet we all know the big issue here.

Should we also be thankful that the EPA set itself up so that protection from harmful refrigerants could only be rendered by the EPA? By the way, it is not just Freon. The EPA banned all CFCs for refrigeration along with a number of CFCs that provide medically needed functions such as the most efficient inhalers for asthmatics, according to doctors.

We have minimally discussed the need for inhalers in other chapters but the banned substance in this chapter (CFC's) is why the EPA thinks it is OK for children to wheeze when they otherwise would be able to gain real comfort. The EPA ordered that the best inhalers all be taken off the market before there was a substitute that could do the job. The irony is the EPA did this theoretically so that we could all breathe better.

Neither the EPA nor Mother Nature was available for comment about the CFC ban for asthmatic inhalers. Perhaps the EPA would say it this way: "Sorry that you are not breathing well! But, a little wheeze may not be all that bad for children if they only knew how much their suffering could benefit Mother Nature."

I too think that is a bit trite but what can you expect from the EPA—the truth? Let's ask Mother Nature, the adopted Mom of the EPA, her opinion! Whoops! She was busy saving arachnids, cornucopia, mosquitoes, spider ants, and loci, and thus was unavailable for comment.

Americans had reason at the time of the bans to trust the EPA since none had yet read this essay. Trusting Americans were unaware of the DuPont connection with the EPA and until recently (Obama Administration), most of us tended to trust most aspects of government. Now, like many, I trust few aspects of government, and I see the EPA being an Obama tool and as treacherous and as deadly as any organization on the planet. It does not serve Americans. How many other connections to big corporations do you suppose there may be?

A few facts:

In this section we discuss the scientific work of Dr. Wm. Robert Johnston. This is not to be confused with Bill Johnson, the candidate for Senate from Kentucky who was vilified improperly in the last chapter.
http://www.johnstonsarchive.net/environment/wrjp365o.ht ml

Dr. Wm. Robert Johnston is a research physicist in the field of Space physics: the study of the space environment, encompassing realms from the ionosphere to the magnetosphere to interplanetary space. His current concentration is in the study of the earth's radiation belts. He is a well respected scientist on the notion of Ozone Depletion. He writes:

"With the phaseout of CFCs, alternative chemicals are being introduced for air conditioners and refrigerators. Several replacement chemicals have been developed, none of which are as efficient as Freon. Many of these are toxic, flammable, or corrosive. Refrigerators and air conditioners are more expensive as a result.

"This will especially affect people in the third world, who need them for health reasons. Even in the United States, the phase-out of CFCs is costing everyone indirectly. Opponents of the CFC ban say that scientifically, the evidence that man is destroying the ozone layer is too weak to justify policy decisions that harm people."

In other words, Johnston, a real expert, thinks the work being done by the EPA is extreme and unnecessary, and he notes that there is no such evidence that the CFCs are hurting the stratosphere.

Other information on Global warming from Dr. Johnston can be found at:
http://www.johnstonsarchive.net/environment/gw.html

When you read Dr. Johnston and the consensus from the scientific (not the environmentalist) community, it is easy to conclude that even if there were issues with Freon and other CFCs, and even CO_2, a human exhalant, the public response by the EPA and other agencies is exaggerated and self-serving. Additionally, the EPA may have the needs of corporations in mind, rather than the needs of the public.

Chapter 31

The Best Solution to the Freon Non-Problem Part I

Oregon Observer and Gary Lindgren

These facts are a continuation of the Oregon Observer story. It is an American Saga, and Gary, now dead, is actually a major hero.

In 1992, Gary Lindgren, just a regular smart guy, a former aerospace engineer, got wind of the opportunity to create a solution to satisfy the fraudulent need for a Freon replacement. So, he began experimenting to see if he could come up with something while working in his home town of Post Falls, Idaho. He was toying with some old refrigerators, which he had lying around—so he had a nice sandbox in which to play.

Like you, I would have had no idea how to conduct any experiments on such dead items. Yet, I respect any scientist who can.

Like many inventors before him, Lindgren hit the jackpot with a combination of chemicals that emitted no Ozone depletion factors, and was well within all of the numbers as specified by the EPA. Moreover, since his formula worked in all the old refrigerators, no major refrigeration unit would have to be replaced when and if his concoction were to replace Freon. R-12 (Freon) could simply be taken out and

Lindgren's OZ-12 (a.k.a. HC-12a) put back in as a replacement, according to the Lindgren studies. Refrigeration experts across the Internet and across the world have certified this as fact. Yet, because DuPont did not like it, the EPA did not like it.

Lindgren had in fact discovered the alternative answer to what was then the looming refrigeration dilemma—an inexpensive, harmless, non-corrosive alternative to Freon. If the EPA ever were inclined to move out of the way, Lindgren's brew would be found to be the safest for all commercial applications. But, we will never know until we move the corrupt EPA, protected by an ideology driven President out of the decision process.

Though Freon still remains scientifically approved outside of the EPA, and it has never been proven to be an Ozone depletion factor, the fact is that the EPA, using what real scientists consider bogus science, banned it and Congress permitted this atrocity to continue.

Our bright lights in Congress also permit harmful CFL lights in our homes v. the long-time Edison incandescent. Unless Congress eliminates the EPA, that ban will hold. Therefore Freon to the chagrin of many who really know, can no longer be used commercially.

To lighten that statement a bit; this made Freon's use problematic at best. Lindgren's solution is actually as efficient as Freon—actually more efficient, and it is far better than the witch's brew DuPont cooked up as its solution. Do you think that the malcontents at the EPA really liked the DuPont brew? Is it possible that there was something else in play?

Knowing this was an important discovery; Lindgren, who was a really smart guy, founded OZ Technology to market his discovery. HC-12a became his answer to the international chlorofluorocarbon (CFC, Freon) ban as per the Montreal

Protocol of 1987, of which the US was a signatory. The intention of the treaty was of course to limit global warming and ozone depletion.

Both of these notions are hocus pocus and in great disrepute, but they have undoubtedly helped Al Gore become a billionaire after leaving the vice presidency with a measly $2 million in assets.

However, the EPA is indefatigable in its insistence that Freon and DDT must not ever be used again, even if facts prove them wrong. It is carved in the precepts of their environmentalism religion. When the EPA is gone, my recommendation is to simply bring back Freon, unless we find Lindgren's solution, when the light of day analysis is permitted, to be even better than Freon. I think it is better! And it is just as cheap.

Lindgren had actually solved a "non-problem" with a wonderful and acceptable solution. This expose shows how the EPA could not accept a non-DuPont solution even though it is still recognized as the best solution of all by other experts and opinionists in the world refrigeration marketplace.

Because the statement is true, we do like to say that there is substantial speculation that Freon was and is not really an air-quality or atmospheric problem, but it did serve as a straw man—a declared problem—to give the EPA a cause to act. Any solution that did not come directly from DuPont to replace Freon apparently was DOA at the EPA. Was it trust in the team or was it simply corruption?

The EPA loved DuPont for its own reasons. The thinking is that the EPA and DuPont had been good bedfellows and the EPA did not like Lindgren's HC-12a because DuPont could not make as much money on it. I am not suggesting the EPA got kickbacks but there is speculation something other than the facts had to create such a love affair. The affair included a disdain for the unrequited lover, with the best solution.

Even the EPA does not take issue with the fact that HC-12a can immediately replace Freon (R-12) without any changes to the refrigeration / AC system. However, since HC-12a is a hydrocarbon blend, it is by definition, flammable.

This is the claimed EPA big issue. Yet scientists and engineers, and even technicians know that all refrigerants in operation are flammable—even Freon. By itself, Freon is non-flammable but it becomes flammable when used.

How flammable is HC-12a? It is in the family of butane and propane and so, by itself, just like the component butane and propane gases, which are used for cooking and for lighters, HC-12a is highly flammable. Before we move from this thought, however, think of all the things in a car that are flammable, including gasoline and motor oil.

Some readers may like to get an immersion education about hydrocarbons. Butane and propane and Lindgren's HC-12a are hydrocarbons, as is OZ-12, the OZ version of HC-12a. For your edification, I found this site to be the most helpful in providing me with a basic knowledge about what the hydrocarbon debates against the EPA are all about. Feel free to take a trip when you can:

Many sources for the first version of this book have disappeared or have been scrubbed from google's potentially biased search engines. Companies saying bad things about the hydrocarbon hoax either magically stopped saying things or are no longer around to say anything.

I once suggested that to learn more about hydrocarbons go to http://www.hydrocarbons21.com/faq.php. This is no longer a hit but if you take faq.php off you do get to a much more docile site. Additionally, Gary Lindgren's 2002 blurb is still there as apparently the CFC ban is now old news and Lindgren is dead so it does not matter anymore-- http://www.oztechnologyinc.com/news2.html

For your information, I have reproduced the hydrocarbon list from this hydrocarbons21 site for your convenience:

The following hydrocarbons can be used as a refrigerant in cooling & heating applications:

- ✓ R170 - ETHANE - C2H6
- ✓ R290 - PROPANE (Dimethylmethane) - C3H8
- ✓ R600 - BUTANE (N-Butane, Butane) - C4H10
- ✓ R600a - ISOBUTANE (2-Methylpropane) - C4H10
- ✓ R1270 - PROPYLENE (Propene) - C3H6
- ✓ R1150 - ETHYLENE - C2H4

However, the most commonly used HC refrigerants are propane (mainly in commercial and industrial freezers, air conditioning and heat pumps), and isobutane (in domestic refrigerators and freezers).

Gary Lindgren's HC-12a is a mixture of hydrocarbons. Gary, who once was an aerospace engineer, used propane (R-290) and Isobutane (R-600a) to create his effective concoction. So, for the EPA, the good news was that this is considered nearly non-ozone-depleting when compared to dichlorodifluoromethane (R-12, Freon-12), the banned substance.

The part the EPA did not like was it was actually more environmentally friendly than the newly adopted compound approved by the EPA known as 1,1,1,2-tetrafluoroethane (R-134a) created by DuPont. Despite its great qualities, the EPA remained unimpressed with Lindgren's solution, though it was very simple to understand.

My perspective is that the EPA should have looked to either Lindgren's solution or a derivative so the world would not now have to deal with the residual effects of R-134a, which are not very pleasant, and which Dupont itself, with no threats from a latent Freon-loving community is not moving to pasture.

HC-12a can directly be used in refrigeration systems designed for R-12. You don't need a new refrigerator or new air conditioner to run it as you do with the oreferred Dupont's R-134a solution. Moreover, it provides substantially better cooling than an R-12 system retrofitted to the approved DuPont R-134a, with much greater energy efficiency as well.

Since 1996, HC-12a has been sold in Canada as Duracool but the EPA ban on HC-12a goes all the way to Canada. It cannot be used in automobiles even in Canada though it is a drop in quick fix with no work involved. HC-12a can be used in commercial units but cannot be used in mobile air conditioners due to the EPA blockage. Why is the EPA so much against the non-DuPont solution? Can it be its non-DuPont-ness?

Energy efficiency has always been very important to the EPA. As of January, 2012, the EPA began its process to eliminate incandescent light bulbs—not because the bulbs have any problem but because the power plants have to work too hard to light them. See Chapter 18. So, why choose a refrigerant that causes a car engine to have to work harder to cool a car? It burns more gas. Isn't that bad for clean air?

Can it be that the playing field is not fair? Though the official word is that HC-12a performs better than R134a (the DuPont blend), unofficially, refrigeration experts will tell you that HC-12a is actually more efficient than Freon (R-12).

Unlike R-134a, the DuPont solution to R-12 (Freon), HC-12a is completely compatible with the hoses and oils used in R-12 systems, making the conversion much easier to accomplish if it were only permitted by the EPA. Though Lindgren did hold a patent for the specific mix, HC-12a was still considered to be patent-free due to its non-synthetic nature. That made it even more desirable as a replacement for Freon. Somehow, the EPA did not buy any of those arguments. Then again, the EPA is the EPA.

The documentation indicates that the flammability characteristics caused the EPA to declare HC-12a illegal to replace R-12 units in vehicles in the United States. It is not illegal to buy HC-12a in the US, but EPA approval is necessary today for corporations to adopt anything. So, nobody is trying to override the EPA even though they should.

The consolation prize for Lindgren is that his HC-12a product may be used legally in refrigeration systems that were not originally charged with R-12. However, using EPA guidelines, there are certain states that prohibit the use of flammable refrigerants in automobiles.

If we were not sure the EPA was pure, we should now think the EPA is not pure.

Those in the refrigeration business think that if Gary Lindgren, who unfortunately died in a fire in his trailer in 2009, was Mr. E. I. DuPont, or even Mr. Gary DuPont, speculators would think that all the stops would have been removed so that he would be able to market HC-12a free and clear. Lindgren, may he rest in peace, was harassed by the EPA until the day he died.

Chapter 32

The Best Solution to the Freon Non-Problem Part II

HFC R-134a

In my career as a Senior Systems Engineer with IBM, I was called upon often to evaluate one system against another over multiple criteria to ultimately determine and present which one was the best for a given situation. Bennett Cycle & Supply in Nashville, Tennessee, formerly Fox Tools Supply Company sells HC-12a in America and they hope to wait it out until this phenomenal replacement for R-12 is in widespread use. http://www.bennettsupply.net/cart/

The company built a matrix very much like the ones I used for comparing computer systems so that it would be easy to see the various characteristics of cfcs and hydrocarbons and how HC-12a compares with the DuPont recommended solution HFC R-134a. Please notice in the chart that both are non-ozone-depleting. That is the only positive characteristic of the DuPont solution, though I do not claim to be a refrigerant expert.

The only real problem with R-12 that the EPA cared about was that they said it was ozone depleting though real scientists do not agree with their premise. If the EPA wanted

non ozone depleting, that is what they got with the DuPont
solution but it comes with a lot of other nasty baggage issues.

If I were you, I would not want to ever touch HFC R-134a.
This Dupont patented non-ozone depleting chemical
concoction is hazardous to the health of human beings and
animals. But, why would the EPA care about that? Perhaps it
is a tool that can be used to aid in population control? I
copied the original Fox Tools chart from their site a few as
the site existed a few years back for our full review: Their
new chart is at this URL:

http://www.bennettsupply.net/hc12vs.htm

The chart on the next page shows the major differences
between the HC refrigerant product and HFC R-134a
Notice the last item in the chart. It is not in the original
document. I added it because from all the literature out there
it is true. It tells you in no uncertain terms that all refrigerants
are flammable when in use. The EPA ruled out HC-12a
because it is flammable. Yet in system, all refrigerants are
flammable so the whole story has not been revealed to the
public?

R-134a (and other refrigerants) is just as flammable as HC-
12a when mixed with refrigerant oil, yet the quantity of
refrigerant and oil in a typical system is so low that the
danger of a fire issue in any case (including HC-12a) is
minimal.

One would have to believe the EPA was asleep when they
approved R-134a or they thought nobody would catch them.
When R-134a is exposed to flame, it releases one of the worst
gasses of all time. Perhaps you already know of the toxic
phosgene gas. Contrast this with HC-12a, which is
completely non-toxic.

In the interest of full disclosure, do you find it strange that the EPA does not discuss the phosgene gas as a problem in case of an auto accident? After all, this colorless gas gained infamy as a chemical weapon during World War I. It is more lethal than mustard gas.

I would like to see burn tests on R-134a. In most refrigerant information sites they offer the same response as the wiki.answers site I reference on the next page:

HC Refrigerant Products such as HC-12a	HFC R-134a
Non Global Warming (GWP negligible)	Global Warming (GWP of 3200 for r134a on Greenpeace calculations and publications. In other words it is a light greenhouse gas.
Non Ozone Depleting	Non Ozone Depleting
Non Toxic	- Animal Testing has indicated that with repeated exposure Benign testicular may develop
	-Postmortem will indicate increased organ weight
	-r134a Human Testing has indicated that with repeated and/or high concentration single exposure humans may experience any of the following: Reduced oxygen intake Temporary alteration of heart's electrical activity Irregular pulse / palpitations Inadequate circulation Heart irregularities Tremors & other Central Nervous System symptoms Unconsciousness or death Thermal decomposition (exposure to open flame, glowing metal surfaces) forms
	"Hazardous" hydrofluoric acid and possible carbonyl fluoride (both of which can cause severe Central Nervous System reactions.)
Compatible with both mineral and synthetic oils including PAG and Ester oils	r134a not compatible with mineral oils. Need ester and PAG only. Ester oils are very hydroscopic. PAG oils are subject to toxic registration in certain states/regions. .
Non Corrosive	r134a Highly Corrosive
Pressure "high side" of MVACS approx. 150 psig	Pressure "high side" of MVACS approx. 300 psig
Energy efficient compared to R-12	r134a not energy efficient compared to R-12
Flammable – non toxic emissions when burning	R-134a (and other refrigerants) appear to be just as flammable as HC-12a when mixed with refrigerant oil, yet the quantity of refrigerant and oil in a typical system is so low that the danger in any case is minimal. Additionally, when R-134a and R-12 is exposed to flame, it releases toxic phosgene gas, whereas HC-12a is completely non-toxic

"R134a, when exposed to a flame, such as from a candle, a cigarette or a gas range, decomposes into phosgene gas, which can be deadly if inhaled in sufficient amounts."

http://wiki.answers.com/Q/Is_it_legal_to_add_freon_to_a_l eaking_air_conditioner

It is strange that the EPA chose to ban HC-12a but permits R-134a. We have noted this before but it helps to look again. Maybe we're missing something. Gasoline is flammable. Motor oil is flammable, and R-134a in system is also flammable.

But, the EPA is right. You are likely not to die of burns in an R-134a equipped vehicle perhaps because the WMD gas released during burning will get you (Phosgene is a deadly WMD gas) before the flames burn any part of your body.

The EPA does not suggest that and it is possible that the amount of phosgene in a potential accident may be minimal or something not to be concerned about but that is a risk not too many would want to take. Why does the EPA not fully explain phosgene gas? Would you rather be burned or would you rather inhale something that would not kill you with certainty until a few weeks after it was inhaled?

Phosgene Gas in WWI

In the first combined chlorine/phosgene attack by Germany in WWI, against British troops at Wieltje near Ypres, Belgium on December 19, 1915, 88 tons of the gas was released from cylinders causing 1069 casualties and 69 deaths. Nobody ever died from HC-12a gas, so you tell me which is more dangerous to humans. Clearly the EPA believes that Freon Gas (R-12) is more deadly to Mother Nature; but what about humans?

If you would like to learn a bit more about air conditioning in very, very, easy to understand terms, feel free to go to http://www.misterfixit.com/aircond.htm. You may not be interested. I too was not interested originally but I am glad I took the trek. It is very revealing.

If you want to learn more about lethal gases used in wars, we have no additional references. However, as you, we are shocked about the notion of phosgene gas close by humans after a decomposition of an AC refrigerant.

Bug spray is flammable

Let me go over this flammability issue one more time and you tell me whether the EPA ought to approve HC-12a since the flammability issue is not as clear-cut as the EPA would like us all to believe.

As discussed, all refrigerants are blended with oil in the actual system, and all refrigerants are violently flammable under catastrophic system breach conditions (refrigerant rushes out, creating aerosol mist of oil—a big flame-ball erupts whether it's R-12, R-134a, OZ-12, or whatever). So, should fire be an issue with HC-12A? It does not seem so.

Is the reason that HC-12a is not approved because it is not very expensive and anybody—not just DuPont can make it? It is a fact that the hydrocarbon blends (HC-12a, etc) are very cheap (about $1.25 for enough to charge a few systems), But they aren't approved by the EPA for use in automotive A/C systems.

I am so suspicious about getting my facts from the EPA that I searched many other sites for corroborating evidence before I came to any conclusions. In the first edition of this book, facts were easier to come by. Is somebody hiding something?

Again, I am not a scientist but I do have a B.S. degree in Information Technology, and this tells me never to accept a poor premise. I was not conducting experiments in my examination. I was assessing analyses done by experts. I would love somebody to do an expose on why HC-12a is really being held up.

Apparently trying to avoid a defamation suit, the Oregon Observer in its expose, danced around the issue as it noted that "There is evidence to suggest that the CFC ban is another enviro-hoax based on bad science so big business can open up a brand new marketplace enforced by an international treaty and rape the people of the world for $billions. The estimated 'chiller change' market in the U.S. alone is $40 billion."

"The actions of the Environmental Protection Agency (EPA), with a self-admitted policy to drive Lindgren and other small hydrocarbon refrigerant producers out of business, make the enviro-hoax evidence all the more compelling."

HFC-134a as documented in the Oregon Observer and as we have shown in the chart has many undesirable properties, but the EPA knew it was an original, patentable product by DuPont. Among its undesirable "retro" characteristics; it was found to be an unstable, expensive, corrosive, toxic, inorganic, greenhouse gas-producing product. Somehow, none of that mattered to the EPA or to DuPont.

To make HFC-134a, any other producer would require a chemical plant that cost at a minimum $2 billion to build. That just about assured DuPont would get all the refrigerant business at the time. HFC-134a was the EPA strategy, and they made sure it worked from a business standpoint for DuPont.

When market entry ($2 Billion) is expensive or difficult, the dominant player gets what the business people call a "monopoly." As a casual observer, my research shows that is exactly what DuPont needed to rescue itself from its malady—lack of Freon profits.

Somehow, a man from OZ became a threat, but he would not have been able to come up with a $2 Billion bogey to beat DuPont in a rigged market. Then again, if DuPont held the patent any plant-building would be moot.

Clearly, patent restrictions as well as hostile market entry terms made it highly unlikely that any other company would ever be able to make the HFC-134a product. So, is it possible that the EPA saw its job as preventing any other "nobody" solution from getting the light of day? Was a big supplier with a big patent required to make the EPA sleep well at night?

Working further on the list of retro characteristics, nobody in the mainstream media will report that 10 percent of the total 134a production volume always ends up as toxic waste. This nasty stuff needs its own disposal methodology.

Besides what appears to be potential corruption in the approval process, I would suggest that the worst part of HFC-134a from a commercial perspective is that it requires those who switch from Freon to suffer through an expensive conversion or get a new air conditioner or refrigerator.

The new box, of course can use any legal EPA approved refrigerant. Moreover, if your Freon unit needs to simply be recharged, the EPA will not permit it. The system needs to be changed and 134a will be your new game. That is a very expensive proposition.

In other words, every refrigeration system in the world had to change so as to accommodate the corrosive nature of HFC-134a. The DuPont invention was really bad overall. DuPont perhaps knew it would be adopted by the EPA regardless of faults, and they may have thought they could come up with something better sooner, but there is no documentation supporting that line of thinking. In a nutshell, HFC-134a, from what analysts report, is a poor product, and America would be better without it.

When it needed to become the product released to market, and it needed to work for consumers, DuPont needed to augment it with some hellish chemicals including expensive, carcinogenic, synthetic compressor oils. The profit motive for some companies is a huge driver of product change. Without the bad stuff, whatever good HFC-134a promised could not be delivered. It could not chill an ice cube.

HC-12a, a product from one smart man's garage, needed none of this extra duty work; but, then again, it was not made by the EPA-friendly DuPont Company.

Most of the people in the refrigeration industry see the CFC ban as a scam and thanks to the Oregon Observer, the late Gary Lindgren and others, now you are one of those people.

Based on what we now know, why should we, the forgotten taxpayers of America, pay the salaries of 18,000 people in this un-American Agency—the EPA. It works against all of US. It costs US $10.5 billion per year, and each time they do anything, we lose!

Regardless of the opinions of ideologues and zealots, the EPA deserves nothing. Hopefully a quick end to its existence will come very soon.

Chapter 33

The EPA Kills Asthmatic Children

Medical Evidence—CFCs Help Asthmatics

The EPA CFC ban used a broad brush on CFCs. Freon and car air conditioners were not the only casualties. Though there was no perfect solution to the CFC ban, there are no exceptions, even if a child's life hung in the balance.

The EPA is all-knowing! No exceptions is the EPA hard-nosed style. Even if your product, based on CFCs, helps living people live better than any other product, the EPA dictate required that it be removed from the marketplace. You see by now I suspect that the EPA is unmoved by human needs, even if as noted, a child's life depends on the EPA doing the right thing. If the EPA thinks X; X it shall be!

Even if your company was using just a few ounces of a CFC for your product, it would still be banned. You would not be permitted to make the device. It does not matter to the EPA that products that use just a miniscule amount of CFCs, which had been proven to be the best products in their marketplace, could actually help people live better lives.

For example, Doctors of asthmatics believe that CFC inhalers are unmatched in their ability to relieve the symptoms of mostly younger Americans.

In other words, in the marketplace, if the EPA were not a participant, the inhaler that helps children the most would be the one that doctors prescribe the most. Can you imagine if the EPA is the agency Obama eventually selects to enforce the medical provisions of Obamacare?

Just like the EPA stopped the Gulf oil spill from being cleaned up in short order, they have stopped the use of the best inhaler for asthmatics, while concurrently claiming through their bloated propaganda advertising budget that their organization is the reason humans can breathe. This is a big, big lie.

The ideological EPA, practicing the worst form of environmentalism—a total disregard for mankind—knows exactly what it is doing. CFC inhalers have been banned forever because the emperor-driven EPA also controls Congress. Despite proof from the medical community that the EPA ban causes deaths and discomfort for young Americans, the EPA continues to be unmoved, and children needlessly suffocate.

The bottom line for the EPA on the CFC ban on inhalers is that in 2015, they are still banned and will continue to be banned as long as the EPA has any say. Children in this case are the ones who suffer while the EPA executes its agenda without scientific proof that a ban is needed. The EPA says "No." to any exception. Congress unfortunately remains powerless as the Obama team controls the Senate even with Republicans in the majority.

The EPA created a medical issue out of its major scheme or as some called it, a scam. The issue they wanted to assure was put out to the public was "CFCs hurt all people." The medical community disagrees with the EPA, but this regulatory body overruled the doctors and nurses and instead won one for the environment at the expense of our children.

Consider the history of the best inhaler medicine ever used. When one day a parent went to the grocery store in December of 2011, to get Primatene Mist, the best of the best inhalers, they quickly learned that the drug store was out of the asthma control medicine Primatene Mist. Moreover, whether they knew or not, the drugstore said that they did not know when or whether they would get any more. Parents were lucky to find one or two packages left on the shelves when the word finally got out that it was better for their children to not breathe than for Mother Nature to be upset.

We all remember the commercials for Primatene Mist but unless we had a kid depending on this to avoid a spell that killed them, we did not know how valuable this treatment was. It was the #1 over the counter medicine to help treat bronchial asthma. It was very helpful in quickly treating asthma attacks. It was marketed by Armstrong Pharmaceutical Inc. It helped relieve shortness of breath, chest tightness and wheezing that was related to bronchial asthma, emphysema and other breathing problems that were diagnosed by a doctor. It widened the airway to make it easier to breathe. The EPA said this was not enough of a reason to not classify it in the same ballpark as Freon.

Doctors and medical practitioners continue to be upset that their calls for a fix have been ignored. They cannot believe that the EPA has placed its agenda over what is good for Americans, especially those with bronchial issues—mostly young people.

Here are some unaltered comments from medical professionals about CFCs. Again, you must make your own decisions: Back in 2011 with the first edition of this book, there was a great site at the following URL:

http://www.savecfcinhalers.org/Doctors_Speak_Out.html

This site is no longer available but I captured a number of quotes back in 2011 that help make the case for asthmatics over the EPA" Ask yourself why this site was taken down? There are no entrails.

Here are the quotes introduced by the site above in 2011.

"I occasionally have bronchospasm after I get a cold, and I personally can say that the HFA version of albuterol doesn't work. My patients say the same thing. How CFC inhalers were banned and more expensive, less effective medications substituted for dependent patients is beyond me. Dr. Howard Schulman, RI #4916

"Many say that they feel like the inhaler isn't delivering the medicine."

Dr. Mario Castro, pulmonologist and associate professor of medicine for Washington University's School of Medicine, December 29, 2008

"During my twenty five years of practicing medicine, I have had occasion to treat hundreds of asthmatics, from mild cases to severe cases requiring hospitalization. I can report that during this time, I had many patients who responded better to the CFC inhalers than to the HFA inhalers. The relief response was faster and more pronounced, and these patients were much more satisfied with the CFC inhalers."

"Fifteen years ago, I developed the sudden onset of adult asthma, which was frequently severe to the point of crisis, requiring oxygen as well as injections of epinephrine and steroids. I feel that the CFC inhalers provide faster and longer lasting relief from difficult breathing than the HFA inhalers."

"The amount of CFC's released into the atmosphere by the MDI's from asthmatics is trivial in comparison to the numerous other causes of contamination, and to withhold an effective therapy for one who feels suffocated and unable to breathe is callous and grossly misdirected. Many physicians feel that there is an emotional component to the causation of asthma."

"Even if studies claim that the two types of inhalers are of equal effectiveness, to deny to an asthmatic in crisis the medication he or she feels is more effective is cruel and might well aggravate the asthmatic symptoms instead of providing the treatment (i.e. CFC's) the asthmatic person feels is more effective."

"CFC's are not available because of the influence of medically untrained persons prevailing upon the legislature to ban them from the marketplace. It has been widely noticed that when a patented drug's patent protection expires, and cheap generics become widely available, the manufacturer of said patent medication immediately produces a new patent-protected medication said to produce much better clinical results. Note that universally, the new medication is considerably more expensive than the former patented drug, and many times more expensive than the generic version."

Here are some others I found at random on the Internet:

At http://www.medicalnewstoday.com/opinions/78601, Hettie Creech' whose daughter paid the ultimate price for the CFC ban posted the following:. "My daughter could not get Primatene Mist and she died from an asthma attack. She had tried other medicines but they did not help. It saddens and disturbs me that her life support was removed from her, and no one cares."

Here is another sad post from the same URL: BS....More money is what it is all about. Posted by Brandi on 10 Feb 2012 at 10:10 pm.

I thought, well if the prescribed inhaler works, great. It doesn't. Makes my husband sick. Doesn't work the same...really crappy. We would add it to the cost of living. It's pure S**t that they are doing this. My dh only uses it during the brutal cold. He uses one inhaler about every 6 months..@ 12.00.

Now we have to go to the emergency room tomorrow, cause he broke his inhaler tonight...so add up that cost for him to simply breathe. Walk in clinics...don't deal with asthma.

In late 2013, June Giacona commented on "FDA bans final two asthma inhalers containing chlorofluorocarbons," an article by Sherry Jacobson—of the Dallas News— sjacobson@dallasnews.com. June's heartfelt opinion is shared by many who think the CFC ban is a hoax that costs asthmatics a lot of time and expense and can actually kill them. Here are her comments:

"This is extremely sad to see these toot your horn articles about the FDA removing all CFC inhalers and how smooth the process was getting the 25 million asthmatics safely transitioned over to an HFA inhaler . Nothing about this article is true."

"If real Asthmatic would have been allowed to be a part of this so called process, CFC inhalers would still be available today. Myself, being a life-long asthmatic, has not found one HFA inhaler that relieves my symptoms; some have made it much worse."

"I can't imagine who was used in the clinical trials for all these inhalers; but there is no way it could have involved real asthmatics. The FDA has received millions of complaints about these HFA inhalers all from serious side effects to them just not working at all to relieve the slightest attacks but that has gone on deaf ears...

"Why? Why isn't an asthmatic's quality of life not taken into consideration during all these processes? Who in this day and age would leave an asthmatic with no over-the-counter medication? There was a safe and effective OTC medication (Primatene Mist) some were Hell bent on removing, finally got that accomplished with the help of Big Pharma, leaving asthmatics with only an expensive emergency room visit option or lay there and suffer option until you could get to a doctor to get another ineffective inhaler. This is a process no one should be put through."

"I can only pray that some wise up; back off the pay outs-- it's only money;, speak up for your fellow humans; you know who you are. Have some compassion for those of us who are suffering. You could be in the same boat someday. Trust me it is not somewhere you want to be..."

"The cats been out of the bag about the CFC inhalers not causing environmental damage, and you continue to beat that drum to cover up one of the biggest blunders in medical history aside from the diethylstilbestrol nightmare that continues today. Please right this wrong! Asthmatics deserve better."

At www.consumeraffairs.com/health/hfa_inhalers.html, Rana of Montgomery, AL posted this on April 12, 2014. She gave her new inhaler a grade of 1 out of 5. "I have had asthma since I can remember. I used to use the white Warrick Albuterol inhaler. It worked great! At the first sign of an attack, the inhaler kicked in within 10 seconds or so. These new HFA inhalers are terrible. I don't care what clinical tests say... Listen to the majority of the consumers. How many medicines pass clinical trials only to be recalled at a later date? Be smart... listen to the majority. And yes, I care about the environment, but I care about people more! What good is the environment to me if I can't breathe? These new inhalers don't work! We asthma sufferers are suffering more!"

Summary

The EPA worships nature and abhors man. The more humans that live on earth, the more unhappy is the EPA. The more comfortable humans are made; the more likely they will want to live longer lives.

Would the EPA care if children with bronchial issues died because of the CFC ban? That is already on the table. If they cared, for the amount of traceable pollution, the ban would be lifted in these circumstances.

Http://www.consumeraffairs.com/health/hfa_inhalers.html, is a site in which there are a number of complaints about inhalers and ironically there are also ads for inhalers. Here are some comments from the site.

"The ProAir brand inhaler does not reach the lungs and does not contain more than 20 doses when it is supposed to contain 200. I and 6 children all have had lifelong asthma and we cannot get relief resulting in many trips to the ER. Every doctor and pharmacy argues with me that they work just fine and they have had no other complaints."

"Type in "ProAir Complaints" on the Internet and complaints come up one after the other. Why is the FDA not correcting this when people are literally dying? And why are these doctors and pharmacists lying to us?"

"All insurance companies will only cover the red ProAir canister and that is usually with a hefty co-pay. Then when they only last a few days, they will not let asthmatics get any more because they insist it was a 30-day supply!

"A few weeks ago there was a big deal made about a college girl who "died from overuse of her inhaler." Her classmates stated that she had been puffing on it more than usual until she finally died. It was all over the news until the comments from those of us that use these inhalers were very negative stating that this poor girl died because she kept trying to puff on her medication, but it was not reaching her lungs and did not stop the attack that killed her. Those comments stopped any reporting of this case and the poor girl's death is just going to go down as her doing something wrong. These cases are too many to mention so they are just being disregarded. This needs to stop!"

Chapter Note

In the war against humankind, in which the EPA may already be engaged, a desirable "end game" would be that 90% less people live on the planet after the war. Mother Nature would finally be appeased. If you buy that, do you think there is any collective weeping in the EPA for a soul that passes on because they could not breathe without help from a banned CFC?

Chapter 34

Some Final Thoughts on the Longevity of the EPA

It is not a Democrat or Republican Issue

You may not be able to tell by my writing, but I am a Democrat who grew up when Democrats were for the good guys, the common man. This was before the Democratic Party leaders had become progressive Marxists.

At the time back in 2011 / 2012, that I wrote the first edition of this book, I was considering a run for the US Senate in the State of Pennsylvania, after having had a semi-success running for Congress two years earlier. Though Pennsylvania Democrats are sick that the progressive notion of the new American Dream is a handout, it is still very difficult to beat machine politics.

While we are still a robust and strong country, it is up to all Americans to stop the encroachment of the redistributive mentality and the socialist zealots and the environmental ideologues and apologists, while we still have an America to save. I think Democrats can do it if we pick new leadership and kick the full can of bad Democrats back home way down the road.

In the meantime, as tough as it is to say, many Republicans, and just about all conservatives, are thinking more clearly, having seen how bad it can be. Therefore we are all better equipped to help America today if we can get past bad leadership. Democrats need to begin demanding more from leadership than abusive regulations and giving American jobs to foreigners; or else we simply need to expel them from Congress.

We have gone way too far left. It is good Democrats who are being hurt by tactics that prevent Americans from finding good jobs. The EPA is one of the greatest examples of a tool the progressive Marxists Democratic leaders use to limit job opportunities for Americans while making the country weak and vulnerable to our enemies. The EPA thinks it does not need the people; but it is really the people who do not need the EPA.

EPA treachery has got to stop. With new leadership in the Democratic Party in the future, there can be both a better Party and a better America. If the Republicans developed some mettle, that too would be good for America. Entrenched sycophant ideologues in government agencies have to get kicked out along with their "yes men,' at the top or bottom of government as well as the Congress.

Conservatives do not really care to which Party we belong as neither represent America or our interests. Maybe a new Party that got the best Democrats and the best Republicans together as in the days of JFK and Ronald Reagan could jolt start America back on course. Maybe it could keep us there for another fifty years before the progressives dared appear again.

I am sure I will be called radical for suggesting that the EPA is an instrument of population control. Yet, the evidence is strong. An honest look at the proof that I present in this book and a moron can see little doubt about it. No other conclusion is likely.

The Internet is loaded with excellent opinion and fact pieces discussing in detail the science and the politics of the EPA. We are witnessing the intentional, systematic destruction of America as well as other countries as a result of the callous creation and the execution of edicts from this too-powerful, corrupt body of regulators.

This Congress won't stop the EPA; The President knows it.

For their attempts to rein in the EPA back in April 2011, and then again in the fall 2011 and even a few times since then, I congratulate the Republicans in Congress. Yet, they failed predictably, and now they no longer try. I blame my Party, the Democrats, for permitting the EPA treachery to continue.

The Republicans tried using legislation to mitigate the damage from the EPA's ban on greenhouse gases, boilers, and basically energy in general. But, the progressive / Marxists in the Senate, including my own Senator Robert P. Casey, Jr. from Pennsylvania defeated their attempts to win one for Americans.

Fraudulent evidence did not stop EPA activists

The EPA had decreed the ban on greenhouse gases long before there was conclusive proof that there was a problem. There still is no proof other than that AL Gore's waist line has grown and his bank account is now so large that lots of folks think Al is a messiah just as the President.

The EPA is definitely out-of-control but since they have the backing of the Democrats in the Senate, they can do as they please and no reasonable person or body can stop them. Republicans are now theoretically in control but they are blood cowards so we can't look to them for a solution to much of anything. Of course we can replace the Democrats in the US Senate and that would be a good start; but let's not do it with the wimpy Republicans that will never choose to do the right thing is there is an opponent.

Greenhouse gas regulations

After the regulations went on the books, the EPA admitted that it had not followed its own protocol. Legally, it had no choice but to follow protocol but the EPA likes to make its own rules. Neither AG Eric Holder nor the next AG are expected to take on Obama's top agency. Meanwhile, the people seem too ready to accept crap for a government.

Instead of facts, the EPA in the greenhouse gas debacle, chose to speculate that the perceived problem was real, and then, without proper authorization issued their ban on greenhouse gasses, including CO_2. Ironically, they miscalculated that the low information Americans would not know what CO_2 was even though all exhale it every day.

Everybody seems to know that we breathe in oxygen and exhale carbon dioxide, (CO_2) as a human exhalent. In other words, they banned the gasses before they had actually gone through all of their own required tests and procedures. Yet, there are no apologies coming from the EPA.

A six-month old Inspector General Report was made public in the fall 2011. It had been swept under the rug until the EPA was forced to push it into the sunlight. The report clearly demonstrates that the EPA does not care if it has all the facts, as long as it can execute a prescription that meets its ideology.

As we noted in Chapter 1 of this book, the EPA was called out on this by the Inspector General long before Congress got involved. Yet, it chose to not reverse its tracks. It is too powerful an agency for our good! Now, in 2015, everybody opposed to anything Obama is for, seems to be looking for the next election cycle. How can this former community organizer be so powerful?

Some may say, so what? However, be cautioned that the EPA enforcers are the last agency to which to say "so what?" They will do as they please and there will be carnage in their wake. The "what," is the survival of a viable America? The economy is being toppled and the EPA is a prime force behind assuring that it collapses. The EPA needs to be sent home and the sooner the better.

EPA regulations work the opposite of attempts to resuscitate the economy and create jobs. No recession in the past had to deal with the countervailing force of a powerful EPA, working to defeat all initiatives intended to get businesses moving again.

EPA v Humans

The EPA does not want a robust economy if it means humans have to be saved and then served; our garbage disposed; CO_2 exhaled; and a broad range of other polluting activities acknowledged. It is better for the EPA for people to be out of work since the activities noted above do not occur when people are out of work. When people are not employed, they also do not create exhaust driving to work. The EPA loves Mother Nature, not mankind. Mankind is a big threat to Mother Nature and the EPA is Obama's personal army protecting "her" from harm.

If this were a cartoon, it might be a nice ending and there could be a big Ha! Ha! But this is real life. The EPA unfortunately for America and Americans would rather you choose to end your life than have your sorry butt around to pollute even one more day.

If you have been through all these thirty-four chapters, by now I suspect after all the confirmations, you believe in my initial premise and resulting conclusion. Keep checking the

312 Kill the EPA

body of work from the EPA and ask yourself continually: "Who is this for?" It is not for you or me. That is for sure.

In early October 2011, a bill trying to curb the EPA's power (the TRAIN act because the EPA train is off the track) did not pass in the Senate 50-50, with 60 votes required. Undaunted, Republicans still passed an identical bill in the House later in the week by a vote of 233-180, mostly along Party lines. They did so even though it had little chance of becoming law so the people could see what was going on.

Democrats owned the Senate until 2015 and now Mitch McConnell on the R side has given the Democrats a free one year lease so they can create more havoc on the US economy. Mitch either did not get the conservative message of the 2014 elections or he simply does not care what conservatives think. What a shame for McConnell and the biggest wimps in the world, today's Republicans.

Democrats, even in the minority still own the EPA. As a Democrat, I take no ownership pride in this monster organization, and I would have voted to kill it if given the opportunity.

By the way, there were four Democrats – Sens. Mary Landrieu of Louisiana, Joe Manchin of West Virginia, Mark Pryor of Arkansas and Ben Nelson of Nebraska who did support the Senate Bill to limit the EPA. One Republican, who insiders have labeled a "RINO," Sen. Susan Collins of Maine, back when it was on the table voted against it.

Will the Republicans try again? I do not think so. RINOS must be replaced in order for good things to happen again in America—unless Democrats see fit to abandon social justice and anti-American sentiments; and choose to be for Americans first.

Hopefully, the EPA will not have reduced the power on our power grids by the time we can get the required important laws passed or perhaps we'll have brownouts or other power disruptions in which we will have no heat or light and perhaps even those big network towers will have to be shut down at times making 24-hr texting a thing of the past.

Nobody is suggesting that we not work for a cleaner environment. We should continue these worthwhile efforts but we should win through science, not through power plant closures. Shutting off power is a radical notion but then again, the EPA is a radical agency.

We do not need to crush the economy to achieve environmental goals. We're all for clean air. What good is clean air, however, if there is no food and no warmth?

The EPA is a long-term tyrannical agency that must be shut down as each day they cause more damage to the country. Most of the recent fuss is about a new EPA rule that was scheduled to be rolled out in November 2011 but it has been postponed by Obama just like Obamacare til after the 2014 elections.

Figure 27-1 Texas Power Plant EPA with EPA Bulls-Eye

AP PHOTO/DAVID J. PHILLI

The W.A. Parish Electric Generating Station in Thompsons, Texas, one of the largest power plants in the United States. A bill passed by the House would delay a requirement that such coal plants slash their mercury emissions.

It requires coal plants to slash 90 percent of their mercury emissions. That rule is required under the terms of the 1990 Clean Air Act. It has been delayed for more than 20 years because the coal plants cannot comply and remain profitable. So, the EPA is OK with shutting them down and removing 40% of that power source from the grid. Most Americans will not stand for that.

EPA encourages a weak economy

The EPA solution is to let the plants close if they do not comply. This agency is made up of uncompromising bullies, and Obama and the Senate have chosen not to rein them in. The best solution is to shut down the EPA but there is a way we all may have our cake and eat it too but the Department of Energy would have to pay the price.

Since the EPA likes to lord over other agencies, and since solar power is a game of chance in which taxpayers always lose, why not consider allocating what may be left (there was once $9 billion) in the DOE budget before they can give more money to companies like Solyndra ($535 million) or SunPower, the proud recipients of $1.2 Billion.

Too much federal money for corrupt industries

As hard as it is for prudent Americans to believe, SunPower got their $1.2billion in guaranteed loans from DOE even after Solyndra had already failed and right after the company (Sun Power) had announced it was building a plant in Mexicali Mexico, and right before it received $900 million in private financing.

The $1.7 billion from Solyndra and SunPower could have been given to coal plants to help make their processes cleaner. I am not for industry subsidies but I am against the government propping up alternative energy companies as an excuse for unfettered crony capitalism.

The 2009 stimulus was the biggest payola to campaign donors since campaign financing became a necessity. You and I may not recall this but in the election of 1828, Andrew Jackson used a campaign staff to help him raise money and secure votes Jackson never dreamed that $80 billion could be taken from the treasury to pay back his biggest donors. Yet, so it was in 2009

The 2009 stimulus set aside a whopping $80 billion just for energy companies. It was then used to subsidize politically preferred energy projects. In 2012, there was 9 Billion left and many of the companies that had received the big checks had already gone out of business, declared bankruptcy, or were currently circling the drain.

The government does not pick winners and losers very well. The job of helping venture capitalists be successful should be left to the venture capitalists and they should use their own money.

There were some little potatoes thrown in the stimulus pie and since 2009, over 1900 investigations into stimulus fraud, waste, and abuse have been opened. Six hundred convictions were made. I am thankful for small things for sure, but just about all the money is gone, and Mr. Obama has nothing to show.

If there is any left, the cash would sure go a long way to clean up the dirty coal plants and reduce their emissions to get them into compliance with the EPA standards. There is no sense in taking whatever is left in DOE, ($9 billion perhaps) and wasting it on another solar or geothermal deal.

The EPA religion needs to be stamped out!

If we remember that the EPA is as much against fossil fuels as it is against DDT and CFCs, the incandescent light bulbs, and unmeasured manure, then we already know why solar projects are destined from the get go to fail. Despite our best efforts, DOE will still get the funding cash while clean coal plant fossil fuel projects that could help America will get nothing. The EPA, the Senate, the Department of Energy, and the President must go.

This can be netted out by saying simply that the inmates are running the asylum, and apparently we can do nothing about it other than throw out our elected representatives, which we will surely do the next chance we get.

Can you imagine even considering taking 40% of the coal power plants off the grid? What would this do to jobs and the economy, the price of energy and the ability of regular people being able to provide light and heat for their homes? Besides delaying the 90% reduction standard for emissions, which is almost impossible, the bill also would have stopped the EPA from implementing a rule known as the cross-state air rule.

This cross-state bill is scheduled to require coal plants to limit toxic emissions that cross state lines and contribute to health and environmental damage. These are all good ideas to implement incrementally when the country has money and when the economy is not already in the toilet.

When you hear Republicans and a few Democrats, talking about job killing regulations imposed by Obama agencies without Congress acting, this is what they are talking about. To please Mother Nature, the EPA sees no problem in shutting down the coal industry, the power industry, or any other industry, few as there may be in today's America. For every job Obama claims to create, the EPA is prepared to take twice as many away.

We go back to the new charter of the EPA which does not include helping humans. It sees its main purpose as to protect nature. So, when EPA actions raise electricity prices, cause plant closures, and eliminate jobs, the EPA as an entity really does not care.

Officially the progressives and the EPA say they are saving lives and protecting public health. They claim that by slashing emissions of toxins that contribute to birth defects, lung disease, premature death, and asthma in young children, the cost to the economy is worth it. Yet, the science on their solutions is not settled and many of the best scientists say the EPA is all wrong.

Recently, the EPA had a chance to specifically help asthmatics. We discussed this in Chapter 33. The big, bad powerful yet, "caring" EPA said "no!" to children. The EPA said "no!" to asthmatics. They are an abysmal group of people.

Rep. Ed Whitfield, R-Ky, who chairs the House Energy and Commerce Subcommittee on Energy and Power spoke on behalf of Americans who will not be able to eat or feed their children or heat their homes if the EPA has its way.

318 Kill the EPA

"Over 14 million Americans are unable to find work and millions more have stopped trying. The breaking pace at which EPA is cranking out new regulations is creating obstacles to job creation in America and also to stimulating the economy."

This is the debate taking place in Congress right now even though the President is prepared to veto anything that helps the American economy. It is good that this debate is occurring but it is not good that Obama has given the EPA the upper hand. Once coal mines go out of business and coal power plants go offline, it will be too late to make sure we have enough energy to run the country.

How clean does air have to be?

If you knew that your air would be, say, .0000000001 cleaner if you used no electrical power at all, would you go ahead and turn off the main switch to your home? I can bet you a dollar to a donut that emissions would not be reduced by even that small amount. Not driving would bring it down even further. So, at what point would you turn off the main? At what point would you stop driving? How much cleaner would your air have to be for you to be willing to turn off the main and use no more power?

Isn't "shuttering power plants," a lot like turning off the main before the power has a chance to reach your house? The difference of course is that you have no choice. It would simply be lights out.

Everything in life is a trade-off but the EPA does not have to trade anything—ever. The EPA has got to go! They can take your job, bankrupt you, turn your lights off, make food prices unaffordable and make you use Chinese light bulbs at ten times the price, and you have nothing to trade. What do you get for that? Well, at least a .0000000001 improvement in air quality. Would a rational person make that trade?

I do not think so.

Would a rational agency ask you to make that trade?

I rest my case.

Together, let's vote out all the bad Senators; the bad representatives; this bad president, and then for good measure to prove we are serious for America, let's kill the EPA!

After God, the power of your vote is the source of all real power in the United States. Use your power.

God bless America, and opposite wishes for the EPA!

Books by Brian W. Kelly
www.letsgopublish.com; Sold at
www.bookhawkers.com
Email info@ letsgopublish.com for specific ordering info. Our titles include the following:

Great Moments in Notre Dame Football The story about the beginning of US football and ND football in the US as well as the great moemnts and great coaches and players ove the years.

Thank You IBM The story of how IBM helped today's technology millionaires and billionaires gain their vast fortunes

WineDiets.Com PresentsThe Wine Diet Learn how to lose weight while having fun. Four specific diets and some great anecdotes fill this book with fun.

Wilkes-Barre, PA; Return to Glory Wilkes-Barre City's return to glory begins with dreams and ideas. Along with plans and actions, this equals leadership.

The Lifetime Guest Plan. This is a plan which if deployed today would immediately solve the problem of 60 million illegal aliens in the United States.

Geoffrey Parsons' Epoch... The Land of Fair Play Better than the original. The greatest re-mastering of the greatest book ever written on American Civics. It was built for all Americans as the best govt. design in the history of the world.

The Bill of Rights 4 Dummmies This is the best book to learn about your rights. Be the first, to have a "Rights Fest" on your block. You will win for sure!

Sol Bloom's Epoch ...Story of the Constitution This work by Sol Bloom was written to commemorate the Sesquicentennial celebration of the Constitution. It has been remastered by Lets Go Publish! – an excellent read!

The Constitution 4 Dummmies This is the best book to learn about the Constitution. Learn all about the fundamental laws of America.

America for Dummmies!
All Americans should read to learn about this great country.

Just Say No to Chris Christie for President!
Discusses the reasons why Chris Christie is a poor choice for US President

The Federalist Papers by Hamilton, Jay, Madison w/ intro by Brian Kelly
Complete unabridged, easier to read version of the original Federalist Papers

Bring On the American Party!
Demonstrates how Americans can be free from Parties of wimps by starting our own national party called the American Party.

Saving America
This how-to book is about saving our country using strong mercantilist principles. These are the same principles that helped the country from its founding.

RRR:

A unique plan for economic recovery and job creation

Kill the EPA
The EPA seems to hate mankind and love nature. They are also making it tough for asthmatics to breathe and for those with malaria to live. It's time they go.

Taxation Without Representation Second Edition
At the time of the Boston Tea Party, there was no representation. Now, there is no representation again but there are "representatives."

Healthcare Accountability
Who should pay for your healthcare? Whose healthcare should you pay for? Is it a lifetime free ride on others or should those once in need of help have to pay it back when their lives improve?

Jobs! Jobs! Jobs!
Where have all the American Jobs gone and how can we get them back?

IBM I Technical Books

The All Everything Operating System:
The story about IBM's finest operating system, its facilities, and how it came to be.

The All-Everything Machine
The story about IBM's finest computer server.

Chip Wars
The story of the ongoing war between Intel and AMD and the upcoming was between Intel and IBM. This book may cause you to buy or sell somebody's stock.

Can the AS/400 Survive IBM?
Exciting book about the AS/400 in an System i5 World.

The IBM i Pocket SQL Guide.
Complete Pocket Guide to SQL as implemented on System i5. A must have for SQL developers new to System i5. It is very compact yet very comprehensive and it is example driven. Written in a part tutorial and part reference style, this book has tons of SQL coding samples, from the simple to the sublime.

The IBM i Pocket Query Guide.
If you have been spending money for years educating your Query users, and you find you are still spending, or you've given up, this book is right for you. This one QuikCourse covers all Query options.

The IBM I Pocket RPG & RPG IV Guide.
Comprehensive RPG & RPGIV Textbook -- Over 900 pages. This is the one RPG book to have if you are not having more than one. All areas of the language covered smartly in a convenient sized book Annotated PowerPoint's available for self-study (extra fee for self-study package)

www.ingramcontent.com/pod-product-compliance
Lightning Source LLC
Chambersburg PA
CBHW072110270326
41931CB00010B/1507